WHY DIDN'T YOU JUST DO WHAT YOU WERE TOLD?

WHY DIDN'T YOU JUST DO WHAT YOU WERE TOLD?

essays

JENNY DISKI

BLOOMSBURY PUBLISHING
LONDON · OXFORD · NEW YORK · NEW DELHI · SYDNEY

BLOOMSBURY PUBLISHING
Bloomsbury Publishing Plc
50 Bedford Square, London, WC1B 3DP, UK
29 Earlsfort Terrace, Dublin 2, Ireland

BLOOMSBURY, BLOOMSBURY PUBLISHING and the Diana logo are
trademarks of Bloomsbury Publishing Plc

First published in Great Britain 2020

ISBN: HB: 978-1-5266-2190-0; eBook: 978-1-5266-2192-4

6 8 10 9 7 5

Typeset by Newgen KnowledgeWorks Pvt. Ltd., Chennai, India
Printed and bound in the U.S.A. by Sheridan, Chelsea, Michigan.

To find out more about our authors and books visit www.bloomsbury.com
and sign up for our newsletters

CONTENTS

CONTENTS

INTRODUCTION

When you think of the 1950s and who was
available in London and Paris to sleep with,
you can only wonder that she made time to do
any work.

Most of us were easier to take when we were
young, especially if we were beautiful.

No one ever mentioned the possibility of a career
as a mariner: hadn't Moses ordered the Red Sea
to part rather than have the Children of Israel get
their feet wet?

Death has a cachet which lends weight to even the
featheriest of lives.

One of the pleasures of reading Jenny Diski, her essays
especially, is that pleasure is such a large part of it.
She wasn't vain, or no more so than average, and she
didn't show off any more than other writers do but she
enjoyed her own thoughts and her sentences as much as
she enjoyed her own company, and she doesn't let that
pleasure go to waste. She entered the life of the *LRB* in
1993. Karl Miller, the paper's first editor, met her at a party
and suggested that I get in touch with her – I was Miller's
deputy. 'You'll get on with her,' he said, 'she's a bit like

you.' By the time of her death – she died of lung cancer in April 2016 – she had written more than two hundred pieces for the *LRB*, reflections on the world and its stories for the most part. And Karl Miller was right: she and I were quite alike, in our manner and even to a degree our appearance, or at any rate the clothes we wore; in the things we found funny and the value we attached to that; in the words we used and how our sentences ran, and, yes, we became friends, very good friends. But there was also an enormous difference between us. Let's just say she was the writer; I was the fan.

Between September 2014 and the end of 2015 she wrote seventeen pieces about herself, her past and the progression of her illness, pieces that became a book called *In Gratitude* – both the gratitude and the ingratitude addressed to Doris Lessing, who'd invited Jenny, then still a schoolgirl, to come and live with her and her son. At the beginning of the new year, as she came to the end of what she had to say, diary and book completed, she started to die. It wasn't a coincidence. Some weeks later she lost the physical ability to write and would ring the *LRB* office to say, each time as if for the first time, that she was sorry but she didn't think she could write any more; she still had the words – and even the sentences – but they were no longer getting through to her fingers. A vital circuit had been cut and dictation couldn't fix it.

When she started writing for the *LRB* she'd published five novels; she also wrote reviews for the *Mail on Sunday* and had a column in the *Sunday Times*. The column was about supermarkets and called 'Off Your Trolley'. The first one was about death (her death), though tinned soup and brands of yoghurt came into it too. The second, more encouragingly, was about mayonnaise, and featured Roger Diski, by now the 'ex-husband': 'A handy ex-husband, just back from France, still with the taste of the real thing in his mouth, nominated himself to test my collection of mayonnaise. I would have double-checked his findings, but I decided against it after seeing him dip a well-sucked finger into each jar.' As he was leaving, he told her that M&S had just started selling caviar and suggested she do a column about it. But the following week – 'bad news for ex-husbands' – they'd sold out.

Her first piece for the *LRB* was also about exes: 'Moving Day. My ex-Live-in-Lover will come this afternoon to move his things out.' Her daughter has gone to Ireland with her father (the ex-husband), where she'll do rural things that Jenny, 'born and raised in the Tottenham Court Road', knows nothing about. The kitten is ill and at the vet's. She will have the flat to herself:

It is a kind of heaven. This is what I was
made for. It *is* doing nothing. A fraud is being
perpetrated: writing is not work, it's doing nothing.
It's not a fraud: doing nothing is what I have to
do to live. Or doing writing is what I have to do
to do nothing; doing nothing is what I have to do
to write. Or: writing is what I have to do to be my
melancholy self. And be alone.

Tuesday, Wednesday and Thursday are the best days:

I get on with the new novel. Smoke. Drink coffee.
Smoke. Write. Stare at ceiling. Smoke. Write. Lie
on the sofa. Drink coffee. Write.

On Monday a man came to talk to her about depression and the difference between clinical depression and melancholia (he was making a documentary). They don't disagree. On Friday she has an appointment at the zoo. A talking orangutan called Jenny is a character in the novel she's writing and there are one or two things she still needs to find out. From what she's told it's clear she is pleased with her choice of primate to impersonate her. Orangs, the keeper tells her, are 'lazy, sullen and devious'; unsociable animals unlike gorillas and chimps. Duty-bound to pay a visit to Suka, 'who'll be Jenny in the novel', she finds her as no doubt she expected to find her, 'as melancholic as you please, dropping handfuls of straw on to her head'.

Jenny liked sleep and often took to her bed; she liked blankness of all kinds: white surfaces, uneventful days. Pointless activity, she said, was better than activity that had a point: no activity was better still. A place that had never been looked at and never would be was best of all. Hence Antarctica ('other landscapes fidget'), which she memorialises (we would now have to say) in a piece entitled 'A Feeling for Ice' that would later become her book *Skating to Antarctica* (1997).

'A Feeling for Ice' was a travel piece that had less to do with travel than with her childhood in a block of flats in Tottenham Court Road called Paramount Court. Both her parents, she now discovered, had tried to kill themselves; so had she, the first time when she was fourteen. 'I came,' she concluded, 'from a family of suicidal hysterics.' What she had been looking for in Antarctica was a place where all that could be ignored, 'a place of safety', 'a white oblivion', somewhere the memory of her parents couldn't reach her.

What she saw first were the penguins.

A legion of black faces and orange beaks point
out to sea facing in our direction, seeming to
observe our arrival. One day, once a year or so,
black rubber dinghies approach and a handful
of people come to the Bay believing that the
penguins are watching them arrive. For the
penguins, it's just another day of standing and
staring. They parted slightly to make way for us
but they still stood looking out to sea. We were
not part of their existence, presented no obvious
danger and were ignored, quite overlooked ...
That was the point, for me, of Antarctica: that it
was simply there, always had been, always would
be, with great tracts of the continent unseen,
unwitnessed, cycling through its two seasons, the
ice rolling slowly from the centre to the edges,
where eventually it breaks off.

For Jenny – maybe not in life but as a writer – there
was no underestimating the therapeutic properties
of indifference. But now that Antarctica is dwindling
and indifference is no longer possible, what would her
response be? Twenty years ago, when she was writing
these pieces, it would still have been possible for a
visitor to Antarctica to see 'a great blank wall of ancient
compacted snow' floating past their window. Is anything
left of it now?

'I'm very good at getting what I want,' Jenny said of
herself, and she was. She also said: 'I'm not entirely ill at
ease with boundaries.' She meant the kind of boundary
you have to observe on your tricycle ('I was a city-bred

child'). What she couldn't control, she kept out of sight. She wrote about herself a lot – almost never didn't, one way or another. That in a sense was the point – 'everything I write is personal' – but she wasn't self-obsessed. She didn't hijack the subject or intrude herself into the middle of it. At the same time, whatever she was writing about – cannibalism ('so far so googleable') or Martha Freud ('housekeeper of a world-shattering theory') – the accounts she gave were ones only she could have given. Rereading her pieces now, I find that almost every sentence I look at is so Jenny-ish without at the same time being attention-seeking or straying from the matter at hand that I worry about things I may have missed out. She said she didn't do narrative, and that also made sense: she didn't have the patience, or what her dodgy father called the stickability.

Jenny and I had a good time. We played cards – a game called Spite and Malice – and fell out: she thought I was a bad loser, I thought she was a bad winner. We went to Valencia and watched a fireworks display that the *Guardian* had asked her to write about (the ground shook); we spent half an hour following a young priest because he was wearing jeans under his cassock and we wondered where he was going; we drove the car round and round a roundabout in southern France because the car was dirty and we thought the water sprinklers might clean it. That sort of thing. That too was Jenny-ish.

Mary-Kay Wilmers

Moving Day

Moving day. My ex-Live-in-Lover will come this afternoon to move his things out, eighteen months after moving in. First thing, I wave the daughter off to Ireland with her dad, for an Easter holiday of dosing sheep and castrating lambs on a friend's farm. Apparently, they use elastic bands. Father and child might be having me on. What do I know, born and raised in the Tottenham Court Road?

I will have three whole weeks alone in my flat. It hasn't happened since L-i-L moved in. I have a scratchy feeling of excitement in my head as I anticipate the next twenty-one days. Is this true? There must be sadness at the break-up; am I telling myself lies? No. The sadness is there, all right, but in a different compartment from the excitement. I put both on hold until the clearing out is done.

In the event, it's a very jovial affair, with all the brittleness and pretence that joviality implies. So, eighteen months after the beginning of the Great Experiment, I do all I can to be amiable and assist. He says he's pleased to see me smile at him. I smile away as we pack things into boxes, disconnect machines, fill black binbags with socks and underpants. We wind leads and flexes into manageable coils, joking about missed sexual opportunities and how it's too late to be inventive now. Like a fast cut between forward and reverse in an old silent comedy, with suits over one arm, and bits of stereo equipment in the other, we put things back into the car from which they emerged something very like a geological age ago.

Two cars were needed, in fact, since by now too much has accumulated to fit into his car alone. Still smiling, I volunteer to help. We drive in convoy to his office, cornering carefully because we don't want anything to break, decant the worldly goods, and settle down in the pub next door for a well-earned gin and tonic or two. I express surprise, as I sip, at how much extra stuff there is after only eighteen months. 'Imagine if it had been eighteen years', he says ruefully.

Such a timespan is beyond my imagination; in much the same way, I cannot grasp the size of the universe. The brain is not equipped for the understanding of mythic quantities. Of space: such as the universe. Or time: such as more than eighteen months of living with someone. My brain goes into spasm. 'They say the universe is set to implode in twenty million (or is it billion?) years,' I reply.

There was only one moment of open disharmony in the whole event. It echoed the tension there had been all along. There was always an inequality of certainty about the project of us living together. He spoke easily about *forever*. I did not consider the week after next a safe bet. In recognition of our different styles I bought him an ironic bottle of wine when he moved in, chosen to be ready to drink in 1997, on my fiftieth birthday. It was partly a small gesture of risk, but mostly I expected to be doing exactly what I was doing with it today: popping it into one of the cardboard boxes of his belongings, well before 1997. We stood in the doorway looking at the bottle in the box on the floor. He said he didn't want it. I said it wasn't mine, and neither did I. The stalemate was broken when I took the bottle by its neck from the box and swung it (I like to think with some elegance) against the stone step by the drain in the front yard. A storm cloud accompanied the crash of breaking glass, and darkened the day with the threat of sudden, electric rage from each of us. It took a dangerous moment to pass over: but it did, and the milder breeziness returned. 'Nice one', he said. 'Thank you,' I smiled, with a warm inner glow of satisfaction at the unlaunching of *us*. No sense crying over spilt claret.

Altogether, a rather civil end to the affair. Refreshments over, I return home, nicely balanced by the gin between a proper sadness and the anticipation of the next three weeks entirely to myself. As I drive, I sing along to the Evs' 'All I Have to Do Is Dream' on the radio. It feels as if the car has acquired power steering, so light and easy is the journey back.

Sunday. I wake to the sound of the kitten being sick on the carpet at the foot of my bed. I hadn't planned for this. It was to be a morning spent repossessing my space. Still, cats are often sick. I get on with my plan.

Taking back one's space is something of a technical operation. It involves moving through the flat, doing what one does, but in a particularly alert frame of mind that follows the activities slightly up and to the left of one's physical body. This watchfulness, this observation of the minutiae of your use of contained space, calls for concentration. Everything is deliberate: breathing, movement, the set of the head. After a little while something else occurs: the splitting-off of a protoplasmic self that insinuates itself into every part of the flat. Like smoke, it wisps into corners and under sofas, investigating places that are too awkward for the body to go, and which never get dusted. It's almost like a dance, a floating self that breathes its way around the place while you only seem to brush your teeth and make a cup of tea. It's a celebration of solitude that won't be broken by people coming in from the outside world with their own stories and their own internal speed. Without that kind of solitude, I get lost. It's as if someone is vacuuming the air out of my lungs. Impossible to live with another person all the time and not begin to scream that they are stopping your breath. For some reason, the other person thinks you're mad, when you're really only being practical and trying to save your life. Then it's time to collect empty cardboard boxes from the off-licence.

All of which is all very well, but the kitten keeps on being sick, and protoplasm won't flow naturally under these conditions. *Worry* sets in. I have a special place devoted to worry that has an insatiable hunger to be filled. When it's empty, it worries anyway about what it's going to worry about. A sick kitten is ideal worry-material.

To the vet. It is every bit the medical emergency I'd been trying to tell myself it wasn't. Darwin's gut has turned inside out. Christ. An unhappy accident. Major abdominal surgery is needed. Now. I don't ask the price. I think of the worst number I can and try very hard not to imagine how many stomachs could be filled by such a sum in far-off places (or nearer by). What am I going to say? Too expensive, kill it, please? Actually, yes. But I can't. So I leave Darwin to the vet and his fate (he might die anyway). I feel wretched; he's been in pain all day, while I've been wafting. What am I going to tell the daughter, whose kitten Darwin is?

I'm furious. I didn't want another cat. Although, perhaps I did. I allowed the daughter to persuade me that three cats aren't any more trouble than two. Now look. God is very strict.

In bed, I cry, which isn't unpleasant, but it is unusual. Is it for Darwin, or Ex-L-i-L? Or is it just an interstitial sort of crying that lives between night and the following morning, between sleeping and waking? It feels like sadness, but not mine; or rather, not a personal sadness, but one of great immensity, and slightly up and to the left of me, where I lie saturating the pillow.

Monday. I call the vet first thing. Darwin has survived the operation and the night. It will be two days before he's out of the woods, but his chances are better. I am hugely relieved, but livid at having to mind so much about a cat, or anything at all, come to that.

As luck would have it, today's the day a man comes from Bristol to talk to me about depression. I giggle maniacally to myself when I remember. He's making a documentary on the subject.

What about being alone? Where did that go? I consider phoning and telling him he can't come. I spend twenty minutes inventing stories about why. An imaginary aunt has just died. I've had my first ever epileptic attack. I have to do an emergency reading in Aberdeen. What about a kitten whose gut has turned inside out? What about I'm too depressed to talk about depression? I give up. Anyway, if he's coming from Bristol, he won't be home answering his phone.

He turns out to be a perfectly nice man and pleasantly acerbic with it. His only obvious fault is that he drives up in an Alfa. We drink coffee and talk. He thinks there's a distinction between depression and melancholia – he's right, there is. He thinks there's a connection between melancholia and writing (or any of that creative stuff) – he's right, there is. But I'm wary of making much of that, because a real bone-deep depression is as painful as cancer, and that's a fact, too. I worry about romanticising it. On the other hand, last night's howling was precisely what he is talking about. Melancholia *is* a curiously different condition from clinical depression, or, at least, a place you can get to if you go through the clinical depression and wait. And it isn't negative. It's more like being in the part of my head that I write from. So, we bat this about a bit, but I still hear myself hissing aggressively about not wanting to make depression or writing seem mystical or magical. They are, of course, in a way. But they're also not. Long may confusion reign. Things are difficult; why shouldn't they be? The nice man nods. It seems we aren't having a disagreement.

Tuesday. Wednesday. Thursday. Nothing. Nothing. Nothing. These are the days. Don't speak to anyone (except the vet on Darwin's progress: all is well). Leave the answering machine on. Don't answer the doorbell (luckily, no one rings it). This is it, then. Me in my space. Me and my melancholy.

I do nothing. I get on with the new novel. Smoke. Drink coffee. Smoke. Write. Stare at ceiling. Smoke. Write. Lie on the sofa. Drink coffee. Write.

It is a kind of heaven. This is what I was made for. It *is* doing nothing. A fraud is being perpetrated: writing is not work, it's doing nothing. It's not a fraud: doing nothing is what I have to do to live. Or: doing writing is what I have to do to do nothing. Or: doing nothing is what I have to do to write. Or: writing is what I have to do to be my melancholy self. And be alone.

Moreover, I don't have to think about food. No one here now finds eating an essential part of their life. In addition to smoking, drinking coffee and writing, I make regular trips to the fridge to gaze on its cosmic emptiness. I adore its lit-up vacancy. No L-i-L, no daughter, needing the fridge full of possible feasts. I haven't been shopping for ten days now. There's a bit of inedible cheese, and a jar of jalapeño chillies that I nibble at when I'm peckish. Every thirty-six hours or so I call in an emergency pizza. Another nice man on a bike brings it round. I do not die of starvation. I continue to drink coffee (sometimes tea), smoke, write and stare at the ceiling.

Pages pile up. I feel guilty. Someone else must have written them. Anyway, even if I did write them, it was too easy. They won't be any good. Uh huh, there's the worry centre activating again. Because Friday, I have to go out.

Friday. A trip to the zoo. I want to know about orangutans for the novel. Mick Carman, the head keeper of the primates, has agreed to talk to me. He's wearing green wellies with khaki trousers tucked into them. He's been at the zoo for twenty-six years. Again, I feel a fraud. I'm planning to write about a talking orang called Jenny. He'll think me frivolous. Cautiously, I tell him I'm just a fiction writer. I need some facts, but I make things up, too. Do I know, he asks without prompting, that the Malays believe orangs can talk, really, but they don't because they think they'll be made to work if the humans find out? I didn't know. Thank you, God, and I love you, too.

We discuss the daily routine. Mick reckons that orangs are closer to humans than gorillas or chimps; he doesn't care what anyone says. I'm delighted to hear this, more grist for my fiction mill. But why? Because they're lazy, sullen and devious, if I see what he means. Oh, yes, I do see. They're by far the most difficult animal to keep in captivity because of this, *and* because they're basically solitary animals, not social like the other apes. They each live in their own territory, defending it vigorously from all comers, except for sexual encounters. It's every orang for himself or herself. Speaking of which, I tell Mick, I read a paper written by a Scandinavian woman anthropologist demanding that 'orangutan' (meaning 'man of the forest') be amended to whatever is the Malay for 'person of the forest'.

Quite right. Quite right. We must defend the personhood of the solitary, female whatevershescalled-utan with all our might. For she is me and I am her, and soon I'm staring through reinforced glass at Suka (meaning The Delightful), who will be Jenny in the novel. She sits in her cage, solitary and morose, and as melancholic as you please, dropping handfuls of straw on to her head. And I wouldn't mind betting that some protoplasmic wisp is nuzzling into the corners of her cage, aching for the curious eyes of the likes of me to piss off and leave her on her own.

28 May 1992

Good Housekeeping

By the age of thirty-one Jeffrey Dahmer had killed seventeen people, all men, none of whom he had known for more than a few hours. He masturbated with the bodies, dissected them, had sex with the viscera and performed fellatio with the opened mouths of severed heads. Not long before he was caught, and while in the process of yet another killing, his flat in Milwaukee contained two corpses in the bath, a headless torso immersed in bleach, several severed heads, hearts and genitalia in the fridge and freezer, and the body of a man killed two days previously under a blanket on the only bed, where, presumably, Dahmer slept until he discovered the head crawling with maggots, and was obliged to cut it off and prepare it for freezing.

Do we need to know about this man and his activities? Is he of intrinsic interest? Wouldn't it be enough to catch him, account for seventeen missing people, and prevent any more deaths by locking him securely away for the rest of his life? It could be useful for specialists – criminologists, psychiatrists – to have the details of Dahmer's life and doings with a view to learning about the causes, and therefore the prevention, of such aberrant behaviour. But is it useful for you and me, with no more than a window-shopper's interest, to know about Jeffrey Dahmer? Brian Masters (in *The*

Shrine of Jeffrey Dahmer) says yes, not only is it useful, it is vital to examine this human being in detail, because he is one of us.

I suppose the world divides into those who look and those who look away. Looking away is easiest, of course, because it requires no justification, implying, as it does, decent sensibility. Looking is altogether a more difficult activity. I doubt that it's ever entirely free of prurience, but the decision to gaze on the abominable – starving children in faraway countries, death and destruction in vicious wars, images and accounts of the Holocaust – might also be a conscious decision to bear witness to the monstrous possibilities of our own humanity. Part of Primo Levi's final depression centred on his belief that fewer and fewer people were listening to what he had witnessed on our behalf. 'Nothing human is alien to me' is more than an affirmation of species togetherness: it's a warning that by denying kinship with the worst of our kind, we may never know ourselves at all. There have been others like Dahmer, but he'll do as the worst.

Masters quotes Colin Wilson: 'The study of murder is not the study of abnormal human nature; it is the study of human nature stained by an act that makes it visible on the microscopic slide.' This is a seductive argument for insatiably curious creatures like ourselves, but why then don't we pick up (or review) with equal relish books about the good, the gentle or the kind? If wickedness is a black hole we peer intently into because we are unable to comprehend it, isn't goodness, actually, as mysterious? Why isn't it as interesting?

Masters is severe with his readers; there is a touch of the moral tutor about him. His study of murder and psychological mayhem is a philosophical enquiry which we are bound to contemplate if we seek the truth. 'I realise, of course, that this is a dangerous undertaking, and there are many who will take refuge in any manner of evasions rather than face it ... The reader must have something of the therapist who "draws on his own psychotic possibilities", or he will flounder in the reassuring soup of "objectivity".' In spite of quoting the dubious authority of R.D. Laing, there is no questioning Masters's intention, which is serious, as it was in his previous book on Dennis Nilsen, another killer whose behaviour was inexplicable to most people.

Murder is the borderline between society and the wilderness. It is the irreversible act which must make the killer an outcast, forever set apart by his or her act. But this does not mean he (or she) is inexplicable to the rest of us. The taking of another life is always terrible, but it is also sometimes understandable. Even the most dreadful of murders, infanticide, is not beyond the comprehension of parents who remember the power that the cries of small babies have to distress. From time to time we have all had to use self-control when faced with the rage other people can create in us. But such feelings, even when acted on, are still *feelings*, and connect us with others. Murder is usually a social crime.

Jeffrey Dahmer is extraordinary (although not alone: Nilsen's affect and motivation are remarkably similar) in that absence of feeling is at the root of his crimes. So absent is the feeling that murder is hardly the crime at all. It only happens to be what he has to be charged with because the law does not recognise his real transgression. The death of others for Dahmer was merely a necessary stage on the way to what he really wanted: lifeless bodies deprived of all volition.

Depersonalised from childhood, he needed to subtract the person from individuals in order to make a relationship with them. In this sense, Dahmer (like Nilsen) was not destroying, but creating: he was making dead bodies which he then, and only then, could have and hold. Before he began habitually killing people, he drugged them insensible even when they were willing to have sex with him. And later, when dead bodies proved so unsatisfying because they could not be kept for very long, he tried, a crazed and ill-informed Dr Frankenstein, to create a living zombie by drilling into a sleeping man's skull and injecting the frontal lobes with acid. Death was not his object: objects were his object.

If we are looking at Dahmer to see our own distorted reflections, there are two essential questions: how did he come to be the way he was? And: was he mad, a monster or evil? In order to answer the first question, Masters details Jeffrey Dahmer's upbringing. A tranquilliser-addicted, neurotic mother, a distant, though not uncaring father, a country-town boyhood. It is not a happy childhood, and like many children of disturbed families, he became withdrawn. The problem here is to make a distinction between Freud's 'ordinary unhappiness' and the devastating turmoil of this particular individual. Masters pinpoints details which, with hindsight, look powerfully significant. The game he invented at the age of eleven was called the Infinity Game, where stick people were annihilated if they came too close to each other, and tightly drawn spirals called Black Holes were the entrances to Infinity, from which nothing returned. He had an early addiction to being drunk. He vented his unhappiness by smashing at trees with an axe in the woods, rather than speaking to anyone. At four, he had the experience of a double hernia operation, and a (presumably subconscious) memory of having his viscera handled, then of waking in such pain that he asked his mother if his penis had been cut off. And he dissected dead animals.

This last was Dahmer's single boyhood enthusiasm. He took roadkill apart, examined the internal organs, let the flesh rot and then tried to reassemble the skeleton. He never killed anything, nor took pleasure in giving pain. It's tempting to think that, finding a void within himself, he was taking living things apart to see what it was he was missing. When he began to kill men he picked up, it was with the intention of keeping them, of not letting them go away. There was something he wanted from them and in all probability, it was life. But like taking a watch to pieces in order to see where the tick is, the thing he was looking for vanished in the searching.

None of these aspects of Dahmer's youth really explains what he became, and even if the combination of all of them signals what he was, there is still no clue as to why. Which, of course, is the real mystery. An early interest in form and structure might turn an adolescent into a sculptor, an architect, a butcher, a biologist. Young boys who have had hernia operations don't regularly become the kind of necrophiliac even necrophiliacs shy away from. Drunkenness might make it easier to do unspeakable things to human beings, but most people who get drunk to overcome their inhibitions do not want to do what Dahmer did. And might not the young inventor of the Infinity Game become an astrophysicist or SF novelist? Masters does suggest (nerve-wrackingly for the inhabitants of North London) that Dahmer's kind of withdrawal has two possible outcomes: if it doesn't make a killer of you, 'it promotes the creative isolation of the artist, who is, in this respect, the antithetical twin of the murderer.'

If we must confront wickedness, we may also have to confront our inability to grasp it in a simple cause-and-effect way. Not long ago someone suggested I read Alice Miller's case study on Hitler, because, she said, 'the way she analyses his childhood makes him completely understandable.' Do we want Hitler's childhood to make him understandable? And could it ever? The fact is, the range of unhappiness in childhood is so vast and so dreadful that I doubt Hitler's home life was worse than that of many another infant who did not grow up as he did. But it is not Hitler, really, who we need as comparison to Jeffrey Dahmer. It is the concentration camp guard we need to wonder at, the man who looked human beings in the eye while he performed the acts which Hitler merely ordered. The mystery is in the absence of shame and humanity on the small scale of Dahmer and his visitors, or you and me. It's at that singular point we can find no other word more appropriate than evil.

The question the jury at Dahmer's trial had to decide on was not guilt or innocence, but whether the man was a mad devil or a sane monster. Technically, did he have a mental disease? Did he have any control over his impulses? Dahmer spoke of being 'compelled' or 'possessed' by the hunger to have bodies. He did not only use the bodies for sexual gratification, but had a black table with skulls and a skeleton arranged on it, which he called his 'shrine', and he also ate human flesh.

Masters makes a good deal of anthropological evidence on the cannibalism/primitive religion nexus, citing the Aztecs, the windigo psychosis of Canadian

Indians who become eaters of human flesh, and of course, the Catholic Mass. Certainly, Dahmer seems to fit in with these notions, as well as the dark area of the psyche which includes werewolves and vampires. The sacrifice of humans and eating people as an act of love, or a desire to partake of their qualities has a long history. Masters speculates on the spiritual plainness of Dahmer's Lutheran religion, and how it might have created a vacancy which hankered after Dionysian excess and primitive ritual. (You almost get the feeling Masters is suggesting that had Dahmer been a Catholic – of the Southern European variety, it would have to be – he might have been all right.) It's important, says Masters, that Dahmer is not a moral idiot. He knows right from wrong. But that is no proof against possession. The Devil only triumphs over a man capable of putting up a fight against him. Corruption must have a decent medium in which its bacilli can multiply. Dahmer was finally taken over, but there were periods when he tried for normality.

In the end the labels seem transferable: what we might call multiple or schizoid personality and feel comfortable with, is surely no more than a current transformation of the ancient idea of possession by spirits. In either case, what the individual feels is that his ordinary social self has been overcome by a force, a will, beyond his control. Call it devilry, call it madness; either way Dahmer was obviously not very well.

Which is not what the jury decided. On all counts of murder Dahmer was found, by ten votes to two, *not* to have a mental disease. It suggests, since there is no death penalty in Wisconsin, that the ten were those who choose to 'look away'. They decided not to have his condition examined, but to lock him away out of sight.

Masters is very likely right to suggest that Jeffrey Dahmer's crimes were extreme versions of our own unacted-on fantasies, on which we prefer not to dwell. A desire to explore the internal labyrinths and possess the interior of a lover's body is not beyond the sexual imagination. Indeed, it is implied in the various acts of penetration people perform with one another. Sexual hunger is visceral; though, unlike Dahmer, most of us settle for dark dreams and do not go beyond the limits of reason.

The danger in this line of thought is that Dahmer becomes an existential hero, the outsider who dares to act on what ordinary mortals can barely think about. But the reality of Dahmer is otherwise. Finally, I doubt that his actions can tell us more than we know already from myth, story and fantasy. The strongest and most awful image of both Dahmer and Nilsen is that of housekeeping in hell. Both come to a point where the bodies pile up around them – Dahmer taking a shower with two corpses in the tub – the smells are intolerable, the logistics of disposal impossible, and they are condemned to a seemingly unending task of dismembering, eviscerating, dissolving, and scrubbing away at the disorder and putrefaction they have created. All the classic images of hell are present in each of those flats, inhabited by the ghost of Hieronymus Bosch and the two increasingly bewildered, dull-minded men, who finally long to be caught so that their nightmare can stop. The question of whether Jeffrey Dahmer is, in the end, of vital interest is addressed by Dahmer himself, and I'm inclined to agree with him: 'This is the grand finale of a life poorly spent ... How it can help anyone, I've no idea.'

11 February 1993

HE COULD AFFORD IT

This is the story of a man who insisted on having precisely twelve peas on his dinner plate every evening. He threaded the peas all in a row on to his fork and ate them, but if one of the peas was too big to fit on the prong with the rest, it was returned to the chef to be replaced by a pea of standard size. Once you know this everything else follows.

Howard Hughes's life is a series of obsessions, each overridden in its turn by a bigger and better fixation. It begins with twelve peas on a plate, and ends with urine stored in Mason jars. Actually, it's not an unusual story as such – the world is full of people dogged by ritual obsessions. What made Hughes remarkable was that he had the money to give absolute licence to every desperate whim. There was no practical reason for him to try to control his madness. The rest of us have to make our neuroses fit in with the world around us – a touch of reality that may trim our unreason. The rich are different from us not just because they can afford to indulge their madnesses, but because they can pay other people to sustain their nightmares.

This is a practical, rather than a moral point, and not one made in Charles Higham's biography *Howard Hughes: The Secret Life*; Higham's moral fervour in telling this wretched story twangs with self-righteousness.

There's talk of 'moral cesspools' and 'man-hungry, tweedy heiresses' – it's a world where God and Charles Higham sit in judgement and everybody gets their just deserts. You might think that a man whose lovers include Katharine Hepburn, Ava Gardner, Claudette Colbert, Bette Davis, Lana Turner, Rita Hayworth, Marlene Dietrich, Tyrone Power, Robert Ryan and Cary Grant must have had some kind of good time, but no one gets to have much fun in Higham's book. Higham explains with nice elaboration that, with women, Hughes 'preferred intermammary intercourse – making love between a woman's breasts – or fellatio to vaginal intromission. With men, he also preferred oral sex.' On the other hand, we're told later that after marrying the virginal Terry Moore on a yacht outside the five-mile limit so that the marriage wouldn't be legal, he 'massaged her clitoris, using a Japanese technique of arousal that overcame her inhibitions'. Unfortunately for inhibited women everywhere (except in Japan), Higham doesn't amplify.

Women are either virgins or sluts to Higham, and he doesn't give much for their strength of character whatever their moral state. Here's how he describes Katharine Hepburn: 'She was no stronger than any other woman when it came to meeting an immensely powerful and wealthy young man with stunning good looks and a lean, hard body who looked vulnerable and anxious to be mothered.' Do you hear the weird sound of simultaneous salivation and teeth-grinding? As a final thrust we're told: 'It never seems to have occurred to her, in her extraordinary state of self-centredness, that she would be sharing Hughes with Cary Grant, Corinne Griffith and any number of unnamed beauties of both sexes.' The slurping and gnashing reach ear-splitting proportions.

But however loud the voice of the moral majority, the tale of Howard Hughes comes across for the miserable, sad thing it was. Not a tragedy. That would require a poor, talented boy who hungers for success, makes good and can't handle it. What we've got is a rich, talented boy who starts off with everything, wants more and handles it well enough, but is unfortunately also a fruitcake. It wasn't just the peas: during the same period, he took to conducting his business conferences on the lavatory. Severe anxiety about constipation had set in. Apparently, the business associates of rich young men do not refuse to meet wherever the rich young men require them to.

What made Howard run? Was it that wicked Uncle Rupert who sodomised young Howard? The late *Photoplay* publisher James Quirk told his nephew Lawrence (who decades later told Mr Higham) that Rupert put pressure on Hughes to go to bed with him. Higham says *they* say that Rupert owned a circular graveyard in New England in which he kept the bodies of people he'd murdered, drowned his daughter, replaced her with a double and made love to his sister. Which is pretty conclusive, and who knows, maybe that was where the funny stuff with the peas – not to mention the constipation – began. Then, thank God, we've got an explanation for the whole sorry mess and we can go about our business safe in the knowledge that once again child abuse is to blame for it all.

Then again, perhaps it was the family holocaust that happened when Hughes was in his late teens and, over a period of less than two years, his germophobic, hypochondriacal mother died under an anaesthetic, his alcoholic aunt hanged herself, and his father fell off his chair and died of an embolism. Or did Hughes's congenital deafness so isolate him that his world shrank to the peas on his plate? Actually, there's no indication that Higham cares to explain why Hughes was the way he was. The family background and tales of his youth are not developed as psychological causes but are merely tossed on an accumulating pile of corruption. Everybody is doomed because everybody, past and present, is contaminated. This is quite Greek, except the chorus is that of the tongue-clicking virtuous – no hint of pity attends this drama.

Of course, sex has nothing to do with Hughes's life. Women were conquests and in that sense not very different from planes – Hughes had a number of record-breaking flying exploits to his name. When one – sadly unnamed – movie star refused to go into his bedroom after weeks of being wined and dined, he went in by himself, leaving the door open so that the astonished woman could see him having sex with a life-size, anatomically correct, rubber replica of herself which he had had made. But by the early 1950s he had given up the real-ish thing and was spending days at a time locked in the Goldwyn studio's screening room, peeing into bottles and masturbating to the bad movies he had RKO make for the purpose. This ended when Otto Preminger screened a rough cut of *Porgy and Bess* in the room, and Hughes, as anti-black as he was antisemitic, refused ever to go there again.

All along, it was about power, and although he seemed not to be very good at business (luckily he was rich enough to stay rich whatever messy deals he made), he had a real talent for buying influence – with

Nixon, the CIA, Somoza, the Mafia and any passing local politician. He was involved in an assassination attempt on Castro, the Watergate break-in and had the US weapons establishment in his pocket. Power is, of course, control, and Hughes accumulated it from the moment he had access to wealth. But it was at the peak of his influence that the obsessive anxieties really took flight. As he wrapped up control of the macroscopic world, the microscopic universe began to control him. His mother's fear of germs re-emerged and he sat naked in air-conditioned hotel suites, touching nothing – doorknobs, telephones – unless his hands were protected by a Kleenex tissue. Sometimes for days on end he'd sit like this, staring at the light bulb in case a fly landed and deposited its germs. Three Mormon aides were employed to work eight-hour shifts exclusively to deal with the threat – which has had the happy result of allowing one of them to write a memoir entitled *I Caught Flies for Howard Hughes*. Magazines were brought in on a trolley by other aides who had to move one step at a time to Hughes's signal so that no dust was disturbed in the room. There had to be three copies of each magazine, and when, eventually, they were within arm's reach, the Kleenex-covered hand would reach out and select the middle copy.

If, from the word go, you have power, but want more and have the means to get it, eventually you get all the power an individual can have. But flies still fly, and germs remain invisible – and so long as something, somewhere in the cosmos is beyond your command, you don't have everything. Nothing you've got is going to make up for the control hole, once you've spotted it. Perhaps there's another way of looking at it: when a man has everything, what is going to keep him alive except the discovery of some recalcitrant aspects of the world he can go on wanting? Hughes needed the flies that didn't need him.

Higham reckons that he has two main contributions to make to the sum of human knowledge: the first is that Hughes died of an early form of Aids. There are certainly coincidences of symptoms over Hughes's long, slow deterioration, though these could be the symptoms of any kind of autoimmune disease. He cites evidence of an English sailor whose frozen blood proved to have been HIV-positive when he died in 1959, which might indicate something, but not that Hughes had Aids, since he refused to allow blood to be taken. Higham asked a retired forensic surgeon if, with his symptoms, Hughes could have had Aids, to which the surgeon replied that he could. In fact, Hughes died of kidney failure brought on by taking too many analgesics in his attempt to control the permanent pain he had been in since a flying accident. Case not exactly proven, I'd say.

Higham's other theory is that, contrary to the rumours of Hughes being non compos mentis and under the evil influence of his Mormon aides, he was meanly and miserably in control right up to the time of his death. This sounds more persuasive. A man as control hungry as Hughes wouldn't let a small detail like dementia or insanity prevent him from keeping tabs on things.

There may have been a moment when Howard Hughes had the chance to be a human being. In his twenties he walked out on his life and hoboed around America. Preston Sturges based *Sullivan's Travels* on the adventure. But what Hughes found out in the real world didn't please him. He came back and settled into his penthouse seclusion. And Preston Sturges, of course, went mad.

7 April 1994

STINKER

It goes against all the currents of current wisdom that a public man should be just what he seems to be. Is there anyone left in the world who doesn't believe at some level or other in the disjunction between appearance and reality? I suppose somewhere deep in the forests where no white man has trod; in the highest, most inaccessible plateaux of some far-flung mountainous region, there might be a few primitive folk left who still think that what they see is what there is. But the rest of us are not completely astonished to discover that nice, ordinary MPs who take decent girls to Tory fundraising dances prefer stockings and electric flex in the privacy of their own kitchens, or that our favourite English poet of quiet suburban gloom had a nasty sense of humour and some unfortunate habits. We know that beneath all exteriors lie subterranean streams and caverns where the private, unknowable self contradicts the stated desires and achievements of the visible life.

A biography, these days, must be a tale of the unexpected. Wouldn't modern readers feel cheated to find that Antonia White and A.A. Milne were wise and devoted parents, or that Larkin only released his bicycle clips in order to sip cocoa in striped pyjamas and have gently sad, humane thoughts before bed? But an authorised biography has little to offer a post-Freudian readership. Isn't it autobiography in disguise: a ventriloquist act where the subject, or their family, pulls the strings and keeps the subterranean firmly underground? The approved biographer is not likely to be the surgeon we require, slicing through the superficial layers with his scalpel.

The prefaced justifications of unauthorised biographers are no more than pious mouthings; who, really, wants to read an authorised biography? So take Jeremy Treglown's apologia at the beginning of his Dahl biography with a pinch of salt. Ophelia Dahl plans to write the authorised version of her father's life, with the approval of his second wife, Felicity, who asked friends and relatives not to co-operate with any other project. Should we worry then that Treglown lacks sources? Hardly. Apart from Felicity and Ophelia, everyone talked, as people will.

Roald Dahl is, however, a different case from the public achiever who turns out to have feet of clay. Nobody who had read his books or heard his opinions could ever have supposed him to be a comfortably wonderful human being. On the whole, it seemed that Roald Dahl was not a very nice man who wrote not very nice, though hugely popular, books and short stories for children and adults. If this biography is disappointing, it is because, in reverse, it offends our assumptions about appearance and reality. Roald Dahl, it emerges, was exactly what he seemed to be, and Jeremy Treglown is hard put to come up with anything surprisingly endearing about the man.

The last time I read Roald Dahl was to my seven-year-old in 1984. I'd got to page 46 of *George's Marvellous Medicine*, beyond the first description of Grandma: 'She was a selfish grumpy old woman. She had pale brown teeth and a small puckered up mouth like a dog's bottom.' I'd managed George's later depictions of Grandma as 'a grumpy old cow', 'a miserable old pig' and his remorse at not being able to cover her with sheep dip: 'how I'd love to ... slosh it all over old Grandma and watch the ticks and fleas go jumping off her. But I can't. I mustn't. So she'll have to drink it instead.' By page 46 George's medicine is ready and I was about to read: 'The old hag opened her small wrinkled mouth, showing disgusting pale brown teeth.' But I'd had enough.

I explained that since she could now read herself, this bedtime story thing ought to be a pleasure for both of us. I turned down the corner of the page, offered to read her anything else and promised to continue buying her books by Roald Dahl. Only she'd have to read them herself. Separate development in the Dahl department worked out well enough. And I now have a handy sixteen-year-old, close enough to back then to recall what it was like being a child and reading Dahl's books. With a surprised blink of childhood pleasure recollected, she explained: 'They were *exactly* what I wanted to be reading. Every one of them. They filled me with ... glee.'

Multiply that pleasure by 11 million paperbacks sold in Britain alone, between 1980 and 1990 (not to mention a print run of 2 million of *Charlie and the Chocolate Factory* in China) and you get a notion of what Dahl meant when he spoke of his 'child power'. He claimed, probably rightly, that he could walk into any house with children in Europe or the US and find himself recognised and welcomed. Compared with that, having his books banned by librarians on the grounds of racism (the original Oompa Loompas were black with fuzzy hair and thick lips), misogyny ('A witch is always a woman. I do not wish to speak badly of women ... On the other hand, a ghoul is always a male. So indeed is a barghest. Both are dangerous. But neither of them is half as dangerous as a *real witch*'), or ageism (see above), was pretty small potatoes.

Children love his stories. They speak to the last overt remains of the disreputable, unsocialised, inelegant parts of themselves the grown-ups are trying so hard to push firmly underground. If they are coarsely written, structurally feeble, morally dubious, so much the better. If the adults can't bear to read them, then childhood nirvana is attained. Adults are to be poisoned and shrunk into nothingness, dragged unwillingly on their deathbed to live in a chocolate factory, and outwitted like the murderous farmers who wait outside Mr Fox's lair only to be trounced by his cunning. Quite right. Dahl has a proper relationship with childish desires and best we keep out of it. Except, perhaps, for the recognition that there are other more gracious childish desires which can also be catered for.

Given that special relationship between Dahl and his readers, and the fact that he wrote two volumes of self-dramatising autobiography for children, what is the function of an adult biography of the man? Jeremy Treglown quotes the American children's writer Eleanor Cameron's attack on *Charlie and the Chocolate Factory*. It's necessary to sort good books from bad she says, but goodness in fiction is also a moral matter depending on 'the goodness of the writer himself, his worth as a human being'. This would seem to be an extraordinary basis for deciding the value of adult fiction; people, like books, are a matter of taste, and if I would find it tiresome to have Dostoevsky round to tea, that doesn't mean *Crime and Punishment* should be swilled down the waste disposal along with the old tea leaves. But perhaps intention *is* important. There is something in us that wants good writers to be good people. There's also something in us that knows pigs can't fly.

Treglown paints a portrait of a young man delirious with his own promise. As a wounded RAF war hero (who actually crashed his plane through inexperience on a routine flight) he was sent to Washington and New York to gossip and gather intelligence about American intentions towards the Allies. He was better at the gossip and excellent at self-promotion. 'He was extremely conceited, saw himself as a creative artist of a high order, and therefore entitled to respect and very special treatment,' says Isaiah Berlin. Brendan Gill remembers him: 'The most conceited man who ever lived in our time in New York City. Vain to the point where it was a kind of natural wonder.'

His attraction to conspicuous wealth and for women resulted in his flashing gifts of gold cigarette cases and lighters at his friends, as well as a gold key to the house of Standard Oil heiress Millicent Rogers. No one, except possibly the heiresses, seems to have had a very high opinion of the young man, apart from Charles Marsh, an older oil tycoon who became a sort of mystical father to Dahl, though not to either man's benefit according to a dining companion: 'Roald and Charles both did a job on each other ... The *bullshit* that washed across the table.' They vied with each other to keep up what Treglown calls 'the high gibberish quotient' of their relationship.

Dashiell Hammett was appalled to hear of Patricia Neal's planned marriage to Dahl, while Leonard

Bernstein told her she was making the biggest mistake of her life. Treglown met and interviewed Neal, divorced from Dahl after thirty years of a marriage during which she survived a series of strokes and a Dahl-enforced recovery, and bore five children, of whom one died and the only son suffered irreversible brain damage in a street accident. Wisely, he did not ask her if Bernstein's prognostication had turned out to be true.

But it is in the domestic life that those contradictory elements we look for are generally found, and Dahl's family life was not short of the kind of challenge that shows up public people for what they really are. Treglown offers a suggestion that the death of his father when Dahl was just four, leaving him to be brought up surrounded by sisters and an adoring if physically remote mother, might have resulted in his perpetually yearning to get back to the power and desires of his childhood. If millions of children all over the world love the subversive, prurient and emotionally capricious stories he told, could that be because he never left his infantile self behind? Those of us old enough to have found out that no one ever really grows up can be grateful to Treglown for the comforting thought that some of us are more grown up than others. Dahl's gambling, boasting, sexual flightiness and public tantrums all point in the direction of arrested emotional development. And look how the antisemitism ('even a stinker like Hitler didn't just pick on them for no reason') comes with a childlike vocabulary. He displays a reaction to personal disaster in which desire to gain control over the situation often appears like a flight mechanism. When his son's life is endangered after his accident because the valve to drain the water from his brain keeps getting clogged,

Dahl more or less absents himself in a search for a new model. When Neal is crippled and rendered speechless, he organises a six-hour daily rota to force her to learn to speak again, though he is not on the rota himself. When she is sunk in despair at her depletions, he insists she goes back to work as an actress, although she has terrible trouble remembering lines and walks with a limp. Somehow, the children become his, and she becomes a depressed and depressing presence to them. Friends felt uneasy at the controlling zeal he displayed, and remarked on his lack of simple kindness to his wife.

But Dahl was a good and attentive father, claims Treglown, with relief you feel at having found some quality to admire in his subject. Even so, this potentially benign quirk is tempered by the adult lives of his daughters, which according to their own stories have been blighted with addiction to drugs, drink and self-destructive neurosis. They speak of him still as god-like and powerful and cast around, apparently, for men who can live up to their fantasies of him. But there is a moment when he becomes human, and Treglown wrenches something moving from his subject. He quotes Tessa Dahl explaining: 'Daddy got so caught up in *making things better*. He used to say: "You've got to get on with it" ... He used to shout, "I want my children to be brave."' There's a note of despair and a touch of courage about this which gives Dahl a shade more substance.

The writing career was curiously sporadic and sparse for one of the world's bestselling authors. There were no adult novels, except for a very early effort he later disowned, and even after the first volume of short stories, *Someone Like You*, he was struggling to come up with ideas to fill the next book, telling Alfred Knopf he feared running out altogether. The *New Yorker* and the BBC turned down more short stories than they printed or broadcast, and for a long time British publishers resisted the charms of his children's writing, which he turned to in the early 1960s after the adult fiction seemed to have dried up. Those stories for adults are clever, cruel and sometimes satisfying in the same way, I imagine, that George poisoning his grandmother is to children. But they are, as Treglown points out, stories that can be extracted from their writing and told, all of them, like bar-room jokes. More than anything they are like those urban myths that go around, which have ghostly hitch-hikers stopping a friend of a friend on a dark country road. They are indeed *tales*, which lose their capacity to shock in their desire to do little more than just that.

The publishing history is hilarious, and happy young Dahl readers should not be told that their favourite books (*Charlie*, *The Witches*, *Fantastic Mr Fox*, *The BFG*) were almost entirely replotted and sometimes rewritten by his various editors, who sweated over his first drafts until such time as his imperious vanity was no longer tolerable. Robert Gottlieb of Knopf finally had to invoke his 'Fuck-You Principle', which held that he'd put up with difficult authors only until he could take no more, and then, business or no business, fuck them. The final straw for Gottlieb was an offensive stream of letters from Dahl in England, announcing he was running out of pencils. They were to get him six dozen Dixon Ticonderoga 1388 – 2–5/10 (Medium) and send them airmail. Unable to find the essential pencils, they sent the best they could find, but received a diatribe. Gottlieb cracked. 'In brief, and as unemotionally as I can state it ... you have behaved to us in a way I can honestly say is unmatched in my experience for overbearingness and utter lack of civility ... unless you start acting civilly to us, there is no possibility of our agreeing to continue to publish you.' Apparently, everyone at Knopf stood on their desks and cheered as the letter went off.

28 April 1994

The Natural Death Centre

For some time now, it's been clear to me that consciousness of death is a kindness bestowed on us by the Great Intelligence, so that even if all else succeeded we would always have something to worry about. This, of course, accounts for pussy cats and lions sleeping eighteen hours a day and therefore failing to invent the fax machine. Us humans, up and anxious about death, have passed the time thinking up civilisation as a way to distract ourselves, or at least to let others know that we're awake, too. Unfortunately, the fax machine having already been invented, I had to settle simply for being up and anxious all bank holiday weekend, brooding darkly and leafing restlessly through the *Gazetteer of London Cemeteries*.

It began when my friend Jenny (not me in my postmodern mode, but someone else entirely) made me the offer of a lifetime. She'd bought a plot in Highgate Cemetery, she told me, which was a mere snip at £700, especially since it accommodated three ex-people. Would I care to share it with her? Not immediately, of course, but when the time came. Highgate Cemetery is a very nice place, and Jenny is an old and dear friend. I was properly honoured; no one else I've known has ever wanted to spend eternity with me – as a rule the occasional supper is sufficient – and I wished to express

WHY DIDN'T YOU JUST DO WHAT YOU WERE TOLD?

my gratitude. But at the same time my heart rate began to speed, and my throat to constrict: classic signs of claustrophobia and panic. I've never been any good at long-term commitment.

'Are you sure?' I asked. 'It's a bit perpetual. What about your children?'

'They can make their own arrangements,' she said darkly.

Jenny is known for going off people – even people who are not her children. She keeps a bottle of Tippex beside her address book to deal with those she's no longer on speaking terms with. I felt that apart from my reservations about making a long-term commitment, we ought to be realistic about the eternal prospects of our friendship.

'I know we get on well, but we have to think practically. Forever's, well, a very long time to be side by side.'

'Actually, one on top of the other. It's a vertical plot.'

There was a lot to think about here. Assuming that things went according to the Great Chronologist's plan, Jenny-who-isn't-me would be tucked in first, since she's twenty years older. On the other hand, I smoke several packs a day and eat salami like sweeties. There was, therefore, no guarantee that I'd get top bunk.

While I was wondering if this mattered, the Heir Apparent shuffled into the room and announced that she had something to say about all this, since, after all, she'd be in charge of arrangements. We'd already had a prior conversation about the disposal of my remains because she's a sensible girl and doesn't like to leave things to the last minute. I'd suggested cremation (so they could play 'Smoke Gets in Your Eyes' while the casket slid behind the modesty curtain) and that my ashes should be scattered over the threshold of the Hampstead branch of Nicole Farhi.

The only other really appealing possibility was a monomaniacal plan of the Victorian architect Thomas Willson, who in 1842 designed a brick and granite sepulchral pyramid with a base area the size of Russell Square to be built on Primrose Hill. Its ninety-four levels (topped by an observatory) would be 'sufficiently capacious to receive five million of the dead, where they may repose in perfect security'. The scheme foundered, but if anyone feels like reviving it, I'd be happy to make a contribution in return for a guaranteed place somewhere near the pinnacle. Failing that, I thought I would after all settle for the shared accommodation on offer in Highgate Cemetery.

'God, you're always changing your mind,' the Heir Apparent said impatiently. 'If you're buried, you'll have to have a headstone. That's more of my inheritance gone, and what's it going to say on it?'

'"Jenny Diski lies here. But tells the truth over there",' I instructed. 'Also, I'd like a dove, a winged angel, an anchor and an open book, properly carved on a nice piece of granite.'

The Heir's eyes narrowed dangerously.

'You get in for nothing if you've got a relative on site. Otherwise it's a pound a head. So there's a saving,' the other Jenny reassured her. 'And there's much more scope for drama in a proper burial. At the last funeral I went to, the grieving mistress tried to throw herself into the grave. Very satisfactory, and not a thing you can do at a cremation without making a nasty stink.'

It looked like it was decided. I wasn't to go up in smoke but would instead fatten the worms which feed the birds which keep the London cats sleek, self-satisfied and asleep for eighteen hours a day. While the other Jenny went off to spend the holiday weekend in Bradford (which gave more pause for thought about spending eternity in such eccentric company), I hunkered down with my *Gazetteer* to apprise myself of the interment possibilities.

It was not so much the fact of death as the quantity of it that struck me. In 1906 the Angel of Death dropped in on houses in London at the rate of once every six minutes. Oddly, London's population has returned to roughly what it was at the beginning of the century, though I suppose that the death rate (Bottomley notwithstanding) must have fallen. I added to my collection of useless but disturbing thoughts the fact that currently the total land used for burial in London is three thousand acres. Anyone with GCSE maths (three thousand acres ÷ six-foot plot × three bodies deep) could work out how many dead are lying around London. I don't have GCSE maths, so I didn't try, but, according to the *Gazetteer*, Highgate has 51,000 plots containing 166,000 bodies. Do the rest of the arithmetic for yourselves. And if you're very keen, how many people *in total* have died since Homo got to its feet? More than everyone alive today? I only wonder because I like large numbers.

I was troubled by the idea of so many people dying as we wake and sleep and go about our business. It's an astonishing feat of human lack of imagination to be able to ignore all those souls up and down our streets, fluttering off minute by minute, all around us. I remembered an incident in the early 1970s (when else) during a community festival in Camden Square's central patch of railed-off greenery. Perhaps it was midsummer, or Easter, or maybe it was just one of those pseudo-spontaneous street parties that were supposed to weld us all together, before we knew the Eighties were coming. Anyway, we had a great bonfire, a lamb roasting on a spit, rock 'n' roll megawatting through monster speakers and the decidedly mixed inhabitants of the square – the teenage villains, prepubescent truants and lawless toddlers of our Free School plus the recent incoming gentry whose houses they regularly broke into. The robbers and the robbed mingled riotously to celebrate the spirit of their community.

Suddenly, someone was standing out on the street, shouting through the railings. 'There's a woman dying at number sixty-five!' he bellowed at us revellers over and over again, and finally made himself heard. 'Hasn't she got the right to die in peace?'

There was a bit of a lull, long enough for any-man's-death-diminishes-me sort of thoughts to start rolling around in my head, before a bearded and bejeaned community hero spoke up for the collective will. He was sorry about the woman, he told her son or husband or friend, but there were a couple of hundred people out here, also belonging to this square, and we were celebrating life. Man! The very shade of Jeremy Bentham hovered over Camden Square for a second, and then a roar of affirmation went up. The utilitarians won the day, the Stones were turned up again to ear-splitting level, and John Donne slunk back with the soon-to-be-bereaved protester to get on with private dying behind closed doors. Logical, of course, but for all that, the lamb tasted raw and rotten to me.

It's possible I take death too seriously. It's always seemed a momentous business, coming, as it generally does, after a lifetime's consideration, unlike, for example, birth, which happens (to the newborn, if not the parents) before one has a chance to consider it, so far as I can tell. For a long time I supposed it only happened to very serious and substantial people, but then my father died when I was seventeen and I was amazed to discover that something as weighty as death could be done by someone so dedicated to evading life's trickier realities. I confess I was, and still am, impressed that he could have done something so committed as to die.

The *Gazetteer*, however, kept all such metaphysical thoughts up in the air where they belong, and my feet on the ground. It quotes from the *Builder* in 1879: 'The principles of proportion and of harmony of grace and form which are required by a well-dressed woman in her costume are equally applicable when she comes to choose a tombstone for her husband.' Though not as much fun, I should think, as burying a husband, thoughts about one's own tomb are just as sartorial. What if Armani and Calvin Klein diversified into the undertaking and stone-dressing business? I could fancy an eternity of decomposition under a layered beige, beautifully cut headstone. But could my cheapskate descendant be trusted not to shop around and dump me in the Monsoon cemetery for dead hippies?

Planning the style of one's burial is also a rather cunning way to avoid thinking about its prerequisite, I discovered. The *Gazetteer* has no mention of people dying or the manner of their death, and in an investigative wander around West Hampstead Cemetery (I thought I'd better wait for Jenny's return from sunny Bradford before visiting my prospective plot) there were very few indications of how the interred got there.

I suppose it doesn't matter unless something extra special carried them off. I'm rather partial to the idea of being *translated*, myself, but mostly the dear departed, sorely missed, tended to fall asleep or pass away.

Except for Tony. *Tony* was carved in six-inch lettering on a slab of black marble and under it was inscribed: *I Had a Lover's Quarrel with the World 1947-1987.* I was moved. Forty-year-old Tony. One of my lot. Postwar Tony, agitated by peace and prosperity, his youth a haze of misremembered sex and drugs and rock and roll, as overfull of romantic aspirations as he was of existential despair, threw in his towel after doing the best he could to compose a resonant if pretty yukky farewell to life. Sadly, when I got home, I found it was a quote from Robert Frost. Even so, Tony didn't just pass away and wanted to be remembered for not doing so. Perhaps he died of disappointment at not even being able to think up an epitaph of his own. Mostly, disappointment of one kind or another is what my generation died young of. If it's any consolation to them, those of us who remain find ourselves with the practicalities of not having died young to attend to.

There is, apparently, a cemetery in Buenos Aires which is a veritable city of the dead, with named avenues lined with scaled-down architected homes for the late lamented. Relatives come and housekeep on Sundays, dusting, polishing and replacing lace doilies while chatting to neighbouring survivors over the fence. This set me brooding about my one-up-one-down resting place in Highgate. What about a mausoleum, I began to wonder. It could be fitted with a wood-burning stove and comfy chairs. I'd leave funds so that a bottle of Scotch and packs of cards would be available in perpetuity, so friends and well-wishers could drop by on gloomy Sundays for a game of poker. The Heir Apparent was not keen on this idea. Quite apart from the drain on her inheritance ('To hell with the expense,' I cried. 'You're so selfish,' she hissed), there was the matter of the earth's resources to consider. She pointed severely to an article on natural death.

'There is some other kind?' I queried.

It turns out there's no legal reason not to bury your dead in the back garden. I was delighted.

'Darling, you can have me around always. Sod Highgate. You can just dig me a nice big hole and pop me under the yucca.'

She explained this wasn't a good idea because it would very likely lower the value of the house when she came to sell it, and she certainly wasn't going to dig me up and take me with her every time she moved.

I called the Natural Death Centre and a Mr Albery explained that their idea is to use European Union set-aside land to inter bodies and create lovely nature reserves full of you and me, while the farmers get paid for not growing anything useful on it. Instead of gravestones, they'll have trees. I could have a plaque if I wanted it, though he didn't sound enthusiastic. No need for embalming. All those chemicals are just to stop what's going to happen anyway from happening for a while. It seems it's perfectly all right to keep an unembalmed body at home for up to three days, and frankly who wants one around longer? And forget about coffins. Mr Albery advises the use of a simple sheet. By now the Heir was smiling broadly; it was all beginning to look like a pretty thrifty exercise.

However, it turned out that for £85 a specially woven natural woollen shroud can be purchased, which has a plank along the middle (to stop that nasty wobbling corpse effect) and four ropes at each corner for lowering it into the grave. A bargain, I thought, though the Heir muttered that one of our old sheets would do perfectly well. Still, I have a terrible dislike of the cold, especially when it gets into the bones. There was something comforting about the prospect of a woollen shroud, and I think she would have relented if just then I hadn't remembered that I have no desire in this life or after it to conserve resources, that I am and always have been an urban dweller and I didn't see why a detail like death should mean I have to end up in some draughty, disorganised, naturally set-aside bit of rustic. What I fancied was a proper old-fashioned pollution-filled London cemetery to rest my wearied bones, and if I couldn't have it, along with an expensively carved headstone and a very long and elaborate funeral, with hymns and popular hits of the 1960s sung, a certain amount of dancing, and my deeds recounted for the edification of all, then the Heir could whistle for her inheritance and I'd leave everything to the Natural Death Centre including my clothes. That did it. A proper interment at Highgate is assured.

23 June 1994

SWEETIE PIES

Denis Thatcher is entirely inventable – as John Wells understood: he comes in a flat-pack with easy-to-follow instructions, all the components familiar general shapes, all parts from stock, no odd angles, no imagination required. When they came up with the idea for Ikea, they used Denis Thatcher as the prototype. You can make him up in the time it would take to boil an egg.

Whether you see Denis Thatcher as a national treasure or as dismal confirmation that stereotypes live and breathe, and it is only our arrogant fantasy that the planet is inhabited by three-dimensional complex life forms, depends, I suppose, on how phlegmatic your temperament is. You can roll with reality and settle down to write the entirely documentary 'Dear Bill' letters, or you can despair, gnash your teeth and rail against the Lord for culpable laziness when he got around to inventing humankind. He was, perhaps, boiling an egg at the time. I'm inclined towards teeth-gnashing but aspire to being a more balanced person, so I alternated reading *Below the Parapet: The Biography of Denis Thatcher* by Carol Thatcher with a rereading of *Moby-Dick*. A dozen pages of Denis ('He was happy in his own skin and had played with a straight bat since the day he was born') over a cup of tea, and then back to Ishmael ('whenever it is a damp, drizzly November in my soul; whenever I find myself involuntarily pausing before coffin warehouses') to cheer myself up.

There may have been a touch of the Ahabs in Denis's genealogy. Thomas Thatcher, grandfather of the present baronet, was a bit of an adventurer, sailing to New Zealand in the 1870s to seek his fortune rather than following his father and grandfather into farming near Swindon. He made his mark, and initiated the Thatcher family business by producing an arsenic-based sheep dip for the Wanganui farmers which turned out to be a very useful wood and leather preservative as well. More interestingly, according to his great-granddaughter, Thomas Thatcher, after returning to England a wealthy man, suffered a nervous breakdown and died in Croydon Mental Hospital aged sixty-three, with the cause of death given as 'melancholia, dilation and fatty degeneration of the heart and circulatory system'. We are told he had a 'bullying, despotic nature' and my spirits quite rose with the possibility of a convergence between the Denis Thatcher story and *Moby-Dick*, but Thomas is as near as the Thatcher dynasty got to Captain Ahab. Though Thomas's son, Jack, was a bit of a gambler, the dubious genes had exhausted themselves by the time they reached Denis.

Denis is clearly a great believer in genetic destiny: 'If you're born shy, you're born shy, aren't you?' and 'I think you're either born with a gambling instinct or you're not.' According to his sister, Joy, Denis was 'born grown up', and at eighteen he joined the family business, now called Atlas and to become eventually 'the largest de-greasing and de-scaling service of its kind in the world'. His father's secretary remembers that, at eighteen, Denis 'was already the man he was to become'.

Common sense, says Carol, has always been his most valuable asset, along with 'pragmatism and homespun logic'. Two of his favourite sayings – 'Any fool can make it: we've got to sell it' and 'If all else fails, read the instructions' – provide a flavour of the Thatcher thrust of mind.

In fact, if one was a serious student of human nature and not a thrill-seeking dilettante, it would be books about Middle England's businessmen and their wives one would read avidly, rather than turning for succour to folderols about high emotions on the high seas. Though the temptation is great, we skip Denis Thatcher's unremarkable life and sayings at our peril, for they are what gave us ten years of radical nastiness while we weren't looking. It is by no coincidence called 'Thatcherism' and not 'Robertsism', for Denis is fully representative of the culture which allowed it to flourish. He married her, the rest of them voted for her, and some of us, foolishly, with our noses in the wrong books and not paying attention to reality didn't even dream that such a thing could happen.

If there is a quirk, it is Denis's tendency to marry Margarets. At any rate, he married the wrong Margaret to start with, though what with there being a war on and his being a bit lacking in experience, it is an understandable error. Certainly, both the first and second Mrs Thatchers have done their best to keep it from preying on his mind. The first Mrs T considerately changed her first name to Margot, while the second and correct Margaret warned her daughter (who until the *Daily Mail* published the story in 1976 had known nothing of her father's first marriage): 'Don't mention it to your father ... He won't talk about it. It was a wartime thing.' Although, according to Lady Hickman, formerly Mrs Thatcher, 'Friends do say we look rather alike,' Carol explains that her mother detests the comparison, wishing to consign the entire affair to history. Denis's memory, however, is quite sharp about that period of his life. When Carol tells her father that she has been to see Margot he gets 'rather misty-eyed' and asks: 'Is she still incredibly beautiful?' 'Yes,' replies Carol and they sit in silence. The awkward moment is retrieved, however, by another of Denis's timeless observations: 'God guided us both. Neither can one, nor would one want to rewrite history.' The guidance that God gave Margaret the First was to have an affair with someone else, while Denis was keeping his staff officer's desk tidy in Sicily. 'It was entirely my fault, and I regret it a lot,' says Margot now. 'The war was a strange time. You never knew what was going to happen. You grabbed happiness while you could.' Even the redoubtable Denis could not entirely avoid the unorthodox events of war, but his fatalism is surely sound: the loss of the initial Margaret must be seen as returning him to the right Margaret and his true destiny.

The romance between Denis Thatcher and the young Margaret Roberts, she of the Tory hats, the unreconstructed hairdo and piping voice, was no rushed affair. They met in February 1949, when Margaret was trying and failing to get into Parliament, and married in December 1951. Having been told by her political mentor Lord Bossom ('What sort of a name is that?' grumbled Winston Churchill. 'It's neither one thing nor the other') that she needed a husband and children to get on in politics, marriage was on Margaret's agenda. Though neither of them can recollect the proposal when asked by their daughter, the honeymoon was, Denis remembers, 'quite pleasant' and they settled into a marriage which their daughter describes as a tacit agreement to get on with their own interests. He was by now wealthy, and spent from early morning to late at night at the office and his winter weekends refereeing rugby. His wife, still lacking a secure constituency, decided to read for the Bar. 'Do what you like, love' was Denis's response, as it would be to all her future plans: it would indeed be the response of all God's Englishmen for some time to come.

If daughters are to be believed on this subject, the Thatchers did not have a close marriage even at the beginning, nor was he deeply moved by the birth of his twins. 'My God, they look like rabbits. Put them back.' As to the impression Margaret gave her daughter about maternity, Carol comments: 'Margaret, who had felt unwell during much of her pregnancy, was relieved that we had arrived safely. As she now had one of each sex, that was the end of it as far as she was concerned.' She'd bagged the full set, as Bossom had instructed, and it was back to work and ambition. Denis would travel abroad for whole months, selling his wares; he rarely wrote a postcard home and never phoned, so he only found out that his wife had finally become an MP from the *Evening Standard* provided on the plane as he returned from a South African trip. Emotional neglect clearly kept the family together, though it isn't something which has seeped down to the next generation, apparently. Mark's then wife, Diane, complained that her husband never phoned during the long periods he was away. 'Well, when I was away, I never rang up,' Denis told her.

The young people were so demanding. When Carol foolishly asked her mother, 'Why can't you be home more?' she was told: 'Darling, you have to understand that you have a lot of benefits that other children don't have: you can come to the Opening of Parliament and have supper at the House of Commons.' When Carol expressed anxiety on the morning of her Bar finals, as it happened the same day as the Tory leadership election, her mother snapped: 'Well, you can't be as nervous as me.' The children grew up learning to put their problems in perspective: that of their parents. It's hardly surprising that Mark got lost in the desert, the only direction he knew was the direction in which his mother was going. There's been loose talk around on publication of this book, suggesting that the Thatchers were a dysfunctional family, but in fact the family was a microcosm of the Thatcher view of how a nation should comport itself. No such thing as society, each individual an emotionally independent capsule getting on with his or her best interests, and no namby-pamby caring. Say what you like about the Thatcher woman, she wasn't all talk.

Once Margaret was elected Prime Minister, however, Denis stood by her. He was, by then, very wealthy indeed and retired, so he had time on his hands for common sense and a kind of stand-offish devotion. He snuck off at weekends to play golf and drink copiously with his male pals, but when his woman needed him, by God he was there. Canniest of all, he never gave interviews. This was just as well, since his opinions were precisely what you would expect them to be. Mistaking a cast member of *Anyone for Denis?* for a real policeman, he praised him: 'You get fuzzy wuzzies going on the rampage down in Brixton, you people sort it out in no time at all.' To critics of the South African regime speaking on TV, he could be heard, in the privacy of the drawing room of Number Ten, to mutter like any retired English gent: 'Bet you don't even know whether Simon's Town [*sic*] is east or west of Cape Town!' A pretty definitive argument against sanctions, you will admit. He wasn't that keen on the Commonwealth, either, and sidled up to his wife after a scathing attack on Thatcherite Britain by a Commonwealth leader, to give advice: 'I'll tell you exactly how to deal with this, Sweetie Pie: cancel all their aid and he can work out how much each minute of that bloody speech cost his country.'

He only let rip in public a handful of times. Once in Delhi at the Heads of Government meeting he failed to take a liking to Indira Gandhi, who he believed had 'chips on both shoulders' and finally let her have it: 'Well, Ma'am, we did build the railways for you and without them India wouldn't be what it is today.' And he was overheard at a cocktail party asking: 'Who do you think is worse, Sonny bloody Ramphal or Ma sodding Gandhi?' Then there was the moment after the Harrods bombing when, seen carrying one of their bags, he shouted across to the press in Downing Street: 'No murdering Irishman is going to stop me doing my Christmas shopping at Harrods.' There's no question that Denis is made of the stuff which made the Empire what it is today. At Mrs Gandhi's funeral, Denis the practical Englishman came to the fore. They had trouble getting the fire under the bier started. 'The bloody fire wouldn't go. And then they start to throw ghee on it – melted butter to you and me ... I thought to myself: why doesn't someone go and get some paraffin and get the bloody thing going. The poor old girl wouldn't burn.'

Unfortunately, we are not given any fly-on-the-wall after-work conversations between the tender-minded Mr Thatcher and his right-minded Prime Minister wife, though Carol is clearly her father's daughter: Africa is still 'the dark continent' and she berates Zambia for providing a 'rather amateur motorcade' and accommodating the VIPs in 'rather pokey prefabs hastily erected to host some previous summit of African leaders'.

Robert Morley consoled Denis when he complained about 'those buggers at *Private Eye*': 'You should be grateful, my darling; they have given you a personality.' The only unusual thing about Denis and his opinions is that he happened to have the ear of a prime minister, though to be fair, according to Carol, he never attempted to sway her to his way of thinking – though to be fairer still, he probably never needed to. Margaret would surely have fully approved of his letter wondering what 'the great Churchill would have said of those who wish to "sell" the House of Commons to Brussels; and what he would have said of Heath, the latter-day appeaser of a latter-day Hitler.'

He was there for Margaret during the tough times; applauding the sinking of the *Belgrano* and backing her during what Carol calls the 'gutless treachery' of the leadership election of 1990. 'Congratulations, Sweetie Pie, you've won; it's just the rules,' he told her with tears trickling down his face as Sweetie Pie failed to win enough votes in the first ballot. And you do begin to warm to his devotion: after all, everybody needs someone they can rely on. Except that once she was out of office, and a suburban housewife at a loss for something to do in Dulwich, Denis made himself scarce.

She sat at home eating TV dinners, while he visited his club every evening. Without the Number Ten staff, she was helpless. When Carol asked why her mother never rang, she answered: 'Because I haven't got your number, dear.' Margaret's diary was blank at first, while Denis's cronies kept his social life at full swing. 'My father's friends stayed with him, rain, hail or shine; Margaret's stopped with politics.'

Happily, she pulled herself together after a while, and now they both go their separate ways, just as they did at the beginning of the marriage. Margaret was unable to attend the launch of her daughter's biography of Denis, being off somewhere on a lecture tour. Carol, who lives in Klosters with a ski instructor, is quoted as saying that she had been to the launch of both her mother's books. Nobody mentioned whether Mark was there, but then it seems that the family is not inclined to mention Mark if at all possible. Thankfully, Denis made it, and the free gin flowed like gin. I wonder if he made his standard speech, the one that ends: 'When the real battle comes we will all up and fight and like the soldiers at Agincourt cry, "God for Margaret, England and St George".'

23 May 1996

A Feeling for Ice

I am not entirely content with the degree of whiteness in my life. My bedroom is white; white walls, icy mirrors, white sheets and pillowcases, white slatted blinds. It's the best I could do. Some lack of courage – I wouldn't want to be thought extreme – has prevented me from having a white bedstead and side tables. They are wood, and they annoy me a little. Opposite my bed, in the very small room, a wall of mirrored cupboards reflects the whiteness back at itself, making it twice the size it thought it was. In the morning, if I arrange myself carefully when I wake, I can open my eyes to nothing but whiteness.

If I trace it back, that wish for whiteout began with the idea of being an inmate in a psychiatric hospital. White hospital sheets seemed to hold out the promise of what I really wanted – a place of safety, a white oblivion. Oblivion, strictly speaking, was what I was after, but white hospital sheets were an approximation, I believed.

Actually, the reality of the hospital in London was rather different, though the sheets were white. The near-demented Sister Winniki (identical twin of Big Nurse) always ripped the crisp white sheets off me at too early an hour in the morning, in the name of mental health. 'Up, up, up, Mees Seemonds. Ve must not lie in bed, it vill make us depressed.' I was depressed and all I wanted was the right conditions for my depression, but we weren't allowed to be depressed in the bin. I had to battle against Sister Winniki to achieve even a modicum of oblivion – but since the whole point of oblivion is that it is total or not at all, I couldn't win.

When hospitalisation failed, I transferred my fantasy to the idea of a monk's cell. But there wasn't anywhere I could go with the fantasy, being both the wrong religion and the wrong sex, so I settled maturely – compromisingly – for making my almost-blank bedroom and achieving at least my morning whiteout. It's something, but not quite enough. Though I'm very good at getting what I want, the world is better at not letting me have more than a taste of it.

Finally, it came to me, effortlessly, as these things seem to come. Suddenly, there's a moment when a thought in your head makes itself known as if it's always been there, as if you've been thinking it forever. Sometimes I think I don't think at all, if thinking means some conscious process of the mind working out the nature and solution of a problem. I'm a little ashamed of this. I wish I thought properly, like proper people seem to think.

I reasoned with myself: throughout the history of the world very, very few people have been to Antarctica; there was no reason why I, just because I fancied it, should be among them. It wouldn't be an outrage if I didn't go to Antarctica, almost everybody didn't. Nothing bad would happen if I reached the end of my life without having been there. But I was, nonetheless, outraged at the idea of not going. Irrationally but unmanageably outraged. This is very important to me, I replied to my reasoning self, but I was unable to explain why.

The Arctic would have been easier, but I had no desire to head North. I wanted white and ice as far as the eye could see, and I wanted it in the one place in the world which was uninhabited. I wanted my white bedroom extended beyond reason. I wanted a place where Sister Winniki couldn't exist. That was Antarctica, and only Antarctica.

It turned out not to be so easy to go to Antarctica. There isn't anywhere exactly to go. But like thoughts that pop into your head, classified advertisements make themselves known when you've got something on your mind. '*Antarctica – the cruise of a lifetime*,' it said. I sent off for the brochure. In the meantime, I called the British Antarctic Survey in Cambridge.

'How can I get to Antarctica?' I asked.

'Are you a scientist?'

'No, I'm a writer.'

It sounded feeble next to the echo of 'scientist'. The woman at the BAS clearly agreed.

'You can't go if you're not a scientist engaged in specific research.' Was she a relative of Sister Winniki?

'Why not?'

'Because the British Antarctic Survey is set up to protect the environment for serious scientific purposes.'

'What about serious writing purposes?'

She said she could arrange for me to interview people who have spent time on British Antarctic bases.

'Have you thought about having a writer in residence?' I wondered.

To say she put the phone down wouldn't be quite true, but the conversation terminated.

I am not averse to disappointment. It has its own special pleasures. Disappointment is the hidden agenda within fantasy, a nugget for the aficionado who might trick up the bland negativity of the word by sliding alphabetically towards *disjunction* and *disparity*. If you could have what you dream about, if I could have Antarctica all white and solitary and boundless, there would finally be no excuse. Imagine, you are exactly where you want to be; and now what? Yes white, yes solitary, yes boundless, but will it, in its icy, empty, immense reality, do? In my head, it does fine: why seek out the final disappointment which the earlier, smaller disappointment only seeks to prevent? The point of desire is desire itself, the essential pleasure in expectation is expectation. The idea that reality is a completion of the wish is fallacious. It is only our dim literal-mindedness that makes us believe that we should try to achieve what we wish for. The disjunction between what I want and what I can have is my friend, my best friend in all likelihood, and I know it. Disappointment is a safety net to be relished in a secret, knowing way by the disappointed. Give thanks for the BAS and all the other preventers of fantasy come true.

The brochure arrived and I reset my daydreams.

Some realities you cannot get away from. I learned that, repeatedly, from the age of two at Queens Ice Rink. An ice rink is a promise made purely for the pleasure of creating disappointment. If you want to skate without stopping you have to go round and round the bounded ice; you can't go on and on, even though the surface permits a gathering of speed which can only be for the purpose of heading forwards without hindrance.

I'm not entirely ill at ease with boundaries. I was a city-bred child and boundaries are the nature of the city. Pavements stopped at kerbs and became roads, requiring a change of direction if I was on my tricycle, or a change of attention if I needed to cross to the next section of pavement. There were stopping places, turning points and breaks in the cityscape on any journey.

I lived on an island on an island. What I knew about the larger island was that if you went on in any direction there was sea at the edge of everywhere – the notion of a change of country without a watery division was astonishing to me. When I was very small, we went to Belgium and drove to Holland one day. I couldn't credit the unreality of it. It was the sea that said a country was a country, not an official checking passports at a border. And where were we, I wanted to know, when the car was halfway across the line dividing Belgium and Holland? 'It depends,' my father riddled, 'whether you're sitting in the front or back seat.' This was interesting, because I always sat in the front passenger seat next to my father when the three of us were in the car. My mother sat in the back. Always. Under the peculiar circumstances of the Belgium/Holland border, my father and I were a nation apart from my mother. I swivelled in my seat at the critical moment as we crossed into Belgium again that evening. 'You're still in Holland,' I told my mother, but even as I spoke she arrived back in Belgium with us.

The island within the greater island was a block of flats on the Tottenham Court Road. Paramount Court. It is still there, I pass it in the car once or twice a week. I lived in Paramount Court with my mother, and, when he was there, my father, from the time I was born until I was just eleven, which is to say 1947 until 1958 or thereabouts. Until I was seven we lived in a two-roomed flat on the third floor, facing the well at the back, then we moved upstairs to the fifth floor, to a three-roomed flat at the front, where I had a room of my own for the first time. Tottenham Court Road has changed. The traffic is one-way now and there's much more of it; the cinema was pulled down years ago and the space remains unplugged, although it's designated for the new hospital which will replace University College Hospital and the Middlesex. There were then, of course, no electronics shops, there being nothing in the way of electronics in the 1950s.

The corridors inside the flats, the back alleyways, the cinema and the skirt of pavement around the island were my playground. It never crossed my mind that my domain was limited in any way. The bareness of the narrow, cream-coloured, empty corridors, the neutral carpet and the unadorned pavement was decorated and redesigned every day with whatever landscape I chose for it. It felt enormous, limitless, available for any purpose I wished to put it to, and filled with both familiarity and surprise. Even now I can't imagine any suburban or country childhood that would have provided me with so much. I spent a lot of time wandering, playing on my own, but there were other children in the block with whom I played in the spaces of the flats. Helen, Jonathan, Susan, whose doors I knocked on, with whom I would have tea sometimes, who, occasionally, would have tea with me in my flat. So, I still dream about getting back to roam in the corridors, to climb the fire escape, to play the games and tell myself the stories I invented in my childspace.

Prince Monolulu, who has since become a pub, lived in Fitzrovia and was a regular passer-by. He was immensely tall and ebony black. He wore exotic flowing robes (exotic, that is, for those days) and always had brilliantly coloured cock feathers in his hair. He was a racetrack bookie and a professional character. When we met on my pavement, he'd yell out his catch phrase 'I got a hoss. I got a hoss.' And we'd fall into each other's arms.

Inside the enclosing walls of Paramount Court I began life with parents who were cash rich. The profitable days of the black market were still making it possible for my father to bring plenty of money home, and the remains of the jewellery my mother had from her first husband were sold off to keep her feeling wealthy when the black market came to an end. For the first three years of my life, my mother's desperate need to display wealth was taken care of. Of all things in her life, I was the best medium for her display – she went abroad for my woollen vests, dressed me in velvet-collared coats like the little prince and princess, and made sure I always wore white gloves and had immaculately ironed satin bows in my hair. When the money dried up, my mother struggled to maintain my appearance – the white gloves were the last thing to go.

As I recall, it was my mother who took me skating. Every day, long before I was old enough to start school. You could skate before you could walk, she would say when I was older. Feet don't skate, but they experience skating. You sense the solidity of the ice through the blade in a way that is quite different from being on any other hard surface. Concrete doesn't feel as ungiving and absolute as ice. And yet, to skate is magical, as you find yourself coasting free and frictionless. The clear distinction between yourself and the ice you are on strengthens the sensation of your own body, and of its capacity both for control and for letting appropriate things happen. And for all the impression of physical mastery, skating is still strange and dreamlike. Dreams of flying are the nearest you get to the feeling of being on the ice.

Every hour the skating stopped and a machine was pushed up and down the ice, like a lawn mower, to smooth it. Underneath was pure, untouched surface again, gleaming, milky-white, virgin, immaculate ice. For fifteen minutes after this the rink was only for serious skating; people practising what they had learned during a lesson, and rehearsing dance routines to the music coming from loudspeakers. In the middle, figures were skated, and I would go on with a handful of others and practise making 2s, 3s, 4s, all the single digits, appear in the silky new ice. This was another kind of skating, not going anywhere, rather meditative, concentrating on the ice at your feet to assess the quality of the marks that were appearing under your blade. These figures were the building blocks of the kind of free and flashy skating I wanted to do, I was told. They would teach me balance and control on the ice. The figure 2 had me turning and leaning so that I could eventually skate in just the way I wanted, but I had to work at it to get the technique right. It was boring making 2 appear over and over again on the surface of the ice when I could have been flying free.

Now, I like the idea of that slow, concentrated, meticulous and pointless activity. Eyes down watching the blade and glancing behind to check on the quality of the mark you have made, seeing it not quite correct, not bulbous enough, or unevenly rounded, finding the tail too elongated, not sharply enough defined, and beginning again to make it better, eventually to make it right. It's that I imagine myself doing now.

My mother didn't find my endlessly practising figures on the ice pointless; she was willing to sit day after day in the chilly seat beside the barrier. The figures were for her, as for my skating teacher, a means to an end. They would make me the new Sonja Henie, the skating champion turned skating movie star. I would be the youngest champion ice skater ever, and she would be the mother of the champion. My mother dreamed of making me into an ice princess, but something went wrong. After a while I refused to practise, and life, in any case, got in the way. What she got, to her bitter disappointment – though I think the irony might have been lost on her – was an ice maiden of another kind altogether.

I last saw my mother on 22 April 1966. I remember it because the last time I saw her was two days after my father died. The date in my memory is the date of his death.

When I was fourteen, I had been admitted, after an overdose, to the mental hospital in Hove, where I stayed for four and a half months, stuck, because the psychiatrist in charge wouldn't let me live with either of my parents. My father was in Banbury, my mother in Hove. The mother of a schoolfriend had heard about me and offered me a home in her house in London, which I, the psychiatrist and both my parents gratefully accepted. When my father died I was still living in her house, aged eighteen, and two months away from taking my A levels.

Two days after my father died, my mother came through the front door and handed me an umbrella. A gift. For April showers and stormy weather. It wasn't any ordinary umbrella, it was pale, powder blue and shaped like a pagoda, its spire rising to a delicate point, and all around the base was a scalloped frill made of a matching powder-blue artificial, chiffon-like material. Look for the chiffon lining – blue skies, nothing but blue skies – on the sunny side of the street – every time it rains it rains pennies from heaven – come rain or come shine.

My mother sat down to lunch. She was almost feverishly elated. *She was pleased he was dead. It served him right for being the bastard he was. And she wasn't a hypocrite. She'd always said, hadn't she always said –* she had always said – *that if she saw him lying dead in the gutter, she'd kick him out of the way and walk by. And that's what she would do if she saw him now lying in his coffin.*

The woman I was living with was present and at this point, thinking I needed something more than a blue umbrella, reminded me about an A-level class I had to get to. I'd better hurry, she said, or I'd miss it. I hurried so much getting out of the house to the non-existent class that I forgot to take any money with me, so I wandered down to Camden High Street and sat in the library, prepared to give it a couple of hours before my mother ran out of steam and went on her way. The library had a large plate-glass window, and my mother, instead of turning left to the nearest Tube and bus stop when she got to the High Street, inexplicably turned right and walked right past it. Not actually past. She was already screaming when she pushed through the doors. I sat in silence while she shrieked and wept, noisily enumerating my faults, not the least of which was being just like him: a liar, deceitful, treacherous, heartless. True, actually, in this context. Then she departed, her aria over, leaving the library in a silence it rarely achieved in the normal course of the day. I never saw her again.

Whenever, in the past thirty years, people asked, as they do in the regular way of introductory conversations, about my parents, I said my father died in 1966 and that I hadn't seen or heard from my mother since the same date. Often, incongruously to my mind, they would ask me if she was still alive. 'I don't know,' I'd reply.

'But don't you want to know?'

'No.'

'You must,' some soul brother or sister of Sister Winniki would insist.

There seems to be no limit to the reach and power of popular psychology. Everyone now knows that mothers are an essential item of equipment in any psyche, and that though relations with mothers may be difficult or even dreadful, attachment to them is mandatory. They also know, as a corollary, that a denial of attachment is a failure to confront the reality of mother-attachment.

'You must find it very disturbing.'

'No, I find it delightful.'

However, I am not immune to the power of popular psychology, for all my doubts and irritations with it. I knew what I felt about my mother's absence, but suspected that what I felt must be an avoidance of the real feelings everyone else supposed I naturally would have. Bad feelings, sad feelings, guilt feelings. Those kinds of feeling. From time to time, in the cause of self-knowledge, I would excavate, try to dig down below my contentment with the situation, but beyond the strong wish for the situation and therefore my contentment to continue, I could find no underlying seismic fault waiting to open up. Of course, psychoanalytic theory has a ready answer to this – how can I possibly know what I don't know I know? There's no argument against this one. Still, there were a few things I did know about myself which might equally have been concealed from me by me, and some of those things gave me pain and difficulty. Perhaps the continuing enigma of my absent mother shielded me from something worse, uncopable with. Indeed it did, it shielded me from her if she happened still to be alive. But if that was the case, then shouldn't I have been grateful to my unconscious for the protection it provided? Surely, it is neurotic to seek pain, where ordinary unhappiness is available? I gave up searching for anguish and settled for naive tranquillity. What I didn't know didn't seem to hurt me.

For the most part, quantum theory has been of little practical use in my life. When shopping in Sainsbury's, trying to get out of bed in the morning, or wondering what to wear, quantum theory is hardly any help. In one area, however, it has had a remarkable relevance. With all due acknowledgement to Erwin Schrödinger, let us do a thought experiment. Imagine a box, inside which is a flask of hydrocyanic acid, some radioactive material, a Geiger counter – and my mother. The apparatus is wired up so that if the radioactive material decays, the Geiger counter will be triggered and will set off a device to shatter the flask and thereby kill my mother. We set the experiment up, shut the lid of the box, and wait until there is a precise 50:50 chance that radioactive decay has occurred. What is the state of my mother *before* we open the lid to look?

Common sense says my mother is either alive or dead, but according to quantum theory, events such as the radioactive decay of an atom and therefore its consequences become real only when they are observed. The case is not decided until someone opens the lid and looks. The condition of the radioactive material in the closed box is known as a *superposition of states*, an inextricable mixture of the decayed and not-decayed possibilities. Once the box is open and we look inside it, one of the options becomes reality, the other disappears. But before we look, everything in the box, including my mother, exists in a superposition of states, so my mother is, in quantum theory terms, both dead and alive at the same time for as long as the box is closed.

Since I came across this thought experiment, it has been my view that whatever psychoanalytic theory might have to say about the matter of my mother, it would have to do battle with the uncertainty principle before it could fully win me over. The choice on offer is the assumption that for thirty years I repressed curiosity about my mother's existence because thoughts of her were intolerable, or that, all unknown to me, I was contentedly, not to say harmoniously, living out a recognised phenomenon of the physical universe.

My daughter, Chloe, was halfway through her A-level course when she asked me one day how you find out if someone is dead. I was evasive: as far as I knew there was only one person whose life or death status was in doubt.

'Find out if there's a death certificate.'

Funny how easy and obvious it was.

'I forbid you to do it.'

'You can't.'

'I know.'

Cabin 532 of the *Akademik Vavilov* was quite as right as could be. Plain white walls, a desk, a bookshelf above it. The bed was a wooden-sided bunk built along the wall opposite the desk, with a pair of beige curtains running across it to close it off from the rest of the cabin. The bedding, to my delight, was all white. Opposite the door was a large rectangular window – porthole, if you must – which opened wide. Nothing else.

While the *Vavilov*'s engines got up to speed, I lay myself down on the bunk, as contented with the prospect of the next two weeks as a cat with its own private radiator. Indolence has always been my most essential quality. 'Essential' in the sense that it is the single quality I am convinced I possess and by which I can be recognised and remembered, and also in the sense that I feel most essentially like myself when I am exercising it. I cannot recollect a time when the idea of going for a walk was not a torment to me; a proposition that endangered my constant wish to stay where I was. I imagine myself, child and adult, curled up in an armchair, reading and being told (as a child) or invited (as an adult) to go out and do something. I cannot think why a person sitting with evident contentment in an armchair causes the desire in others for their immediate activity. As a child I would leave the flat when the cries became insistent and find a safe haven on the back stairs, or at the furthest end of the corridor next to the bronze, latticed radiator, and resume my non-activity. As an adult, especially when visiting people, I used to make an effort, with considerable distress, put down my book, pull on jumpers, jacket and boots (it is always cold when visiting friends) and go for the proposed walk, every step of which seemed a terrible waste of good sitting time. These days, maturity has enabled me to say a firm *no, thank you* to the proposition. The aim on these walks is to get cold and damp and head for the pleasure of some cosy pub or café before setting off again into the cold and damp to return to the warm, satisfactory haven we had abandoned in the first place. I understand that people like to make distinctions, that to enjoy this they have to interrupt it with that, but I've never found it necessary. I cannot see the point of interrupting something which is going very nicely. There is also the matter of landscape, the beauty of it, the freshness of the air, the sense of being part of the natural world – even the sense of being part of the urban world. I do like landscape, but I am quite content to watch it through a window while curled up in my armchair. I wholly approve of rooms with good views. As to the freshness of the air, I'm not so eager for it. Though it is invigorating, I admit, I very rarely have the desire to be invigorated. As to the desire to be part of the natural or urban world: much of the time I know I am part of it, except when I am not sure, but I have not found that walking through a landscape or along a crowded street has ever firmed up my conviction in this area. I've lived long enough to know it is a fact that most people find activity useful and confirming, but I am not one of those people; on the contrary, I find it alarming and alienating.

As things stand at present, a phone call initiating activity is never so welcome as the one cancelling it. It's not routine as such that I cannot abide. There is a kind of intrinsic routine that is the very essence of satisfactory times. When I am alone, at home, I get up, work, eat, sleep, work, sleep, eat, in a pleasurable round dictated by my physical needs. I'm hungry, I eat. I'm sleepy, I sleep. And work, especially the long haul of a full-length manuscript, is not an intrusion, but lives well enough with the physical requirements.

Once I gave it five minutes' practical thought, it was as easy to get access to the corridors of Paramount Court, about which I had been dreaming for so long, as it would be to find a death certificate, or the lack of one. I phoned the head porter and explained that I had once lived there and was now wanting to write about the place.

'You won't be knocking on any doors, will you?' he asked when I arrived. 'We've got a lot of old people here.'

I explained it was just the corridors I was after, but while I was standing in his office, I noticed a board on the wall with the names of the occupiers of each flat. The names Rosen and Levine jumped out at me.

It was a couple of weeks before I looked up their names in the phone book and found their numbers, and a while after that before I picked up the phone.

I introduced myself as Jenny Diski and explained who my parents were and which flats we had lived in. I then reintroduced myself in the silence. 'Jenny Diski – Jenny Simmonds, I used to play with Jonathan. You are Jonathan's mother, aren't you?'

That was when she said, 'Jennifer,' and I felt an odd wooziness come over me. I almost said no, not recognising myself by that name. But I had been Jennifer when I was small, though for the life of me, I only really remember being Jenny. I said, yes, but felt fraudulent, which was curious because I never really like being called Jenny. *Diski* feels more accurately like me, though it is an entirely invented name to which both Roger-the-Ex and I changed when we got married. There was a gasp and then a brief silence.

'How are you?'

I was eleven when she had last known me, but what else was there to say?

'I'm well, thank you.'

I explained that I was a writer these days and was thinking about doing a book in part about my mother, that I didn't know anyone who knew us when we were a family at Paramount Court; would it be possible for me to come and talk to her, to get, as it were, an outside view of what went on?

'Mrs Levine and Mrs Gold are still here. Do you remember Helen Levine and Marianne Gold, you used to play together? You're a writer you say? You're all right, then?'

'Yes. I'd really like to come and talk to you about my parents.'

There was an awkward pause. I liked the sound of her voice. London Jewish, parents foreign-speaking, brought up in the East End. She sounded alert and thoughtful, you could hear her remembering and considering what she remembered.

'Well, we were friends of your mother, of course. But ... I'm afraid you didn't have a very happy childhood.' This last was said hesitantly, telling me there were things she thought I'd better not know.

'No, it was a bit of a mess, wasn't it?'

'Oh, you remember it, do you? You had a terrible time. I thought you would have forgotten. Well, in that case ...'

The sound of my parents fighting in our two-roomed flat on the third floor echoed through the corridors of Paramount Court, my father leaving several times, my mother being stretchered away to hospital, the furniture and fittings being confiscated by debt collectors when we were on the fifth floor: these were all public events, but somehow, it was assumed, I wouldn't retain a memory of those things. Adults experience, children don't.

I remember Jennifer with about the same clarity that I remember the young Jane Eyre, Mary from *The Secret Garden*, Peter Pan and Alice. Rather less clarity, in fact, since the last four are readily available on my bookshelves and I have reacquainted myself with them quite regularly. Jennifer, I've merely remembered from time to time over an increasing distance of years, and with each remembering, each re-remembering, the living, flesh and blood fact of her slips incrementally from my grasp. As a person, she is far less substantial than Tinkerbell, who can be brought back into existence through the will of others. Jennifer does not light up when I clap my hands in recollection; she retains only a dim inner illumination. She did not even preserve her name until very recently.

The thing about Jennifer is that there has been no corroborating evidence for her existence these past thirty years. There are no pictures, no written words; no other person who, remembering her, has spoken to me of her. She has existed exclusively inside my head, only exiting into the world like characters (of whom sometimes she is one) in the novels I write. She is no more certain than any other figment of my imagination. I might have made her up – I did make her up from time to time.

Jennifer began to fade when my father died and my mother disappeared. After that there was no one I knew who had known her, apart from myself. Perhaps the fading was not the first thing that happened. Jennifer became detached, became a separate character, someone with a story of her own. Although intellectually I knew that she and I were one and the same, emotionally she grew distant, acquiring a complete and finished life of her own, related structurally to me but existentially separate. I could recollect her environment with a greater clarity than I could her lived experience. I knew stories about her, incidents that had occurred in her life and I could review them as a series of tableaux, but she was a separate incarnation, not a present remembering self. They say the body undergoes a complete cell change every seven years, and this felt true to me. Jennifer inhabited her own existence, physically other, not me, not part of the continuum of me. I had to doubt the thoughts I thought I remembered her having, even the feelings; perhaps my remembering of Jennifer was like the animation of a puppet, my present retrospection pulling her strings and seeming to bring her to life. Who knows what Jennifer was like, with only my memory as a guide?

My picture of any event occurring to Jennifer always includes Jennifer in the frame. The image is not from her eyes – which is how a 'real' memory should be recalled, if such a thing as a 'real' memory could be said to exist – but seen from the outside, from some eyes beyond the frame and therefore, unless they are God's, not actually present at the time of the event. Treacherous, if there is no one to confirm or deny the facts of the event. 'I' seem to be remembering an occasion which I, as someone forty years removed from Jennifer, could not possibly have witnessed. Jennifer witnessed and participated in the event, but now she has become part of the image and not the seeing eye she must originally have been. Who is remembering what? When I think of Jennifer sitting on her father's lap, I see the back of Jennifer, her arms squeezing tight around a silver-haired, moustached, handsome man who is laughing and teasing her. What the hell I was doing there (if that actual moment ever existed and is not just a representation of a general memory), standing to one side, at a little distance from the armchair the two of them are sitting in, no more substantial than a pair of observing and possibly ironic eyes, I cannot say. Jennifer was frightened of ghosts. Perhaps she had every right to be.

Three spruce elderly women in their late seventies and early eighties sat in matching white leather armchairs. I, aged forty-eight, shared the sofa with the one remaining husband. Their hair was dressed, waved and blown dry and their faces lipsticked and powdered. They were formidably well and at ease with themselves. Teatime. These four, and the two departed husbands, have sat like this, taking tea and chatting, since they moved into the flats in 1940. My mother, at times, would have been among them.

'Ninety per cent of these flats were Jewish,' Nathan tells me.

'Why?' I wondered. Why this block of flats?

'The flats had a shelter in the basement. The Jews know how to take care of themselves,' laughed Mrs Rosen. 'And there was the rag trade around Great Portland Street, it was convenient for the tailors.'

And the war? The knowledge that the Nazis were just a few miles away, across the Channel? How did that impinge on their daily life?

'We felt safe here. We were all just twenty, and at that age it didn't bother us. We went to business as usual. To tell you the truth, we didn't really think about it.'

Mrs Levine recalled an incident that happened on a Thursday afternoon, her afternoon off. It started the ball rolling.

'Your mother came to my door that afternoon. Somebody was desperately ill, she said, or something like that. I can't remember. She came up and asked me if I'd like to go to church. I said: why would I want to go to church? But she went. To a church in Trafalgar Square.'

Nathan asked: 'Why not a synagogue?'

'I don't know. She had a reason for going to church. It wasn't a religious reason, I don't think. But I don't know any more about it. It was my afternoon off.'

In fact, she took me instead. I stood outside South Africa House waiting, while she disappeared into St Martin-in-the-Fields. I hadn't the faintest idea what she was doing and she didn't tell me. I used it as a key scene in my novel *The Dream Mistress*. I remember it very clearly. Even so, it was a jolt to hear it being confirmed by someone else. Confirmed, but not explained.

My mother was a woman whose behaviour was often inexplicable. Living with her, day by day, was like skating on newly formed ice. It constantly shattered, every day, but there was no alternative, no other place to go.

'I can tell you something else,' Mrs Gold jumped in eagerly. 'Your father rented a room in Albany Street. You didn't know that, did you? He was a charmer. But he was a confidence man.'

Mrs Levine looked a little alarmed.

'Doesn't she mind?' she asked Mrs Rosen, meaning me.

'No,' explained Mrs Rosen, 'she wants to know. She said so.'

'Well, Jimmy was a confidence man,' Mrs Gold continued. 'He rented this room in Albany Street – on top of the woman who made the curtains – what was her name?

'Anyway,' said Mrs Gold. 'He did a lot of confidence tricks in this place. He had money sent to him. He wrote letters out. He used the room as a postal address. And the woman became a very wealthy woman, she had a curtain place in Vivian Avenue.'

'I had her here to estimate for curtains,' Mrs Rosen remembered.

'That's right. And Jimmy was named as a co-respondent while he was living in Paramount Court.'

Whether he was named as co-respondent to the curtain woman's divorce, or one of the women from whom he extorted money in return for romance, was not made clear. The recollections were all like this, sharp and hazy simultaneously.

I had known my father was something of a villain in a black-marketeering, womanising sort of way. I hadn't known that he was a con artist by profession, with an office and everything. This was, if not entirely new information, a shift of emphasis.

'Was he caught?' I asked.

'I remember he was in prison, for what reason I cannot tell you, but it was whispered behind your mother's back that it was through these letters. You would have been tiny, about three. Then soon after that this tragedy happened.' Mrs Gold was well into her stride. 'Maybe it was before he went to prison, because he knew he was going to be caught. Or after. I don't remember, but he came into our shop in Great Portland Street one morning and asked my husband to go horse racing with him. I said, why does he suddenly want to go horse racing with you, coming round out of the blue, on a working day? My husband told him he couldn't leave the shop. Then he went to Epping Forest, but he was saved.'

'Pardon?' I said.

'He was found in the car in Epping Forest, with the exhaust pipe. You know?'

'Of course, that wasn't the only time.' Mrs Rosen added. 'He tried to do it again. I don't know where.'

I remember one occasion when a policeman arrived at the flat and told my mother that my father had been found in his car with a pipe from the exhaust leading through the window. I hadn't known he'd made a habit of it.

On an impulse I asked: 'Did my mother try to commit suicide, ever?'

'Not that I know of,' said kindly Mrs Rosen, rather quickly.

'I think she did,' corrected Mrs Gold. 'She did. An overdose. How old were you then? Five, I think.'

I'm washing down this family history of social crime and multiple suiciding with my second cup of tea. Still, Mrs Rosen wishes I would have another piece of cake. But I've got a small appetite.

'He had a head of silver hair,' remembered Mrs Gold. 'He was so handsome. And charming.'

'Absolutely charming. A perfect gentleman.'

'He did have something about him,' cooed Mrs Gold.

The three old ladies lost themselves in a rhapsody to the charms of my father.

'Where did your mother find him?' wondered Mrs Gold jarringly, a little rasp in her voice.

'He could talk anybody into anything. He had that personality. The way he spoke, you had to listen to him.'

'Anybody would have been taken in,' Nathan Rosen added quietly.

'He had personality, didn't he? As soon as you spoke to him you felt you'd known him all your life.'

'He was very generous. Always the first to put his hand in his pocket. You had to love him.'

'Maybe too much,' said Nathan, quietly again, bringing the song to an end.

After a moment Mrs Rosen asked hesitantly, lowering her voice: 'Tell me, did he ever abuse you, your father?'

What flashed into my mind, as I considered what to say next, were those nights, many of them, when my naked mother (both my parents slept naked) would enter my room in the fifth-floor flat one door down from where I now sat taking tea, and shake me awake, telling me I had to go and sleep with my father because she wasn't going to sleep in the same bed as him. He would put his arms around me and hold me against his hairy chest, rocking me for, I suppose, both our comforts. And pleasure. Certainly mine: I loved the feel and smell of his warm body, nuzzling into his hairy chest, squeezing myself tight up against his beating heart. I adored being held in his arms and feeling his big hands stroking me. Stroking me where? Everywhere, I think. I took in his physical affection like draughts of delicious drink. I don't ever recall feeling anything but safe and loved in this private midnight comforting.

There was a game both my parents used to play when I was small on the occasions when they were in accord. Usually after an evening bath, I would dry myself in the living room and then run naked between them as each, on opposite sides of the room, reached out for my vagina and tried to tickle it. When they caught me, their fingers at my vulva, I would squeal and shriek and wriggle with the equivocal agony tickling causes, and the game would go on until I was exhausted and they weak with laughter. It was my family's way of having a good time, and there were so few good times that these occasions have a golden haze over them as I recollect them. Looking back, it's clear to what extent I was a conduit between them, in good times and bad, a lightning rod for their excitement and their misery. But those dark nights in bed with my father felt like a private exchange between me and him. They weren't, of course; it was just a child's misreading of herself as the centre of the universe. I was sent to sleep with my father by my mother, and while, as a child, I supposed that they had had another argument in bed, what more likely happened was my mother's (or my father's) sexual refusal, and her replacement by myself. The same pattern as the living-room game.

It was only later, with the arrival of a sense of sexual privacy when I was fourteen, that I responded in what might now be considered an appropriate way. I had run away from my father in Banbury, and gone to my mother, who was living in a single room in Hove. On the night of my arrival, I was curled up facing away from her, when she climbed under the covers of the small bed we had to share. I wasn't asleep, but she thought I was. She slipped a hand around my pelvis and down between my legs, and began to caress me. I was mortified.

'Don't do that,' I snapped.

'It's all right,' she said. 'You're my little girl. My baby. There's nothing wrong with your mummy touching her little baby.'

'Stop it,' I shouted, terribly embarrassed, and pulled away from her. With a tut of irritation, she turned her back in a familiar sulk. I didn't sleep that night. We argued all the next day about where I would live, and in the evening I swallowed a handful of Nembutal I found in her drawer. By the following day, I was an inmate in the Hove psychiatric hospital, and my mother and father would meet each other for the first time for years over my hospital bed, each shouting at me, 'How could you do this to me?' as I lay between them and pulled the covers over my head and began to scream.

'Do you mean, did he hit me?' I asked Mrs Rosen, cautiously.

'Yes,' she said, looking sympathetic. 'I know he hit your mother. Did he ever lift his hand to you?'

'They both smacked me sometimes. They would get into rages and slap my face, but it wasn't a big thing. Nothing special,' I assured her.

Warm-hearted Mrs Rosen looked genuinely relieved. The rules. *One hand for the ship* applied at all times: always keep a hand free to hang on to safety rails, inside and on deck. Get to meals on time. All wet gear was to be left in the Mud Room on Deck One: no muddy boots in corridors or cabins. During landings, keep within sight of an expedition leader and return to the meeting place immediately if called. Never take anything, not a stone, not a discarded feather, from any of the landing places. Do not leave anything behind on land. Comply exactly with the crew's instructions and use the sailor's handshake – hands to wrists – when getting on or off the Zodiacs (the black rubber motorised dinghies on which we will go ashore). We were welcome to go at any time to the bridge, but we must keep our voices down and not interfere with the work of the Russian crew on watch.

Our first stop was to be South Georgia, eight hundred miles to the south-east of Ushuaia, our starting point at the tip of Tierra del Fuego: and there was not a thing between, only sea, sky and space. At this point on the planet you could travel its span without bumping into a single piece of land before returning to where you started. It's the cause of the winds and storms that whip up tempests in these latitudes; there's nothing to stop them rolling round the world picking up velocity like an ice skater. I was in no hurry to see land.

Our journey to South Georgia was almost the same length as Shackleton's open-boat voyage from Elephant Island. I spared him a thought or two as I rocked blissfully in my bunk. A video of the surviving film taken by Frank Hurley of the *Endurance* expedition was shown the evening before we landed at South Georgia. Hurley's moving pictures only got as far as the moment when the *Endurance* finally sank and they took off on an ice floe. Shackleton ordered the men to ditch as much as possible – he threw away the Bible, apart from the flyleaf signed by Queen Alexandra, Psalm 23 and the page from the Book of Job containing the lines:

> Out of whose womb came the ice? and the hoary
> frost of heaven, who hath gendered it?
> The waters are hid as *with* a stone, and the face
> of the deep is frozen. (Job 38:29)

Hurley's cumbersome cinematograph didn't last long, so there is only still photography to record his time on Elephant Island. He kept the film as best he could, but even with modern restoration it looked as ancient as papyrus. The ship beset in the ice was covered with rime, looking monumental, like a sculpture: it's a famous picture, but the movie version of the *Endurance* breaking up, creaking, wailing, sometimes seeming to scream, as it buckles at the centre, the main mast crashing to the deck and the whole thing finally sinking beneath the ice, is heart-stopping. When it was clear that the ship couldn't withstand the pressure, the dogs were dropped over the side on to a slide made out of a sail – a precursor to the emergency slide of planes. The dogs whined and barked, and slithered all out of control as the men below caught them, like fairground barkers, getting them on to the ice, where the dogs shook themselves in relief and ran rings around each other and the crew. Earlier, a scene showed the crew desperately trying to find a way through the closing ice. While some men hacked at the edges of the pack to make a split in the floe, others hauled on a rope to drag the ship through the narrow way that had been cut. The film was so frail at this point that the line of men and the rope between them seemed to bleed darkly into each other, blurring the individuals until they appeared to be umbilically attached to their own shadows. We watched a final shot of Shackleton, on his last voyage, shampooing his pet Alsatian on the deck, sleeves rolled up, enjoying himself hugely. The next morning we would arrive at Grytviken, the place where, just days later, he was buried after he died of a heart attack on his next Antarctic expedition.

South Georgia's only inhabited place, Grytviken, a whaling station from 1904 to 1965, has been preserved, after a fashion, as a museum of whaling and as the site of Shackleton's burial. If derelict landscapes like the murkier parts of King's Cross and the old unreconstructed Docklands appeal, then Grytviken is a pearl of desolation. A rust-bucket ghost town, left to rot in its own beautiful way.

We were greeted by a ruddy-faced Englishman in a fisherman's sweater and his hearty wife, though my attention was gripped by the surreal sight of three soldiers in camouflage fatigues yomping past, holding fierce-looking automatic weapons at the ready. It looked like news film of troop manoeuvres in Northern Ireland. The soldiers flashed past as it was my turn to receive a rugged handshake from the ruddy-faced man. He was the curator of the museum, the only spick-and-span building in town. We were warned to be careful where we walked, because floors and ceilings were likely to cave in, and not to walk towards the cluster of buildings a mile to the right, on King Edward Point, which was the British garrison and a military secret. How many soldiers were stationed there? This was a military secret, too. 'Very hush-hush,' said the ruddy-faced curator solemnly.

As far as I could see South Georgia is further away from anywhere than anywhere else in the world. It's 1,100 miles from South America. The Antarctic Peninsula is just two days away from Ushuaia, while it had taken three days and nights to get here. Though – as the British Government sees it – it's part of the Falklands Dependencies, it's actually 1,290 miles from the Falkland Islands. As a whaling station it thrived, but it's a mystery why anyone would go to war over it once whaling was over, until you remember the oil in the surrounding waters (as well as around the Peninsula), and that the hands-off clause in the Antarctic Treaty runs out in twenty years' time. South Georgia's convenience for processing and distributing the liquid billions is obvious.

I walked along the shore towards the hill half a mile to the left, which sported a low white picket fence, of the sort that surrounds an English country garden. On the way, I encountered my first elephant seals, which lay dotted in small crowds and sometimes alone along the shore.

We were warned not to get closer than six feet to any of the animals we might come across, but the bulls were so still on the sand, it was sometimes impossible to spot them, and once or twice I found myself within a foot or two of a boulder that suddenly opened its eyes, raised its head, making the trunk swing obscenely, and then yawned a silent threat at me to keep my distance. Nothing is so red, moist and fleshy as the inside of the mouth of an elephant seal. With the trunk flapping above the scarlet cavern of its mouth, the story of sexual reproduction is laid bare. When the bulls do make a deliberate noise – while they're mating and fighting – they produce from the depths of their blubbery quivering throats a cracking belch so sonorous and amplified that it echoes off the sides of the mountains.

Elephant seals being what they are, and modern travellers being what they are, the photography has begun in earnest. The debate about taking a camera with me on this trip raged for weeks. I've never owned a camera, never taken one on holiday. Roger-the-Ex, however, is a fervent and committed photographer. He and Chloe, and just about everyone else, insisted that I take a camera with me.

Roger brought round what he called a really simple camera. It weighed as much as a single-decker bus, had two bulky lenses which had to be screwed on and off the camera body according to the subject, and had enough scales of numbers for this and that to calculate the trajectory of the stars. I intended to be good and take it, but when I tried to practise the elementary changing of the lenses, I failed. It's just a knack, Roger explained. I didn't have it. When no one was looking, I hid the camera in its small padded suitcase behind the Hoover under the stairs and took off without it. My courage failed at the airport. I bought the smallest, most automatic camera that the duty free shop could sell me. It zoomed itself, adjusted itself for light and focus and wound itself on. It also fitted into my pocket. A compromise. So far, I hadn't used it.

I have a single photograph of my mother. It was taken after we had left Paramount Court, before the social workers and the University College Hospital shrinks sent me to boarding school, when she and I were living in a room in Mornington Crescent. We are in Trafalgar Square. I would have been eleven. The photograph was taken by one of those professional photographers who snap tourists. My mother and I are standing shoulder to shoulder, my left, her right arm around each other's back. Already I am as tall as her, she was barely five foot. I am, in the photo, what I was supposed to be. My hair is in plaits falling on to the front of my shoulders. The end of each plait is tied with wide ribbon into a bow. I have on a pale shirtwaister dress which falls below my knees, and a cardigan over it. I'm wearing thonged sandals so it must have been a sunny day, but for all that, my hands are covered in short white gloves. Very smart, very nice, my mother would have thought. She is in a floral frock, belted at the waist and falling almost to her ankles, as all her dresses did to hide the scar on one of her legs which was left after a road accident that happened before I was born. Her hair is dark and permed short, and she is wearing wrist-length white gloves like me. Around us pigeons are walking about, and the square is dotted with people in summer frocks and shirt sleeves. The black and white photo is faded and our faces are in shadow from the late afternoon sun behind us. My face is long and angular, hers is more rounded – now I think about it, she called it heart-shaped – but there is something sharp about her features. She is smiling directly into the camera, a posterity smile, a mother who is content to be with her daughter. My head is tipped slightly down, my chin towards my chest, and I am looking up, I now realise, with that Princess of Wales upward glance – shy or sly, hard to decide. I think there is the ghost of a smile on my face, but it's more shadowed than my mother's and it is a little difficult to tell. At our feet, extending along the ground and uninterrupted by pigeons, our shadows form a single elongated blot on the otherwise sunny macadam. It is a single shadow, we are standing too close for the sun to slip between our bodies. Her shadow and mine blur together into a unified shape, as umbilical as the creaky film of Shackleton's roped-together men trying to pull the *Endurance* through the ice floe.

Just before this picture was taken, I had been in a local authority home for a month or six weeks, somewhere by the sea, I don't remember where, but I recall walking in crocodile formation along cliffs with the sea to my right. I was there to give my mother a chance to get sorted out, said the social worker who took me there on the train. My mother was signed up for Social Security by the social worker and found the bedsitting room.

They also persuaded her that it would be a good idea if I went to the boarding school. A progressive, co-ed, vegetarian Quaker private school which took a few problem children paid for by their local authorities who were deemed too bright to go to the authority's schools for maladjusted children. It didn't work out so well. My mother kept turning up at the school in Hertfordshire and screaming either at me or at the staff about them keeping me from her and about me deserting her. After a term and a half, they asked me to leave because they couldn't deal with the disruption my mother caused. Later, at thirteen, when I went to live with my lost-and-found father, I went back to the school. That didn't work out so well, either. I was expelled, this time on my own account, for general waywardness, after eighteen months. Thereafter to Banbury to my father, then off to my mother, then into the hospital in Hove.

None of this is evident in the photo of my mother and me in Trafalgar Square on a sunny day, except perhaps in the shadows on our faces, but that, of course, is nothing more than a retrospective conceit.

'What more do you want to know?' asked Mrs Rosen when I phoned her a couple of weeks later and asked if I could see her again. 'We kept ourselves to ourselves. We don't know much.' It wasn't unkindly said, only defensive. I should have let it go, but I'd got home after the first meeting with them and spent several days in bed brooding. Not so much thinking about it, as shaken, as I hadn't expected to be, by the reality of my past in the reflection of their memories.

I knew that my parents were histrionic, but the slant on my father – not just a bit of a rogue, not just a bastard as my mother said, but a professional con man, not just a bad husband and womaniser, but as inclined to suicide attempts as my mother – gave me a fright. Between nature and nurture, it looked quite grim. I've been, for some time, as I put it to myself, all right. But how all right could I be, genetically and psychologically, with parents like that? I came from a family of suicidal hysterics. I'd been suicidal and hysterical in my time, then taken stock and made a decision, or just grown out of it, but now I felt, as I walked back to the car, that I might not have the choice of being anything else; that for years I had been deluding myself into the notion that I had a choice. What sent me to bed was the thought – no, the conviction – that I was the sum of those two people, that under the pretence of an achieved balance, more or less, I hadn't got a hope in hell of being other than what they were. I felt myself to have been all along skating over the thinnest sliver of ice; believing that it was solid when it was only ever a brittle and probably diminishing floe.

My father's emotional vulnerability was far more concealed, at least from me, than my mother's. When I was still very small, he was as beguiling to me as he had been to the ladies of Paramount Court. I adored him; he adored me. At weekends the two of us would roam London, take possession of it. Saturday mornings watching the Changing of the Guard, patting the horses standing guard in the street, my father egged me on to try to make the guardsmen laugh. In the afternoon, we would explore the museums; the British Museum, or the museums in Exhibition Road, roaming the Natural History, Geology and Science Museums, while he made up stories about the exhibits, ad-lib comedies that split my sides with laughter. *What a talker, such a charmer,* the old women had said, sighing. Sunday mornings at Petticoat Lane, buying pickled cucumbers, bagels and cream cheese, and then, after a Chinese lunch in Soho, an afternoon spent at the cinema, first at the news and cartoon house in the Charing Cross Road, and then to Leicester Square for a proper film, in the dark, the long tunnel of dusty light over our heads, his arm around me, my head against his shoulder.

I knew he loved me, and even after he had left the last of several times without making contact with me, I knew he *had* loved me. Now, after visiting the old women, there was a new thought: I had been charmed by a man who made his living charming women. I saw myself suddenly as another of his conquests. *Anybody would be taken in ... You had to love him,* the old people had said. This was a radical change of perspective; a brand-new loss. My father practising his skills on me. Some people cannot help but make people love them.

The first time I remember him leaving, I was about six or seven. 'He's gone, he's left,' my mother said. There's no way to convey the flatness, the despair in her words. You've heard it from time to time in the movie tones of Marlene Dietrich or Bette Davis. It was late, I'd been in bed for some time. I pretended to be asleep when she walked into the dark room and told me. I didn't know what to say, and I was frightened by what would happen to the voice if it was encouraged to go on. Besides, I had a despair of my own. He'd gone, he'd left.

It may have been the next day, or perhaps several days or weeks later, I can't remember, but I came home from school to find the bedroom door shut. My mother was often in bed.

I opened the door to a daylight-darkened room, the curtains closed, lights off, an artificial dusk. There was a noise, a moaning, a weird wailing and I saw my mother lying in bed. She was naked, but she always slept naked. Only she wasn't asleep. She was rolling frantically from side to side in the bed, the covers in turmoil, like someone with a high-grade fever. Spittle dribbled from the corners of her mouth. All the while she was rambling. Talking to God, complaining about her life, crying 'Help me, help me,' muttering maledictions.

I called 'Mummy' from the doorway, reluctant to go nearer, but she didn't answer, or notice that I was in the room, so I had to go closer to the bed.

'What's the matter?' I asked her, touching her clammy skin.

She flinched and stared wildly at me. A crazy woman.

'Don't you touch me,' she screamed. 'Who are you? Get out. I don't know you.'

What I remember is feeling nothing, just turning sharply to leave the flat, and businesslike, ringing the bell on the door opposite. We didn't know them, but a woman answered the door and I said, politely: 'My mother's ill, can you help, please?' A very practical kid. A bit of a cold fish, she must have thought when she entered the bedroom and found my mad mother writhing and keening in delirium.

They carried her off on a stretcher and someone in the flats, not Mrs Gold, Rosen or Levine, sent me to stay with a relative of theirs. Then I went to live with a family who I'd never met before, who it only lately occurred to me was a foster family, but who I was told were 'cousins'. Then my father turned up. Out of the blue as far as I was concerned. He took me back to the flat in

Paramount Court on that first visit, sat me on a dining chair and positioned himself on the floor in front of me, on his knees. He wept – this was the only time I saw his vulnerability and I hated it – begged my forgiveness, and made a solemn and formal promise through the tears (they dripped off the end of his nose, to my exquisite embarrassment) that he would never, never leave me again. Then we went back to the tenement flats – he couldn't look after me himself yet, he told me.

After that he came once a week and we went, not to Petticoat Lane, Exhibition Road or Leicester Square, but to visit my mother in the hospital. There was a lengthy bus ride and then what seemed a very long walk along a tree-lined suburban road. Invariably, during this walk I needed to pee, so each week we would knock at a different house and ask if I could use the bathroom. It became a game, a kind of roulette. I discovered all manner of different toilets, and best of all, one with a musical toilet roll. We were never refused, and sometimes we ended up having a cup of tea with the householders. The charming father and his young daughter were given tea and biscuits by extraordinarily kind and trusting people who, while I was on the loo, were doubtless told of our visit to the ailing wife and mother in the mental hospital up the road. I suppose they thought it was a shame, and such a nice man, poor child. Those brief visits were adventures into unknown worlds, to people whose houses and lives looked to me so solid and stable. Settled houses for real families with chintzy covered furniture that had the quality of eternity about it, and silver-plated teapots waiting in glass cupboards and brought out for visitors. Other lives. But frozen by a single visit into comfortable certainty. It was like going to the movies, too, and slipping through the light beams into the lives on the screen.

Until, of course, the reason for our being there could be put off no longer, and, for me, the price of being with my father had to be paid for by seeing my mother. She wasn't dramatically mad any more; she was a shell now, an emptiness, either drugged or semi-catatonic, or both, which passively received our bunch of flowers from the nurse, who took them from my hand and made approving noises as she placed them on my mother's lap, where they lay pointlessly until the nurse more practically went off with them to find a vase.

It seemed, however, that only with my mother's recovery was I going to get my father back. We would 'all live together again', my father assured me, when my mother got better. And it would be different, he said, there wouldn't be the terrible rows, and he would never leave me again. I'm sure it was put in terms of leaving me, and not my mother.

It took a while, but eventually she started to know who we were and managed a limp smile when we arrived. Soon there were stiff little visits to a back room in a local tea shop, and an occasion when both my mother and my father came and had tea with me at the foster woman's house. When we all went to live back in the flat, it was explained to me that Mummy was very fragile and I must be very careful about what I said. In fact, I always had been, but now the surface of the world itself had turned to delicate ice and we all tiptoed over it, my mother, too, pretending that everything was all right. Within a few months things returned to normal.

My father took me by the shoulders one day when I was almost eleven and almost finished at primary school. He told me that he was leaving for good. 'This time, I'm never coming back. Do you want to come with me, or stay with Mummy?' I have no idea why, except I didn't know where he was going, but I said hardly without a pause that I would stay with her. The decision remains a mystery, but I suppose it's reaching to call it a decision. It was more like a nervous reaction to a sudden announcement that life was going to change again, and to the nonsensical requirement that I state my preference there and then for good and all. His bags were already packed and in the hallway. My preference had always been for my father. I chose to stay with my mother and watched him disappear through the door with his suitcase. I don't know why.

Waiting again. For weeks we lived in the empty flat, while my mother sat helplessly in the armchair the bailiffs had left, telling me that when they finally came and threw us out we would go and live on the street – under the arches of Charing Cross, to be precise. We would practise, as she dragged me by the arm and whisked us out of the flat as if we were never going to return. 'What's the point of waiting to be thrown out? Now, we're on the streets.' And we'd walk around as if there was nowhere to go, as indeed, there soon wouldn't be, in the rain. I remember it as always raining on these occasions. Probably it wasn't always raining.

This time I couldn't stand the uncertainty. I had just started at grammar school, and went every day as if nothing unusual was happening. 'Don't say anything to anyone,' my mother instructed. 'If anyone asks about your father, say he's dead.' I did as I was told. Better a dead father than to admit to desertion. I wondered how I was going to manage going to school when we were living under the arches. I failed, repeatedly, to arrive at maths lessons with a geometry set. The cost was out of the question. I didn't even mention it to my mother. But every day at the beginning of maths, I had to stand up and confess that I still didn't have a geometry set. It became a class joke, whipped up by the archetypal sarcasm of the maths mistress. One morning, instead of leaving the flat and going to school, I lay down on the floorboards and started to scream. Two weeks later the social workers arrived, alerted to my non-attendance at school. I'd short-circuited the waiting.

'What more do you want to know?' asked Mrs Rosen, at the beginning of my second visit to Paramount Court.

I wanted to know what I had forgotten to ask about the first time.

'I wonder how you remember me as a child.'

'As a child,' she told me, 'you were very bright. You were the youngest of all our kids. You were the baby. But you were up to it. You were the cleverest. What they did, you could do, maybe better. You could talk! You could argue! You kept up with them. You could stand up to the others. You always knew how to stand up for yourself.'

There was a real atavistic, mother and child moment of satisfaction for me when Mrs Rosen offered me four-year-old Jennifer standing up for herself. It passed, but still the picture of obdurate, unputdownable Jennifer aged four pleased me. It also chimed with other memories of my childhood. Mostly, they were memories of being in trouble, of refusing to back down, of demanding my rights. There was a tough child, right from the start, with a sense of herself: a survivor, to put against the flaky genes and the training in hopelessness. I suppose, with the threat of my live or dead mother suddenly coming back into my life, I had gone to Mrs Rosen to find out just that. To check that there had once been and always was that survivor. And Mrs Rosen, inadvertently or not, gave her to me in an unexpected moment of good mothering.

The white picket fence surrounded Grytviken's graveyard, where past whalers were buried under neat white low headstones. I had climbed the hill to see Shackleton's grave, and it was immediately obvious, with its tall hewn granite post and 'Ernest Henry Shackleton, Explorer' carved on it and fresh alpine flowers at its foot. But another grave caught my eye, at right angles to Shackleton's. It had a low white headstone, but unlike the rest had a rough wooden cross standing over it. It too had fresh pink flowers and was the only other grave to have been regularly and carefully tended. The words burned into the wooden cross read:

RIP
FELIX 26.04.82 ARTUSO

Beneath the horizontal under the RIP there was a small painted rectangle made of a single white stripe sandwiched between two pale blue ones.

At the museum building, two soldiers sat on the steps leading up to the doorway. I said hello as I passed.

'You're English,' one of them declared, as a shipwrecked British traveller might greet his rescuer.

He was in his mid-twenties and his name was Andy (his friend's name was Scot, which I was to remember is spelled with one t).

I asked why they were patrolling with guns.

'Making sure they can be seen,' Andy told me.

'By whom?'

'The Argies. There's been a rumour going around that the troops here don't have any guns, so we've been making them visible.'

I looked around at the bay, which was deserted apart from the two half-sunken whalers and our white ship waiting for our return.

'Who's looking?'

'Spies on the ships. We've got to let them know not to mess with us.'

I asked Andy about Felix Artuso, up on the hill. He reminded me that South Georgia had been taken by a small group of Argentinian soldiers posing as scrap-metal merchants. Fourteen marines went into hiding and then fought them off. Fifteen Argentinians were killed, according to Andy, though the official number was three. Young Felix Artuso was one of them. A marine came face to face with him and, thinking he was going for a gun, shot first. It turned out that Felix was unarmed.

'It's what happens in war,' said Andy sorrowfully, speaking very respectfully of Artuso, like a fallen comrade. 'His parents wanted him to be buried on South Georgia. The Brits buried him with full military honours. It's the way we do things.'

Since the war, three soldiers had died on South Georgia. One saved his two-can allowances of beer for a Friday piss-up and thought he could swim across the bay. He froze to death in about seven minutes. Another also got drunk and fell during an inadvisable walk in the middle of the night, dying of exposure. An Irish Ranger died from cold and injuries while trying to climb one of the mountains on his own.

'The boredom gets to you,' explains Andy. 'It was really nice to talk to someone from home.'

In the museum I got three copies of a postcard of Shackleton, his hair parted in the middle and slicked down, looking uncomfortable in front of the camera, but wonderfully handsome in a rugged way. He looked as roguish as he seems to have been. A bit of a con man, who took off on the *Endurance* expedition before the money was actually available, leaving others to sort out the mess. Something of a ladies' man, he was, in his charming Irish way. Brother Frank went the whole way and was actually imprisoned for some financial shenanigans with the English aristocracy.

It was beginning to rain, and the sky was darkening. The glorious sunshine instantly became a thing of the past. I began to see that things might be surprisingly changeable around these parts. As the wind got up, suddenly Grytviken was a dour, deserted place. For the first time I started to feel cold and damp. It happened from one moment to the next. A small shiver of bleakness that was not entirely related to the weather ran through me. I felt quite happy to get into one of the first returning Zodiacs and head back for cabin 532. My first landing hadn't been either white or solitary.

By the afternoon, the world had turned industrial grey. While we were having lunch, the ship sailed a short distance south, lurching through a disturbed sea, down to St Andrew's Bay for our second scheduled landing. St Andrew's Bay was the great penguin treat of the trip. We were warned that the landing would be cut short if the wind got any worse. It took about fifteen minutes to get to the shore as the dinghy tacked and swerved to avoid the worst of the head-on wind. It was, however, the most exhilarating ride I've ever had, fast and furious, the motor buzzing angrily against a wind that howled past my ears and made my eyes water salt tears to match the salt spray covering my face. We were so close to it, intimate now with the movement of the waves, the weather, the Antarctic sea. When not lying on my bunk or staring out from the bridge, I'd choose this. From time to time when we smacked into a big wave, I laughed out loud.

As we approached the slightly protected Bay, the wind let up a little and it was possible to look up, straight ahead towards the land. We were being watched. The long shoreline and the beach right back to the glacier and mountains were packed so tight with penguins that they formed a continuous carpet. A legion of black faces and orange beaks pointed out to sea facing in our direction, seeming to observe our arrival. One day, once a year or so, black rubber dinghies approach, and a handful of people come to the Bay, believing that the penguins are watching them arrive. For the penguins, it's just another day of standing and staring. They parted slightly to make way for us, but they still stood looking out to sea. We were not part of their existence, presented no obvious danger and therefore were ignored, quite overlooked. If you stood in their way as they waddled along their track from nest to sea to feed, they stopped a few inches from your feet and made a small, semi-circular detour around you, as they would if they found a boulder in their way. If you got down on your knees and faced them eyeball to eyeball, they looked back, turning an eye towards you, but deciding what you were not, lost interest rapidly.

I was very taken with this timeless standing, unwitnessed, unwitnessing, that we were interrupting, though only barely. That was the point, for me, of Antarctica; that it was simply there, always had been, always would be, with great tracts of the continent unseen, unwitnessed, cycling though its two seasons, the ice rolling slowly from the centre to the edges, where eventually it breaks off.

The weather had worsened. It was now dark, as if dusk had fallen, a twilight that in this Antarctic summer does not occur. After fifteen or twenty minutes' walking along the beach, the wet and icy blasts began to seep through the layers as if they were merely gauze. When it reached the flesh, I felt I had an inkling of what it means to be cold, but then it went deeper, and after half an hour it had gone beyond the skin and directly into the bones. My very marrow was chilled, I felt iced and saturated from head to foot. It was as if the wind, having got my measure, was denying my existence and simply rattling through me. I have never felt so unprotected in my life as in that bleak, dark landscape where there is absolutely nowhere to shelter. Only in those dreams where you find yourself walking naked down a busy street, have I felt as vulnerable.

The next morning around 6.15, I lay shivery in my bunk with a sore throat. I had a streaming, screaming head cold and felt ghastly. I had woken at four to the unrelenting daylight feeling a bit dispirited, a small damp weight inside of me. A tiny blueness. When I thought about it, perhaps it was a moment of panic at being out of reach of anywhere, hundreds of miles out of sight of land. Now I got my achey self up to look out of the window. The sky was dove grey with heavy, snow-laden cloud, and the snow was falling softly, making the windswept wilderness of the Antarctic sea as silent as any suburban winter garden. The horizon was a very long way away. I skipped breakfast and both of the day's lectures designed to help fill our at-sea time, devoting the day to my cold, my bunk, my book and the view from my window. Sleeping, reading and staring out at the snow and sea. I could have done this forever. No Sister Winniki to nag. Just left alone to take all the pleasure I wanted in indolence. What more could anyone want?

And then in the evening the first iceberg floated by my window.

The iceberg emerged before my lazy gaze like a mirage, a dream appearance, a matte white edifice ghostly in the misty grey light and falling snow. A sudden, smoothly gliding event in the great empty sea under the great empty sky. I blinked at it. There was none of the disappointing familiarity of something seen too often on TV or in picture books. This startled with its brand-new reality, with its quality of not-like-anything-else. Even the birds seemed to have hushed for our entrance into the land of ice. The tannoy squawked into life, and Butch, our leader (well, no, he wasn't really called that, but he'll always be Butch to me), announced: 'Ladies and gentlemen, we have icebergs.'

Time to get up. I pulled on a track suit and headed up to the bridge, where I discovered that, like a momentous theatrical production, we were proceeding into real Antarctica through a corridor of icebergs. As far as the eye could see, to either side of us, icebergs lined our route. We'd arrived in iceberg alley. It was absurdly symmetrical, like a boulevard in space. The bergs were tabular, exactly as described, flat as a table on top, as if someone had planed away their peaks, too smooth to be real, too real to be true. It took about an hour before we had sailed through iceberg alley, and all the time we stood and watched in silence.

The icebergs close up, even quite far away, were not daydream white at all. Blue. Icebergs are blue. At their bluest, they are the colour of David Hockney swimming pools, Californian blue, neon blue, Daz blue-whiteness blue, sometimes even indigo. They were deepest blue at sea level, and where cracks and crevices gave a view of the inside of the berg, where the ice was the oldest and so compacted that all the air had been forced out.

These floating mountains of blue ice shaded with white, white ice shaded blue, were not slick and shiny like ice-rink ice. They were dense islands of compressed icing sugar. Confections that lit up the lead-coloured sea and sky. All night they floated along, carved into ancient shapes: ships, castles, monuments, mythic creatures – none of the explorers who described them managed to avoid these descriptions. But sometimes, and most impressively, they were simply vast walls of ice, passing so near to my window that they cut out the rest of the world. A great blank wall of ancient compacted snow that had travelled from the blank centre of the Antarctic continent for centuries – the deepest ice is ten thousand years old – to its edges, to become a tongue of glacier or the very periphery of the ice cap, and has finally broken off ('calved' is the correct term) to sail away on its own. The bergs head north and west at a rate of five miles a day, until they reach the Convergence, where the Antarctic meets warmer seas. Some of them last for ten years, until the sea erodes and melts them to nothing.

I went back to bed at breakfast-time and slept through until late morning. I woke feeling rotten. Everything ached, my head was thick and I still felt sick and crampy. I couldn't move, not even to take a pill, not even to check out the state of the icebergs.

What was going to happen to my Antarctic adventure if I sank for days into my bunk? We were coming into Admiralty Bay, where humpback whales were supposed to hang out. Well, I could look out of the window if there were any sightings. Though only if they were on my side of the ship. I didn't want to see whales with a whole bunch of people on the bridge or the deck. I didn't want to be in a crowd watching whales, even if it meant missing them. I wanted to see my own whale out of my own window, all by myself. I imagined explaining to friends on my return to England how I didn't manage to see a whale. Wrong side of the ship. Didn't get up. Oh dear.

Another morning, and the tannoy announced that we were as far south as we were going to get: 63.42°S, 55.57°W. We had arrived in the early hours at the Antarctic Sound and Butch had arranged a Zodiac cruise around the masses and masses of icebergs we were surrounded by. The sun blazing beyond my window, and the sea glacially still. There wasn't a ripple to be seen on the turquoise surface, nothing but the sharp reflections of the bergs. Suddenly, I felt a bit better. Time to get up. I very much wanted to get close up to the icing-sugar mountains, and down near the surface of the brilliant sea.

To be at the base of an iceberg, rocking on the sea is a remarkable feeling. The cold radiated off the wall of the berg and I peered into crevices that went to the heart of the ice. Everything was flat and still except for the bergs ranged about us as we weaved in and out between them. The ship at anchor, as white and still as a berg, belonged, another mythic shape in the landscape, and didn't seem to impose itself. It was uncanny and peaceful, but deceptive. This was not a place, though it was a position on a navigation chart. Nothing about this area would be quite the same again, as floes and bergs floated and melted, winds whipped up the presently calm sea, seals made temporary lodging, and flotillas of penguins porpoised around the ship in the distance like flying fish. Everything about this seascape would change, but it would also remain essentially the same, its elements merely rejiggled. It was so untroubled by itself that the heart ached. Other landscapes fidget – rainforests full of plants and creatures clamouring for a living, moors troubled and ruffled by scathing, distorting winds, mountains trembling with the weight of snow – but this was truly a dream place where melting and movement seemed only to increase immutability. Nothing stays the same, but nothing changes.

The afternoon arrives and with a moving determination to get their passengers on to the landmass of Antarctica (even though it isn't really – the Peninsula is connected to the mainland of Antarctica by a permanent ice bridge), Butch and Captain Kalashnikov have found a place to land. Hope Bay. Butch grabs our arms in his sailor's handshake and welcomes each of us on to the seventh continent. Here is the snowy landscape, as rugged and mountainous as those places we've landed before, but here is permanent snow which crunches crisply under the sole of my Wellington boot, until, as if to prove that I too am here, one leg disappears down a crevasse. It's not much of a crevasse, I only go down up to my thigh. Not the kind of chasm that swallowed several of Shackleton's dogs and left them swinging in space while the men desperately tried to pull them up, but an assurance, nevertheless, that I am where I am. I am heartily congratulated as helping hands get me up, and then the excitement shifts to another woman, who while standing still on a small prominence, gazing around, has just been swept off her feet and blown flat on her back by the wind.

'Well,' she says, a mite peppery, as she brushes herself off. 'Well! What a thing!'

There is, Butch informs us, a katabatic wind accompanying the clear skies, in the order of forty-five knots. Along with our landing party there are once again a hundred thousand or so penguins, chinstraps this time, spread over a kilometre of snowy land. At the shore an astonishing game is being played, which even the expedition crew are hypnotised by. A crowd of penguins are standing in a line waiting their turn to leap on to a small ice shelf, one by one. Once on the shelf they dive into the sea and then vault back on to the ice shelf, then on to land to go to the back of the queue and have another go. There is no purpose in this, other than that it looks like a lot of fun. We sit for half an hour or so watching the penguins splashing and leaping in their own private playpool.

The snow I have been waiting for is there all right, even the southern summer doesn't melt it down here, but it is hardly white, covered as it is with the green, pink and yellow droppings of tens of thousands of penguins. The sky is once again darkening, but although the wind is strong, it doesn't feel threatening. I follow a penguin track along the perimeter of the small cliff above the beach and then head down, clambering round the rocks to a tiny isolated cove. There are hunks of ice washed up on its beach, a few sleeping seals, and a couple of penguins standing around. One penguin is asleep with its head under its wing, the other is lying flat out on its stomach. I find a handy rock to sit on and suddenly here I am, just where I want to be, in a snowy, lonely place. It's possible that nobody has ever sat on this rock, that no one will ever sit in this precise place ever again. Petrels and skuas cry overhead and the wind blows around the corner of the cove. The sea around the shore is churned up with ice, broken into small pieces that bob about in the water. A penguin pops out of the sea, as if from nowhere, stops for an instant as it sees me, an unexpected sight, but nothing bad happens, so it carries on and joins the other two on the beach. I sit on for another hour, doing nothing, just leaning back against the rock, being on the beach with the penguins and seals. Very briefly, living their life.

The house was empty when I got home. I like the silence of an empty flat after I've been away, it gives a chance to repossess the place. Piles of post on the kitchen table with a note from Chloe saying she'd opened anything interesting looking, and it turned out nothing was. On my desk in the study was a small pile of papers topped by another note from Chloe. 'About your Mum – I went to Hove with Dad to your Mum's house.'

Chloe had been busy while I was away. On top of the pile was a certificate. It stated that Rachel Simmonds, otherwise Rene Simmonds, maiden name unknown, had died on 28 March 1988 at the Royal Sussex Hospital, Brighton. The cause of death was: a) subdural haemorrhage; b) carcinomatosis and c) carcinoma of the pancreas. Someone called Betty Young had reported the death officially and caused the body to be cremated. The last address of the deceased was 3 Third Avenue, Hove, East Sussex.

What Chloe had discovered on her sleuthing trip to Hove was that, in her last years, my mother had lived with a man called Jack. 'One of the men in the flat remembered her. He said that your mother and Jack were always at each other's throats, the house shook with their fights. But after Jack died, he said she seemed to lose the will to live, had nothing to live for ... She didn't seem to have changed much from when you knew her. Are you upset?' Chloe wondered in her note.

It was terrible, I suppose, but I was relieved to find that she had remained just as I remembered her – or that she had been as I remembered her. Not fair on her – as ever. But starting to read Chloe's note, I had a sharp moment of anxiety that everything I recalled might have been imagined, fantasised, fictioned. Or, perhaps, that having got rid of a wicked and ungrateful daughter, she might have become another, renewed person. How would I have felt about that? Pleased for her, if I were halfway decent. But I'm not. I preferred my mother's continued unhappiness to finding myself to have been deluded all these years.

I've tried from time to time to give her her due. She wasn't a neglectful mother: erratic, demanding, helpless, alarming, but not neglectful. She was devoted to me, to how I looked, to my health, to what I ate, to my progress at school. And perhaps she loved me. I don't know how you would define that in these circumstances. I know she thought having a child guaranteed that she would be loved. That was what she found so unnatural about me. Sometimes she said: 'I have to love you, you are my daughter.' Love was obligation, and in saying that, she reminded me of my obligation to her – which I was too sullen and obstinate to fulfil. I would have preferred to have been loved for some reason, some quality other than the accident of birth. But very likely she meant what most people mean when they talk about the unconditional love parents have for their children. It could have been a kind of assurance, but it didn't assure me. She even had a story, not thousands, like my father, but just one which she told me at bedtime if my father wasn't back, and when I was ill and she sat through the night with me and my fever. It was a version of *The Water-Babies* without the water, but with Tom the boy sweep, befriended by a girl, by Jennifer, who took care of him and saved him from his wicked father. I relished this story in which I was the hero, and always wanted to hear it. This is the warmth I remember, when I make a special effort not to deny my mother her emotional rights.

What struck me most forcibly, though, was not that she was dead, but that she had been alive for twenty years after I had last seen her. That is, been *alive* all that time while I had been living my life. It was as if the painting of my past had acquired a shadow, a new presence, separate but lurking darkly around corners. The past became more cluttered than I had pictured it up to then. There had been the possibility, the retrospective possibility, that she might have made contact, might, as in my worst early hours anxiety, have turned up in my life. She hadn't; she might have. Only for the last eight years had she truly not existed; only since 1988 had I been orphaned, really safe.

2 January 1997

The Girl in the Attic

I wonder if to be Jewish is to be by definition lonely in the world – not as a result of the history, but on account of the theology. If ardent young men attending the yeshiva have traditionally engaged each other in intense arguments nagging at the nicer points of interpreting the Torah, it is surely because the Jewish God is notorious for evading questions directed at him. Was there ever such a one for sliding out of an argument as Jahweh? The last time he responded to a direct question must have been when the blameless Job, suffering a foreshadowing of the twentieth century with the loss of his children, his worldly goods and afflicted with all manner of physical ills, demanded – quite politely under the circumstances – to know why of his maker. 'Where,' boomed the Lord, 'wast thou when I laid the foundations of the earth? ... Hath the rain a father? ... Out of whose womb came the ice? ... Canst thou draw out leviathan with a hook?' All interesting questions, but not really to Job's point. God does not seem to be a good communicator. Too busy with the overall scheme of things, perhaps. He'll give out ten blanket rules, but he won't tell you why your life seems to be so bloody difficult lately. The problem of the senior executive without the common touch. Catholicism seems to have understood the Almighty's failing and provided its faithful with a bevy of more approachable undermanagers, each with their own speciality, willing and able to intercede with on high on behalf of the baffled individual. A Catholic knows exactly who to apply to when hoping for better health, safe travel, release from drudgery or persecution. There is a saint for almost everything that ails you. For the Jews, however, there is only a single very busy, self-important and fractious God. So it seemed to me when I was young. I was troubled by the unreliability of prayer, rather as one feels anxious about sending important letters to large organisations.

Anne Frank is the only Jewish saint. I first read the diary of Anne Frank when I was about the same age as she was when she began to write it. She seemed to me to fit the bill perfectly as a possible intercessor. Perhaps, in the years after the war, young Jewish girls all over Europe discovered her as a saint all their own: someone to share the miseries of pre-adolescence, someone to turn to in times of aching solitariness within their raucous families, who would without doubt understand. She sounded so like oneself, and yet she was dead, which gave her a necessary gravitas. She may have personified the Holocaust for millions of adults – the diary is the most widely read non-fiction book after the Bible – but for me, aged twelve or thirteen, she simply told the story of what it is like to be twelve or thirteen in a world where no one seems to be listening to you. Read the diary without hindsight (impossible for any adult, of course, but not so difficult when you are a child looking for a literary friend) and it is a masterly description of the sorrows and turmoil of any bright, raging, self-dramatising young girl. Read in this way, in the way I first read it, the sequestration becomes peripheral, the fear of capture secondary. 'I don't fit in with them' is an early and continuous complaint that for me, at the time, quite overrode Anne Frank's particular circumstances. Being locked in an attic in fear of one's life was, to my mind, just another version of being trapped with the family. What counted was someone who looked not very different from me, saying precisely what was on my mind. Anne Frank, wanting to be a writer, precocious, isolated, furiously adolescent and angry with her family, was the point.

> Last night I went downstairs in the dark, all by myself ... I stood at the top of the stairs while German planes flew back and forth, and I knew I was on my own, that I couldn't count on others for support. My fear vanished. I looked up at the sky and trusted in God. I have an intense need to be alone. Father noticed I'm not my usual self, but I can't tell him what's bothering me. All I want to do is scream: 'Let me be, leave me alone!'

I knew that the war, the Holocaust and the tragedy of a young and pointless death was what I was supposed to be reading the diary for, but I was far too engaged with her inner story to pay much attention to the other stuff. Now, of course, reading it from the other end of the age telescope the story looks a little ambiguous. Quite a good family, as families go: liberal, affectionate, willing to tolerate the moods of a difficult adolescent, and under an unimaginable pressure. There's a new sympathy for Mrs Frank as she turns away from her daughter, who has refused to allow her to listen to her prayers instead of her father: '"I don't want to be angry with you. I can't make you love me!" A few tears slid down her cheeks as she went out of the door.' Anne's main complaint against Mrs Frank is that she doesn't take her seriously. 'The truth is that she has rejected me,' she writes after this incident. 'She's the one whose tactless comments and cruel jokes about matters I don't think are funny have made me insensitive to any sign of love on her part.' Everybody behaving just how they are supposed to, I think now. A good enough family under any circumstances, let alone theirs.

But imagine the liberation of reading at the age of twelve or thirteen:

> I simply can't stand Mother ... I don't know why
> I've taken such a terrible dislike to her. Daddy says
> that if Mother isn't feeling well or has a headache,
> I should volunteer to help her, but I'm not going
> to because I don't love her and don't enjoy doing
> it. I can imagine Mother dying someday, but
> Daddy's death seems inconceivable. It's very mean
> of me, but that's how I feel. I hope Mother will
> *never* read this or anything else I've written.

In fact, I didn't read that the first time. That passage from the entry of 3 October 1942 was heavily edited by her father, Otto Frank. The entry I read concluded: 'Daddy would like me to offer to help Mummy sometimes, when she doesn't feel well or has a headache, but I won't. I am working hard at my French and am now reading *La Belle Nivernaise*.' This is not just a new translation, but The Definitive Edition of *The Diary of a Young Girl*. That 'but I won't' was quite thrilling, it suggested a fervent obstinacy which was very attractive, but 'because I don't love her and don't enjoy doing it' would have offered more than a stubborn young girl, would have given me and the world an Anne Frank who had the horrible honesty of a writer who says what there is to be said, even if it is unspeakable. Niceness was not her project; describing how things were was what she was doing, at first for herself and later with the idea of publication. There are three versions of the diary: Version A is the first unedited diary; Version B is her own edited variant, worked on when, in 1944, Gerrit Bolkestein, a member of the Dutch government in exile, broadcast from London his wish to collect eyewitness accounts of the Dutch Occupation and publish them after the war; Version C is the one Otto Frank cut and culled from Versions A and B and what we have read. There is a Critical Edition which lays out all three versions side by side, so the Definitive Edition is not new, but culled itself, adding about a third more material, but also dropping some of the text. This is the kind of publishing history you might expect of the testimony of a saint; authorised, unauthorised and apocrypha.

It was perfectly reasonable for Otto Frank to censor his daughter's diaries. Of the eight people in hiding he was the only survivor and Anne's pent-up peevishness about her mother, sister and the Van Daans – who shared the secret Annexe with the Frank family – did not serve the purpose he intended in publishing his dead daughter's diary. In a schools' version (Otto Frank's version, edited by Christopher Martin) published by Longman's to commemorate the first national Anne Frank Day on 12 June 1996, the inside front cover states: 'By thinking about Anne Frank and her message to the world, it is hoped that the day will enhance young people's spiritual, moral, social and cultural development.' This is not exactly the personal saint I envisaged, but a Jewish version of St Thérèse of Lisieux, the Little White Flower, who was canonised in spite of a complete absence of the usual mandatory miracles, for dying an early death and struggling with her dislike of some of the Sisters in her Carmelite convent. St Anne, like St Thérèse, was offered to the world as an example. Each put up with their respective lots: the Nazis and tuberculosis. What father, and what champion of martyrdom, is going to include his daughter's detailed description of her vulva ('In the upper part, between the outer labia, there's a fold of skin that, on second thought, looks like a kind of blister. That's the clitoris'), or her haughty dismissal of her mother ('I need my mother to set a good example and be a person I can respect, but in most matters she's an example of what *not* to do') or her irritation at her father ('Father's fondness for talking about farting and going to the lavatory is disgusting'). There are moments of saint-like repentance, but they rarely come without a sting in the tale.

> I was offended, took it far too much to heart and was insolent and beastly to her, which, in turn, made her unhappy ... The period of tearfully passing judgment on Mother is over. I've grown wiser and Mother's nerves are a bit steadier. Most of the time I manage to hold my tongue when I'm annoyed, and she does too ... but there's one thing I can't do, and that's to love Mother with the devotion of a child.

Right from the start, the diary was personified. 'To enhance the image of the long-awaited friend in my imagination, I don't want to jot down the facts in this diary the way most people would do, but I want the diary to be my friend, and I'm going to call this friend *Kitty*.' 'Dearest Kitty' is how all the entries begin, and they end, 'Yours Anne', or later, 'Yours Anne M. Frank'. It enables her not just to grumble about her parents and the other members of the Annexe, but also to practise a heroic jauntiness, a public voice: 'I look upon our life in hiding as an interesting adventure, full of danger and romance, and every privation as an amusing addition to my diary.' She apologises and tries for distance when a previous entry has sounded depressed, and makes sure that Kitty gets a thorough and up-to-date picture of everyday life in hiding. The beginning of the entry for 13 December 1942 is disturbingly vivid, but also literary, reminiscent of young Jane Eyre reading alone behind the curtains in the window seat: 'I'm sitting here nice and cosy in the front office, peering out through a chink in the heavy curtains. It's dark, but there's just enough light to write by.' Making the diary her reader allows Anne Frank to be a writer, to get a sense of the overall work, to balance it, to convey a mood, to reach for an effect.

> To Father, peeling potatoes is not a chore, but precision work. When he reads, he has a deep wrinkle in the back of his head. But when he's preparing potatoes, beans or vegetables, he seems to be totally absorbed in his task. He puts on his potato-peeling face, and when it's set in that particular way, it would be impossible for him to turn out anything less than a perfectly peeled potato.

This is Anne with her public-writing face on, and there's pleasure and great sadness in witnessing her working like this. 'I've made up my mind to lead a different life from other girls, and not to become an ordinary housewife later on.'

Her burgeoning love for Peter van Daan is also part of the work. She creates a romance out of poor material, but all there is to hand. Peter, whose name is the same as that of a boy she had a crush on before they went into hiding, serves to practise on. At first he seems to lack qualities of mind and personality she would prefer, but Anne is undaunted and begins to perceive all manner of gentleness and shyness that she can use to transform him into a suitable first love. They sit close and alone watching the stars. The first kiss is breathlessly described to Kitty: 'How I suddenly made the right movement, I don't know, but before we went downstairs, he gave me a kiss, through my hair, half on my left cheek and half on my ear. I tore downstairs without looking back, and I long so much for today.' And then, just a few pages later, the falling away of a passion she couldn't, and under normal circumstances wouldn't, be expected to sustain: 'I forced Peter, more than he realises, to get close to me, and now he's holding on for dear life. I honestly don't see any effective way of shaking him off ... I soon realised he would never be a kindred spirit.'

The diary ends with an entry for Tuesday, 1 August 1944, in which she describes herself as a bundle of contradictions, wondering who she would be if she could be truly herself: 'if only there were no other people in the world.' Two days later the SS arrive and we are briefly informed in an afterword of the final fate of the members of the Annexe. There's a curious hiatus here.

We have witnessed Anne Frank's life and development over a period of two years, then we hear how, seven months later, she died of typhus in Bergen-Belsen just a few days after her sister Margot, and a month before the camp was liberated. But from the moment of discovery in the attic, to her final illness, Anne, who has been so vividly herself, disappears into the mass. We've followed her fears, first love, anger and joy, but it is impossible to follow her imaginatively as she is transported across Europe, when the irritations of family, the hormonal ups and downs, the dreams all disappear in a fearful reality that she refused to imagine in her letters to Kitty. Later, thanks to one of her Dutch protectors finding and saving the diary, she was to become the most famous victim of the Holocaust, and does achieve her ambition: 'I can't imagine having to live like Mother, Mrs van Daan and all the women who go about their work and are then forgotten ... I don't want to have lived in vain like most people. I want to be useful or bring enjoyment to all people, even those I've never met. I want to go on living even after my death.' But there is something haunting about her absence during those first weeks after she was discovered and the diary was silenced. She disappears into a fog of cattle trucks too full of humanity to see any one individual clearly. She becomes part of a mass disaster, and as alone as it is possible to be. It is in her sudden anonymity that Anne Frank becomes most emblematic of all the individuals caught up in the midst of an immense tragedy.

6 March 1997

Mrs Straus's Devotion

We are moved but not overwrought at the fate of those who died at Pompeii, with the sinking of the *Mary Rose*, during the San Francisco earthquake and at the collapse of the Tay Bridge. We respond much more uneasily to the sinking of the *Herald of Free Enterprise*, the *Estonia* and the *Marchioness*. Lives cut short are less poignant once, to paraphrase Beckett, they would have died anyway. We are on the cusp of having the emotional load of the sinking of the *Titanic* lightened, but not quite there yet. As I write, there are at least two, and possibly seven, very elderly survivors of the disaster still alive, but late twentieth-century impatience – with age, with taste, for trivia – has made us run a little ahead of ourselves. So it is with unconcealed regret that the authors of the *Titanic* cookbook point out that there is no way of knowing exactly what was on the menu at the super-first class à la carte restaurant on the evening of 14 April 1912, because 'unfortunately, none of the surviving passengers who ate there on the last evening tucked a copy of the menu into the pocket of a dinner-jacket, so we can only surmise what the bill of fare included.' That would not be an insurmountable obstacle in itself: one of the less fortunate passengers might have provided the clue. A damaged but still partly legible menu from 12 April 'recovered from the body of a third-class passenger' is given a full-page reproduction (porridge, smoked herrings and jacket potatoes for breakfast), to prove the authenticity of the small steerage-class recipe section that follows.

The problem here is modern longevity. It is, after all, eighty-five years since the unsinkable liner sank; how long are we expected to wait before we can get down to building the *Titanic* theme park? Now, with this glossy volume, the *Titanic* experience can be yours – at least the dry part of it. Along with the recipes for the dishes served that night in first, second and steerage class, there are complete instructions for hosting a *Titanic* dinner party: 'The more you can choreograph the evening to create a period atmosphere, the more you and your guests will feel as though you've travelled back in time to the evening of 14 April 1912.' In order to get fully into the spirit of things, formal invitations and dress advice should be sent out weeks in advance on facsimiles of actual cabin tickets 'filled out with their names, the number of servants accompanying them, and the number of cubic feet of luggage to be taken'. Apparently, the compilers of *Last Dinner on the 'Titanic'* are not anticipating that many readers will re-enact the last meal in steerage, though a perfectly edible supper of vegetable soup, roasted pork with sage and pearl onions and plum pudding with sweet sauce is included for the down-market fantasists among us. This is perhaps the first of a series of last suppers, to include recipes and suggestions for staging a Hiroshima sashimi evening, a Dresden barbecue, the *Marchioness* cocktail party, and God knows what they munched with the Marquis during the 120 days of Sodom, but I dare say they rustled up something on day 119 that we could recreate in our own dining rooms.

Fantasy and cultural myth-making have been the main responses to the sinking of the *Titanic* almost from the moment the news was received in the wider world. *Titanic* has abounded in meaning, the actual event almost submerged by its multiple suitability as social metaphor. Analogy is irresistible when a vast floating city is scuppered in a glacially calm sea by the overlooked remnants of an off-the-beaten-track iceberg. The *Titanic* foundered because the sea was calm: no one expected trouble and the smoothness of the waves concealed the jagged lump of ice that would have been tossed and therefore made visible in a stormier ocean. The ship, hailed as the apotheosis of progress and modern engineering, sank so rapidly as a result of brittle fracture, the low-grade steel of the period breaking violently when chilled. The bald meteorological and technological facts are overwhelmed by the irony of calm waters and fragile steel scuttling the complacency of the very rich in first class, and the hopes of the dispossessed in steerage. The *Titanic* was a ship of fools. As John Wilson Foster tells us (in *The 'Titanic' Complex*), the grand staircase came in William and Mary style, though the balustrade was Louis XIV; the first-class dining saloon and reception rooms were Jacobean, the restaurant Louis XVI, the lounge Louis XV (Versailles), the reading and writing room late Georgian, the smoking room early Georgian. The women's clothes were newly purchased from Paris couture houses; and tucked into a pocket of whatever finely cut suit the bibliophile Harry Widener was wearing (for all we know, along with that elusive à la carte menu) was a 1598 edition – possibly the only copy – of Bacon's essays. 'If he was lost at sea,' he had promised the London dealer, 'the Bacon would go down clasped to his heart.' In keeping with common ideas of the behaviour of the very rich, the *Titanic* cookbook explains that the à la carte restaurant, whose food and service were superior even to the first-class dining room, was not part of the White Star liner's inclusive price. Passengers who took their meals there instead of the first-class saloon, paid at the time for what they ate, though they were entitled to apply for a rebate at the end of the voyage. After the sinking of the *Titanic*, several survivors put in their claims for a rebate, confirming, we are told by the cookbook's authors, who know how to extrapolate what is important from such details, 'that the restaurant had become an immediate hit'. One longs to know whether the applications were merely for their own extra expenditure on food, or if they included the bills of their lost loved ones' gourmet feasts.

Of all the emblematic themes that surrounded the sinking of the *Titanic*, the apparent obedience to the principle of 'women and children first' was the most engaging. It confirmed not just the idea of the difference between the sexes, but also the innate nobility of the upper classes, for a world on the brink of the Great War. The survivor statistics offered by Steven Biel in *Down with the Old Canoe* tell something of the gender story: 94 per cent of first-cabin women and children survived compared to 31 per cent of first-cabin men; 81 per cent of second-cabin and 47 per cent of steerage women survived against 10 per cent and 14 per cent respectively of men in those two classes. As a story of social class rather than gender, the overall figures show that 60 per cent of first-cabin passengers, 44 per cent of second-cabin and 25 per cent of steerage passengers survived.

'Does not the heart of every true American woman go out in tender loyalty to those brave men of the *Titanic* who yielded their valuable lives that the weak and helpless might live?' asked a letter writer in the *New York Times*. There is more here than a mere paean to old-world chivalry and one in the eye for the army of suffragists demanding equal rights: there is a note of regret that such financial and industrial eminences as John Jacob Astor, Benjamin Guggenheim, Isidor Straus and Harry Widener should have given up their lives not just to their own women, but to impoverished foreigners – the Guggenheims and Strauses apparently being accorded an honorary Aryanness for the occasion. The *San Francisco Examiner* eulogised the heroes whose place in the lifeboats and in the world was taken 'by some sabot-shod, shawl-enshrouded, illiterate and penniless woman of Europe'. The essential nobility of the rich and famous, indeed the natural rightness of their wealth and fame, was confirmed by the public image of these men standing on the deck in tuxedos, smoking elegant cigarettes while the *Titanic* slipped ineluctably under the water. For the virulently anti-suffragist and those especially alarmed by suffragist demands for more liberal divorce laws, Ida Straus, the wife of the Macy's executive, became a feminine icon as she refused her place in the lifeboat, choosing instead to stay and die with her husband. 'In this day of frequent and scandalous divorces,' declaimed one editorial, 'when the marriage tie once held so sacred to all is too lightly regarded, the wifely devotion and love of Mrs Straus for her partner of a lifetime stand out in noble contrast.'

The *Titanic* was known to be unsinkable, however. The slowness to react of everyone from the crew to the passengers testifies to the lack of alarm. It is entirely possible that the men who waited on the deck with such aplomb did not believe their lives to be in imminent danger. The ship sank astonishingly fast after what seemed a minor collision with a small iceberg. The visible evidence of damage was minimal. As Biel points out, 'the attitude of the first-cabin male passengers might just as well have been complacency as heroic calm.' One surviving passenger remembered that at the time he left the *Titanic* there was difficulty in filling all the lifeboats, as the danger had not yet been fully realised by the passengers. It might well have seemed that a place in the lifeboat was no more than an extra safety precaution, and further, Biel suggests, the chances of the women surviving in the freezing waters of the North Atlantic in an open lifeboat were considerably less than those of the men waiting on deck for the crisis to blow over. If we aren't happy at the suggestion that the heroes of the *Titanic* might have been doing little more than paying lip service to chivalry, and were in fact in what they thought, until it was too late, was the optimum situation, then perhaps our times are less transgressive than they seem. But perhaps this interpretation makes a dismal modern sense of apparently altruistic behaviour. Moreover, the Strauses' example of marital fidelity was balanced by several clandestine liaisons. The two sons of a wealthy Frenchman from Nice were saved. Their father had run off with their governess and, changing his name to Hoffman, sailed from Cherbourg on the *Titanic*. Kate Phillips was nineteen and pregnant by her wealthy employer, Henry Morley. He, too, had abandoned his wife and he and his lover sailed under the name of Mr and Mrs Marshall. He died, she was saved, and the surviving daughter is campaigning to have Henry Morley legally identified as her father. The playboy John Jacob Astor, reinstated as a hero after the sinking, had been in poor public favour in the States, having ditched his wife for a much younger woman, with whom he had fled to France to avoid the scandal. He was 'the world's greatest monument to unearned income'; Harry Widener, whose accumulation of priceless antiquarian books kept him occupied and sailing the oceans in search of further acquisitions, came a close second.

Biel is American and his admirable investigation of the cultural history of the *Titanic* has a transatlantic skew – not unreasonably, since a large proportion of the passengers were either American or emigrants from Europe, heading for a new life there. The Americanness of his approach takes a bit of getting used to if, like me, all you had previously known about the *Titanic* had come from the 1958 film *A Night to Remember*. It's years since I saw it, but the overwhelming impression I have of it is the immaculate Britishness of the event, all black and white, clipped accents, Kenneth More and the evening-suited band on the sinking deck playing 'Nearer My God to Thee' (they didn't, it was actually something called 'Songe d'Automne', just as elegiac but possibly not as catchy). The American film industry has only now appropriated the story with James Cameron's as-yet-unreleased movie (a Broadway musical version had to be postponed this spring when the stage *Titanic* refused to sink), but there are clear echoes of the *Titanic* in the very wonderful 1972 *Poseidon Adventure*, an upside-down version of nemesis at sea, and in the greatest disaster movie of them all, *The Towering*

Inferno, which is clearly a vertical, dry-land trope for the engulfing of the *Titanic*. All the elements are there. Fire replaces water, but isolation and greed are the central themes: the design shortcuts of the skyscraper representing the lack of lifeboats, the idle rich at their unreachable penthouse party; death in fancy dress and with gourmet food, the sacrifice of male lives in favour of elegantly clad women and the occasional cad who gets his just deserts after attempting to save his own skin.

Although no black people were on board, the *Titanic* has somehow managed to include racial tension among its meanings. The contemporary newspaper account of a white but grimy stoker attempting to steal the lifebelt of a radio operator who had heroically remained behind to continue calling for help, rapidly became a story of a murderous Negro stoker with a knife. But black Americans made their own contributions to *Titanic* mythology with bluesman Leadbelly composing a song that had the world heavyweight champion, Jack Johnson, bidding a gleeful farewell to the doomed ship from the dock, having tried to board and been told by Captain Smith: 'I ain't hauling no coal.' Biel describes how the *Titanic* disaster became part of black urban folklore in the mythic person of 'Shine', the apocryphal stoker, who in numerous narrative poems is the only person on board capable of swimming to safety and refuses to help the whites who offer him all the treasures they have laid up on earth:

> When all them white folks went to heaven,
> Shine was in Sugar Ray's bar drinking
> Seagram's Seven

The *Titanic* belonged to everyone. Bob Dylan uses it in 'Desolation Row', which depicts 'a rock vision of contemporary apocalypse':

Praise be to Nero's Neptune
The *Titanic* sails at dawn
Everybody's shouting
Which side are you on?

It was, of course, a gift for those who saw disaster in modernity. The ship was supposed to be the slickest, fastest vessel ever. The maiden trip was an attempt to break the record for an Atlantic crossing, which is one reason so many notables were on board. Yet, as Biel points out, it was one of the last occasions when death on the move permitted a degree of gentility. For all the speed with which the ship sank, it still took two hours and forty minutes to go down. It was precisely this time lapse that allowed decisions to be made about the manner of living and dying. Heroism, or even cowardice, is hardly possible under modern circumstances. *The Times* ended its review of *A Night to Remember*: 'This air age, when death commonly comes too swiftly for heroism or with no survivors to record it, can still turn with wonder to an age before yesterday when a thousand deaths at sea seemed the very worst the world must suffer.' By the late 1950s the nuclear age had begun and death in fancy dress looked like a luxury. And if the world hasn't become classless in the ensuing decades, no one can feel reassured that the purchase of a first-class ticket on an airliner will give them a statistical survival advantage over economy passengers.

Still, none of this quite accounts for the fervour which the eighty-five-year-old disaster still produces. Collectors of memorabilia, amateur historians, curators of private museums, writers of innumerable websites, regular visitors to conventions form a kind of religious cult for which the *Titanic* is the sacred text. There are passionate arguments about salvaging the wreckage, now possible with our own leading-edge technology. There are those who simply hanker after memorabilia, some who approve a memorial museum, yet others who regard the sunken hulk and its contents as lying in consecrated ground. There is even a schism: the *Titanic* Historical Society, with headquarters in landlocked Indian Orchard, Massachusetts, suffered a breakaway and the founding of *Titanic* International, whose supporters claimed that the election of THS officers was undemocratic and the leadership of Ed Kamuda despotic. The *Titanic* buffs are in the grip of an all-consuming, nostalgic, trainspotting passion for the past. 'Today everything's tourist class,' moans Kamuda, who along with the evils of classlessness, also cites feminism as responsible for contemporary social turmoil and decline. The *Titanic*, he says, represents the loss of 'a way of life which I and others long for'. Like believers in reincarnation who don't doubt that in previous lives they were pharaohs and potentates rather than slaves and serfs, so the dreamers of *Titanic* days assume their places would have been in the first-class smoking room rather than the boiler room. That's what the past, if not history, is for. If, ultimately, we are all passengers on the *Titanic* (the cosmic implications of a ship lost in the void of an empty sea are not easily resisted), at least we can go down with our dreams of exquisitely adorned heroism intact. Or as the authors of the *Titanic* cookbook put it, contrasting a criticism by Charles Dickens of the poor first-class fare aboard Cunard's *Britannia* in 1842, 'no such complaints are recorded from any of the *Titanic*'s survivors.'

5 June 1997

Did Jesus Walk on Water Because He Couldn't Swim?

The Children of Noah: Jewish Seafaring in Ancient Times.
The title startles. The children of Noah were tower-raisers, nomads, farmers, slaves, desert wanderers, war mongers, city dwellers, poets and musicians even, but sailors? *Jewish* seafaring? Jewish *seafaring?* Certainly, there were family days out at the seaside: my father would roll his trousers up to his calves, and my mother discard her shoes to sit on their deckchairs, but neither of them ever ventured seaward beyond the darker, wetter stretch of sand. I was taught to swim (not by my parents, who I never saw buoyant), though, as I understood it, the lessons were so that I could get out of the sea, should I ever be so foolish and unfortunate as to find myself in it. For even non-practising Jews like us, the sea didn't seem kosher. Jewish people I knew were tailors or shopkeepers, their children were supposed to become businessmen, doctors, lawyers, academics, no one ever mentioned the possibility of a career as a mariner. It made traditional sense to me: hadn't Moses ordered the Red Sea to part rather than have the Children of Israel get their feet wet?

The late Raphael Patai's book is, it must be said, a slim volume, and it was over sixty years in the making, whereas his work on the more plausible Jewish alchemists took only ten years to publish. There is no evidence that any of the four great Biblical travellers on water – Noah, Moses, Jonah and Jesus – had what you could call a vocation for the sea.

Boatbuilding in the Bible, and indeed in the other early flood narratives, is not a skill discovered or intuited by humanity, Patai says. Both the need for boats and the ability to make them are bestowed on mankind from on high. When Atrahasis, in one Akkadian text, is instructed by the god Ea to build a ship, he's at a loss: 'I have never built a ship; draw a design of it on the ground, that, seeing the design, I may build a ship.' Utnapishtim, the Babylonian Noah of the *Epic of Gilgamesh*, also has to receive detailed information from Ea on the construction of his ship. Noah is the only shipbuilder in the Bible, and he, too, gets divine instruction: 'Make thee an ark of gopher wood; with rooms shalt thou make the ark, and shalt pitch it within and without with pitch. And this is how thou shalt make it: the length of the ark three hundred cubits, the breadth of it fifty cubits, and the height of it thirty cubits.' So far as boats are concerned, God, not the Devil, is in the detail.

Neither Noah, nor the ten generations that preceded him back to Adam's time, had any need for boats. Adam is named for the earth from which he was created. His heirs were tillers of soil, and builders of cities. Before Noah, the only time that the sea gets a mention is at the beginning of Genesis, when the spirit of God moved on the face of the waters, which it seems were already there before the start of things. The waters are, Patai explains, according to Talmudic cosmology, *tohu*, of the *tohu bohu* translated in the King James Bible as 'without form and void'; an essential part of the chaos which was all there was before God separated and ordered the world into existence. These were the seas that contained Rahab, Leviathan and other sea monsters which, sings the Psalmist, God defeated before he made the world: 'Thou didst break the sea in pieces by Thy strength, Thou didst shatter the heads of the sea monsters in the waters, Thou did crush the heads of Leviathan, Thou gavest him to be food to the sharks of the sea.' God, it seemed, on some accounts (Psalm 107, the Book of Job, and rabbinical commentaries on Genesis), did not just make the world, he fought with the sea to make it. And having overmastered the waters, when he wanted to annihilate the world he regretted making, it was the waters he used to destroy it. 'I will cause it to rain upon the earth forty days and forty nights; and every living substance that I have made will I destroy from off the face of the earth.' (The rabbis, wishing to take God's word as gospel, worried about the problem of fish, who clearly would not be erased from the world by a flood. It was solved when one rabbi decided that the waters that rained down were boiling, thus doing for the fish, and allowing God to keep his word to the letter.)

Little wonder that the Jews had no taste for the sea. Noah is silent. Unlike later chosen ones who questioned and debated with God about his plans, even changing his mind, Noah never speaks. He simply 'did according unto all that the Lord had commanded him'. He is a survivor, not a sailor. The waters rise, the world dies and, locked up in the box God designed for him, he endures the wait. But Patai detects at least one element of seamanship in him. He refers to a study by James Hornell entitled *The Role of Birds in Early Navigation* which adduces reference to the practice of carrying aboard several 'shore-sighting birds' among the ancient Hindu merchants (fifth-century BCE) when sailing on overseas voyages, 'used to locate the nearest land when the ship's position became doubtful'. The same practice is mentioned in the Buddhist *Kevaddha Sutta* of Digha. Five centuries later, Pliny mentions the same custom as practised by the seamen of Ceylon when making sea voyages, as they were unable to steer by the stars.

The raven and the dove give Noah a certain credibility as a sailor, although Midrashic sources suggest that he spent all his seagoing time learning what and when to feed the animals in his charge. So much so, says one, that he never closed his eyes for one minute during his 150 days afloat. As a sailor, Noah became expert in animal husbandry. Back on land, Noah showed no further interest in the sea: he took up farming and planted the world's first vineyard. Though in becoming also the world's first drunk, he may have been exhibiting an elemental trait of the old seadog.

Moses, too, floated to salvation in an ark, though by now, it seems, boatbuilding skills had been acquired and there was no need for direct guidance from God. When the mother of Moses 'could not longer hide him, she took for him an ark of bulrushes, and daubed it with slime and with pitch, and put the child therein; and she laid it in the flags by the river brink.' This is more river than seafaring, but it's an oddly watery start for a prophet whose life was dominated by mountain and desert. Neither Noah nor Moses journeys on the water for the purpose of trade or discovery. The Bible refers on both occasions to the ark as *tevah*, that is, a chest or box, and not a ship (*oniyah*).

Though Patai doesn't mention him, Jacob is another who, like my parents, exhibits a reluctance when faced with water. At Jabbok, needing to ford the Jordan, he sent his wives and worldly goods across, but remained behind for the night during which he encountered the wrestling angel who would change his name to Israel. For all that scholars might suggest his motive was anxiety about facing his brother, Esau, whose birthright and blessing he had stolen, it seems to me possible that he was in a watery funk. Only an extremely unpleasant night sent him wading across the river the next morning.

Jonah, too, becomes a seafarer through a greater fear of something else. Rather than proclaim against the city of Nineveh, as God wishes, he takes flight and buys a passage on a ship about to sail across the Mediterranean from Joppa (Jaffa) to Tarshish, which is thought to be on the Iberian Peninsula. The crew of this ship are not Jewish, and when the Hebrew God foments a storm, they show both proper seagoing superstition and seamanship by crying 'every man unto his god, and they cast forth the wares that were in the ship into the sea, to lighten it unto them'. Jonah, strangely, sleeps through the whole thing, perhaps because he is such a landlubber that he doesn't know it's time to panic, or because he's such a landlubber that he's been rendered barely conscious by seasickness.

Jesus also sleeps through a storm aboard a boat in the Sea of Gennesareth. The disciples cry: '"Master, carest thou not that we perish?" And he awoke and rebuked the wind, and said unto the sea, "Peace, be still!"' Of course, Jesus is more concerned here with being the Son of God than a Jew in his casual mastery over the sea. Possibly overcoming a dislike of water was part of the new teaching. When he walked on the water, it was with the overt purpose of testing Peter's faith, but it suggests to me a lack of swimming skills on both their parts.

However, if none of these Biblical characters convinces me of a longstanding Jewish attraction to going down to the sea in ships, the fact remains that ancient Palestine had ports on its long Mediterranean coastline, and that there was certainly much to-ing and fro-ing, warring and trading in the area. Of Solomon, we are told in 1 Kings 10.22, 'For the king had at sea a navy of Tarshish with the navy of Hiram: once in three years came the navy of Tarshish, bringing gold, and silver ivory, and apes, and peacocks.' It's not at all clear whether the ships were built by Solomon's men, but in Judah, King Jehoshaphat 'made Tarshish ships to go to Ophir for gold', although Jewish shipbuilding skills are thrown into doubt when we find out that these ships 'were broken at Ezion-Gever' either by a storm or because they were inexpertly built. Whether it was at this moment that Jehoshaphat jumped we are not told.

According to the Mormons, however, Jewish seafaring was an ancient tradition. America, claimed Joseph Smith, was populated by a remnant of seafaring Jews. *The Book of Mormon* tells of a group of Jews living in the early sixth century BCE under King Zedekiah in Jerusalem, who, in an attempt to escape from an unfriendly government, sailed, via the Strait of Gibraltar, across the Atlantic Ocean, to arrive somewhere on the American continent 344 days after starting out. So perhaps seafaring is a lost Jewish art, after all.

Patai offers plentiful evidence in the form of religious laws for life at sea, Midrashic commentary on the Hebrew Bible, and folklore to suggest that the Jews, reluctantly or otherwise, were indeed a seagoing lot. But this doesn't necessarily mean they liked it. The commentating rabbis were ambivalent about sailors, though they weren't enthusiastic about other professions, either: 'Let a man not teach his son to become a donkey driver, a camel driver, a potter, sailor, shepherd, or shopkeeper, for their trade is the trade of robbers,' the Babylonian Talmud warns. Patai paraphrases the great Rashi, on the other hand, saying 'that sailors live in constant danger, and therefore their hearts are inclined toward their Father in Heaven; they travel to places of much danger and are always trembling at the perils that beset them.' The distaste for the sea continues. Were it not for divine dispensation, says a Midrash on the Book of Leviticus, 'every man who goes down to the sea would die at once'.

Sea journeys had become an unfortunate necessity and laws were established for seagoing Jews. The Sabbath had to be kept at sea, during which time no riding or sitting in any vehicle is permitted, so the laws state that journeys had to start no later than Wednesday and that a Jewish traveller had to come to an agreement with the skipper that he would break the voyage for the Sabbath. This was highly unlikely, but it allowed the Jew to blame the Gentile for breaking his word. Not that all skippers were Gentile. Patai gives an account of the fourth-century Jewish shipmaster Amarantus Navicularius, with whom Bishop Sinesius sailed from Alexandria to Corynna. In spite of his Latinised name, Captain Amarantus was not so assimilated into Alexandrian culture that he failed to observe orthodox Jewish law. The Jewish-owned and manned ship was recalled by the Bishop:

All the sailors of the ship, their number being
twelve, and together with the captain thirteen,
were Jews, the children of that accursed nation
which thinks it is doing a good deed by causing
death to the Greeks ... They were all deformed
in one or another part of their bodies. As long as
we were not in danger they amused themselves
by calling one another not by their proper names
but by their bodily defects: Lame, Ruptured, Left-
handed, Squint, and so forth ... We were about
fifty passengers on board; among us a third part
were women, mostly beautiful and charming.
But, nevertheless, you should not envy me. Even
Priapus himself would have behaved piously in
a ship steered by Amarantus, who did not allow
us even one short hour of pleasure in which to be
free of mortal fear.

The problem was a storm that blew up as the Jewish
Sabbath arrived with Friday's sunset:

When Amarantus perceived that the sun had gone
down, he dropped the steering rudder from his
hands. The passengers thought that he had done
thus because of despair. When it became known
to them what the real reason was ... and all their
requests that he should return to the rudder were
in vain – because as we entreated him to save
the ship from danger he only continued to read
his book – they tried to threaten him. One brave
soldier ... drew his sword and threatened to cut
off the man's head unless he instantly took the
rudder again into his hands. But the captain, like a

true Maccabean, could not be moved to transgress the commandments of his religion. Later, however, at midnight, he returned to the rudder voluntarily, saying, 'Now our law permits it to me, because there is a danger of life.'

The Talmud states that when life is at risk, Sabbath rules are suspended, but what pleasure Amarantus clearly has at the Bishop's expense in keeping to the letter of the law. Here, at last, is an honest to God Jewish seafarer.

20 August 1998

Perfectly Human

Whatever the truth of the appealing though dubious proposition that by forty everyone has the face they deserve, it looks as if getting the biographer you deserve post-mortem is pretty much pot luck. Here are two beautiful, displaced, canny women with a powerful sense of their own purpose. For Stacy Schiff, the Véra Nabokov she introduces is 'the figure in the carpet ... Hers was a life lived in the margins, but then as Nabokov teaches us – sometimes the commentary *is* the story.' Laura Beatty – in *Lillie Langtry: Manners, Masks and Morals* – however (including the word 'Morals' in the title for more than mere alliterative satisfaction), prefaces her tale of Lillie Langtry with the following deadly judgement: 'Motivation is the key to character, and Lillie's reasons for doing the things she did, range through panic and muddle to greed and plain wrong-thinking. She was after all seduced, and it will not be possible to exonerate her from the ultimate charges of corruption and betrayal of self ... The genius is the only type of human whose agenda is pure enough for his [*sic*] motives to be incontrovertible. Lillie was not a genius.'

One of these women devoted her accidental gift of beauty to carving out a vivid, hectic and erratic life of her own, the other used her accidental gift of intelligence to support and protect the genius of the man in her life.

Both women died quite sad and lonely, but then, dying sad and lonely is for humans close to tautologous; it proves, as Schiff understands and Beatty certainly doesn't, nothing much about the moral quality of a life.

It never becomes clear how, exactly, Lillie Langtry betrayed her self, or what the pure self she betrayed consisted of. In fact, self seems in Beatty's understanding to be coterminous with soul, an even more slippery notion, but one which enables what Nabokov called the biograffitist to thunder on both counts with all the moral fervour at her disposal that Lillie had 'sold her soul' and in the very first line that 'this is the story of a woman who sold her human nature for a legend.' The legend, essentially, is the one in Beatty's fevered mind of a Faustian compact, a Dorian Gray-like perversion of human destiny. But Lillie was just trying to make the best of things under the circumstances: a perfectly human way to proceed, I should have thought. As for her soul – who's to say?

Lillie had the good fortune not just to be born physically attractive ('What woman would not be beautiful if she had the chance?' she demands), but to have a philandering, radical Nonconformist Dean of Jersey as a father, who would have scorned the cant in the pages of his daughter's biography. Lillie herself showed a proper disrespect for moral outrage in the inscription she had written on the minstrels' gallery of the house the Prince of Wales had designed for her: 'They say – What say they? Let them say.' She was allowed to ramble carelessly through her childhood around the countryside with her six brothers, and then in 1874, at the age of nineteen, made the understandable error – wishing for something more than rural domesticity – of marrying the wrong man. Ned Langtry, then in his thirties, was neither as rich nor as fascinating as she had imagined, and the longed-for broadening of her provincial life turned out to be a charmless house on the fringes of Southampton, the social isolation of being a wife, and a near-fatal bout of typhoid. The doctor, egged on by his patient, prescribed London for the convalescent, and the convalescent prescribed for herself the great daily parade of seeing and being seen in Rotten Row, while Ned stayed home to begin his career of drink and debt. She was seen.

At first glance it seemed a very young and slender girl, dowdily dressed in black and wearing a small, close fitting black bonnet: she might have been a milliner's assistant ... or a poorly paid governess hurrying to her pupils. As I drew near the pavement the girl looked up and I all but sat flat down in the road. For the first and only time in my life I beheld perfect beauty. The face was that of the lost Venus of Praxiteles, and of all the copies handed down to us must have been incomparably the best, yet Nature had not been satisfied and had thrown in two or three subtle improvements.

Doubtless the model-agency scout who spotted Kate Moss on a plane would have thought much the same as the painter Graham Robertson when he noticed Langtry walking past Apsley House. Lillie began her career as muse, model and archetype to the likes of Millais, Whistler, Burne-Jones, Watts and Poynter within the month. Society was just as quick to take her up. *Vanity*

Fair gushed in 1877: 'All male London is going wild about the Beautiful Lady who has come to us from the Channel Islands ... She has a husband to make her happy, but still awaits a poet to make her known.' Her husband most certainly did not make her happy, but Oscar Wilde volunteered for the poet's position and spent a night composing a poem to her on the steps of her house – 'To Helen, formerly of Troy, now of London' – and tutored her in Latin and Greek (essential languages for a goddess).

But it looks very much as if the plain black dress – and Langtry's grasp of the nature of style – was the key to her social triumph. When she arrived in London she was in mourning for her favourite brother, and due to poverty, that black dress was the only one she had. London society, coutured to within an inch of its life and bored to distraction, was enchanted by such stark simplicity, unable to imagine the condition of having no alternative. The Prince of Wales and all her other lovers adored it. Lillie's genius was in retaining the dress for as long as she could, collar turned in or out according to the time of day, until it was deliberately borrowed and trashed by her friend Lady Cornwallis-West, when she had another black dress made. Her first downfall was a failure of style, not soul. She put herself into irreparable debt and lost her uniqueness when she finally ordered a full and fashionable wardrobe of frocks to die for.

What lies at the heart of Laura Beatty's condemnation, however, is the notion that she exchanged true love for a career. Beatty's contribution to Langtry's biography is the discovery of letters to her lover Arthur Jones. Most of what we know of the woman is gossip-column scandal and her own heavily massaged memoirs. She destroyed her own papers and told her story as she wished it to be heard. Arthur Jones may or may not have been the father of her secret child; it was just as likely that Jeanne was the daughter of the Prince of Wales or Louis Battenberg. But he accepted the role, from something of a distance, and while she hid in Jersey she wrote the letters that suggest to Beatty that he was the real love of her life.

> You *won't* go back my darling till you know what
> I am going to do. *Please* promise not to. If you
> love me you can't be so unkind as to leave me ...
> You are very unkind not to write to me ... The sea
> is dreadfully rough. Do come Artie for Heaven's
> sake if you care for me ... You must try to get back
> to help me more ... won't you darling. I always
> have you at all events darling haven't I? To care
> for me whatever happens.

Given the circumstances (the Prince of Wales supplied money and kept the bamboozled husband out of the way, but he was not going to admit paternity; Battenberg was sent overseas for a year by his alarmed family), it could as well have been that she was desperate to keep him standing by her and the baby. In the end, however, she knew from her experience of going home to find the bailiffs sitting in the hallway and Ned dead drunk upstairs, that someone had to earn a living, and if it was to be her it would be at the expense of romantic love. Jones was no better a bet than her other lovers – she had execrable taste in men or had the misfortune to be the taste of execrable men – gambling and drinking and making vague promises of his presence while she begged him to visit her in her seclusion and depression and take charge of her life.

So Jones faded out and Lillie pulled herself together. This, Beatty claims, was her 'terrible exchange: money and fame for the security of self'. It was, you might think, no more than survival, what anyone must do when there is no one and nothing to fall back on. When her social and artistic triumph waned, she took acting lessons from Ellen Terry, knowing herself to be no natural on stage, but marketing her beauty and notoriety as she had to. She took off for and stormed America and its cattle and railroad millionaires, and when that palled, she returned home, adjusted to reality yet again and played the music halls. Finally, in her fifties, exchanging a fading mask of beauty for a mask of masculinity, she took up a life of racing. Since the Jockey Club only admitted men, she became Mr Jersey in order to race her stable of horses. Beatty, positively smacking her lips, sees some form of nemesis in this: 'Photographs at this time' – 1910 – 'show her mouth set, at her most masculine, in an attempt to drown out the voices of her lost past. She towers, inappropriately in white lace, over slight young men at Goodwood, or stamps down the London pavements military style, lantern-jawed, heavily upholstered, arms swinging, toes turned out. Gone are the soft smile, the curves and the sleepily sensuous eyes. Now she is angry and huge and male.' Not only beauty, but independence and achievement, too, are indeed in the eye of the beholder.

Doubtless, Laura Beatty would have approved of Véra Nabokov, who grew more beautiful with age and remained a wisp of a thing. Proof perhaps that devotion of the heart is good for the complexion. There was nothing monstrous about Véra, except perhaps her capacity to divest herself of herself. 'She had both the good and the ill fortune to recognise another's gift; her devotion to it allowed her to exempt herself from her own life while founding a very solid existence on that very selflessness.' Or if she is a monster, she is a Nabokovian monster, and is well served by Stacy Schiff, who understands mirrors, magicians and doppelgängers well enough to appreciate the double creation that was VN and VN, and who has the wit and style to eschew moral judgement for something more perceptive. 'Véra saw her husband always before her; he saw her image of him. This optics-defying arrangement sustained them at a time and in a place when little else did; it was the first in what was to be a repertoire of deceptive techniques, for which the couple had only begun their magic act.'

Véra wore an actual mask at their first rendezvous – a promise to the man she had clearly studied of what was to come. Thereafter for more than fifty years she earned money, typed, edited, corrected, corresponded for, drove, agented, protected, cleared snow from the car, and wholeheartedly agreed about everything with the man of whom she made her life. She was, according to friends, 'the international champion in the Wife-of-Writer Competition', 'the Saint Sebastian of wives'. The marriage and Vladimir's artistic greatness, as they both perceived it, was the only real country to which either of them belonged once each had been geographically exiled. Their son, Dmitri, was given residential rights, though he must have felt an exile of another kind. They never settled anywhere (their final thirty years in a hotel in Montreux was to both of them provisional) except with each other. Véra was the keeper of the flame, the muse who was 'the shadowy figure in the foreground' of Vladimir's life and work. When a friend suggested she needed a rest she responded: 'V. is the one who works very hard (I do write an enormous number of letters, also an occasional contract, and I read proofs and translations, but this is nothing compared to his work).' Vladimir was her sense of self, and if that sticks in the onlooker's craw, her power was more than felt by those who tried to get in touch with the great man, professionals, fans, friends or even family. She conducted his life with the world at large; sometimes she signed his name to letters she wrote, at others it was V. Nabokov, Mrs Vladimir Nabokov, Véra Nabokov and for special occasions, J.G. Smith. Those in the know addressed themselves to the complete set: 'Dear V and V'.

Véra's individuality was most publicly evident in her Jewishness. Unlike her husband, she was a double exile: a refugee from the Bolsheviks and from Russian antisemitism. She lost no opportunity to remind the Gentile world that she was Jewish. In prewar Berlin she was advised to apply for a stenographer's job in the office of a German minister organising an international congress. 'I said "they won't engage me, don't forget I'm Jewish."' When she applied and got the job, she recalled querying the decision: '"but are you sure you want me? I'm Jewish" ... "Oh," he said, "but it does not make *any* difference. We pay no attention to such things. Who told you we did?"' In 1958 she wrote to the *New York Post*: 'In your article you describe me as an émigré of the *Russian* aristocratic class. I am very proud of my ancestry which actually is Jewish.' When she was asked if she was Russian, she replied: 'Yes, Russian and Jewish.' She was appalled when her sister Lena, living in Sweden, renounced her Judaism, or as one family member happily put it, had 'gone the whole hog into Catholicism'. When, in 1959, not having seen Lena for years, she considered making a visit, Véra wrote first: 'I have one question to ask you. Does Michaël' – Lena's son – 'know that you are Jewish, and that consequently he is half-Jewish himself? ... I must admit that if M. does not know who he is there would be no sense in my coming to see you, since for me no relationship would be possible unless based on complete truth and sincerity ... Please answer this question frankly. It is a very important one for me.' Lena wrote back fiercely that Michaël knew very well who his ancestors were, but that Véra had escaped much of the difficulty when she left Europe in 1940. 'You were not involved in the war. You didn't see people die, or be tortured. You don't understand what it is to barely escape a violent death. I did that twice. You don't know what it is to, alone, build a life for two.' The sisters remained estranged.

The editing of past events that Laura Beatty so disapproves of in Lillie Langtry, is taken to its highest form by Véra Nabokov. 'She engaged in a veritable cult of denials. She swore up and down that she had never said a single word Boyd quoted her as saying; she abjured all marginal notes, even those in her firm hand; she went so far as to deny to a reporter that she was proud of Dmitri.' The perfect marriage was not without its troubles. Fourteen years into it, Nabokov fell passionately in love with Irina Guadanini in Paris and wrote extensively to tell her so. Véra, living with his confession and the reality of his affair, dealt with it by never mentioning Irina. 'I know what she is thinking,' Nabokov wrote to Irina. 'She is convincing herself and me (without words) that you are a hallucination.' The affair came to an end when Vladimir, deciding as any sensible genius would to go for reliability, announced to Irina that 'he could not slam the door on the rest of his life.' Véra attempted to deny the whole event to Brian Boyd until he told her that Guadanini, more concerned about her own life than Véra could imagine, had kept the letters in spite of Vladimir's own attempt to expunge reality by asking for them back and claiming that they contained 'mostly fictions'. At Wellesley, Vladimir mooned over several of his students, 'kissing and fondling' one young woman, who testified: 'He did like young girls. Not just *little* girls.' She claimed he told her: 'I like small-breasted women.' In the margins of Andrew Field's biography, where this is cited, Véra – displaying the makings of a sense of humour – denies the truth of the quote: 'No, never! Impossible for a Russian.'

What counted for Véra was the fiction. The suppression of fact was merely in the cause of that overarching good. In this sense, Véra was not so much the sorcerer's apprentice as the magician herself. Vladimir had little patience with his own reality, explaining, as Schiff says, that 'the living, breathing breakfasting Nabokov was but the poor relation of the writer, only too happy to refer to himself as "the person I usually impersonate in Montreux".' 'It is a false idea to imagine a real Nabokov,' their friend Jason Epstein concluded. The reality of the life was for the two of them alone, only the writing and the selling of the books mattered, and Véra attended to that with the tenacity of a literary Rottweiler. 'It was her fervent and unreasonable conviction that books should be accurately translated, properly printed, appropriately jacketed, aggressively marketed, energetically advertised

... she seemed to believe that [royalty statements] should be intelligible and arrive punctually.' This was Véra's life, and Schiff contends plausibly that it was only different in detail from that of any other good wife: 'It has been noted that women are accustomed to tending to chores that are repetitive in nature, tasks that are undone as soon as they are accomplished. The pursuit of the accurate royalty statement, of the carefully proofread manuscript, were not the Sisyphean labours those who first observed this phenomenon had in mind. But they constituted the dusting and vacuuming of Véra Nabokov's life.' Véra is the devoted wife that all writers, regardless of gender, long for and for whom the most passionate believer in the right of individuals to pursue their own destiny might well give up his or her principles. Who knows what lurked underneath her passion for her husband's art, what might have been? She was a kind of art form herself. Seconds after Vladimir Nabokov died, 'a Lausanne nurse precipitated herself bodily upon Véra with condolences. Véra pushed her away with an acid, "S'il vous plaît, Madame."' And yet, after her son drove her back from the hospital that day, Véra sat in silence in his car for a few minutes and 'then uttered the one desperate line Dmitri ever heard escape her lips: "Let's rent an airplane and crash."'

1 July 1999

STINKING RICH

I find myself nostalgic for the time, long ago, when one thing the very rich and very famous could be relied on to do was shut up. Paul Getty, Jacqueline Kennedy Onassis, Princess Grace of Monaco wrapped their money around themselves in the form of impenetrable walls and/or designer sunglasses and kept silent while the world wondered and chattered. And you would imagine that if money could do anything for you it would be to insulate you from having to care what other people thought. The people don't have to vote for you, they don't have to love you. But even princesses and tycoons have to seem to be democratic and loveable these days. They have to sell their brand by selling themselves. Sometimes their brand is themselves. There are power lists and personalities of the year, decade and century, and however filthy with wealth you are, you have to worry about 'the people', you have to care what they think of you. We've had our people's princess, desperate to become the queen of people's hearts, and we still have the people's tycoon noisily committed to running the People's Lottery, apparently free of charge. The pitch is to demand to be seen as ordinary, just like you and me, only richer and more glamorous, of course, because it does the populace a power of good to see heightened images of what they might have been, kitted out in fine frocks and indulging in dangerous sports no one else can afford. And they want it known, these rich people, that in spite of their morale-boosting high life, they devote themselves to the well-being of others, and the greater benefit of the nation. They nurture, they improve, they innovate, they care. They are also – well, they *are* modern icons – consummate moaners. They complain loudly and publicly about being misunderstood, underappreciated, and afflicted on all sides by the forces of repression, tradition and evil. Since they're on the side of the people, any attack on them is tantamount to an attack on the ordinary folk they would like us to believe they represent. They are, it turns out, latter-day saints, deflecting and taking on themselves the slights and assaults of the elitist, convention-bound enemy, becoming martyrs and shields of the people. And my God how they whine, how they snivel, how they demand our attention and sympathy.

Still riding on a wave of sentiment that may not have had much more energy left in it, the Princess of Wales timed her exit impeccably. It is tempting to think that Richard Branson also understood, if only unconsciously, that public adulation is likely to tire and turn into its own opposite. Blonde, blue-eyed, apparently artless – like the Princess – he took what seemed to be life-threatening risks by boat and balloon, and nearly came a cropper once or twice, so that he, too, might have gone while the going was still good. As luck (or his carefully chosen fellow adventurers) would have it, however, he has survived, and it may be that he is about to outlive his popular acclaim. It seemed appropriate that Branson's grinning face, on the cover of Virgin Publishing's ghosted autobiography, was seen in virtually every episode of *Big*

Brother, and while the graspingly hopeful housemates came and went, the Branson book stayed, to be taken up by the decreasing remainder as a favourite read. Surely it must have been the devious, miscalculating and ultimately naive Nick who brought it into the house? Nick got sussed by the public and eventually his fellow inmates. Is the same thing going to happen to Richard Branson? He who lives by public relations will die by public relations.

There have, of course, always been those who had their doubts about Richard Branson's status as a millionaire with a heart of gold, and who have declined on principle to fly on Virgin planes, drink Virgin Cola or wine, invest in Virgin life insurance, wear a Virgin wedding dress, ride a Virgin train or speak on a Virgin mobile. Among these hold-outs, I wouldn't be surprised, might have been Tom Bower, who tells us that halfway through writing this biography he found himself in receipt of a writ for defamation after an article he wrote in the *Evening Standard*. One way or another Virgin gets into your life, though Virgin Writs is not, so far as I know, registered at Companies House. The writ arrived after Branson failed to get Bower to agree to submit his unfinished manuscript to him before publication; it was addressed to Bower rather than the *Evening Standard*. A ploy, Bower believes, to discredit him and therefore the biography. The case comes to court next year.

Bower has some important books to his credit. He takes a responsible and well-researched interest in the hidden dealings of the rich and powerful. Tiny Rowland, Mohamed al-Fayed and Robert Maxwell have all received the treatment and been carefully scrutinised. His account of Maxwell's affairs delved into the murky depths, but he also kept a wary eye on the dubious ethics of the business world around the man, and produced an interestingly complex account of Maxwell's psychology. The investigation of Branson's business activities is thorough and compelling, but what is missing, for the satisfaction of the reader and perhaps the writer, too, is the slightest indication of complexity or depth of character in its protagonist. Either Bower has missed it, or Branson is that shallow: a rich man who is of no interest at all. That the self-aggrandising prankster who races to court at every opportunity and continually complains of being done down is lacking substance isn't news, but still it's disappointing to find that there is nothing more to him than one thought.

It's evident that Bower doesn't like his subject – and not unreasonable of him given that the subject is suing him. The smiling golden boy on the cover of Branson's autobiography is replaced on Bower's account by a cold-eyed and menacing prince of darkness. The dislike is much more visible in this book than in others Bower has written. Branson is berated for lacking conscience when at twenty-three he became a millionaire, although 'wealth troubled many in that socialist era.' There were also many it did not trouble. Youthful millionaires who started with a more than decent financial base are not often afflicted by bad conscience, one imagines. Those who are prone to it probably don't do what has to be done in order to accumulate wealth. It seems almost unreasonable to berate Branson in particular for having the qualities that failed to prevent him from becoming and remaining wealthy. He is accused in the early pages of an untroubled conscience, a 'lust for fame and fortune', a preoccupation with earning money, a disdain for authority and intellectuals, an oily ability to treat and charm susceptible journalists, a canny use of offshore trusts, a ruthlessness that allowed him to dump those who were no longer of use to him: all or some of these must be attributes of anyone who makes a great deal of money (and of many besides). Sometimes Bower seems quite disingenuous in his apparent belief that it is possible to make and keep large sums of money while maintaining the personality of a Poor Clare. It is, after all, precisely that fond and fruitless wish in all of us that Branson plays on as he attempts to maintain the fiction that he is Britain's favourite do-gooding, fun-loving, once-hippie, now-laddish millionaire.

He is, of course, a millionaire. The unexpectedly colossal sales of Mike Oldfield's dreary *Tubular Bells* saw to that in 1973. The money was salted away in offshore family trusts, which have ensured Branson's own wealth no matter how dire the difficulty his companies might be in. Even at the time only the very gullible imagined he would be using the money to improve the lot of the poor. He's always been a guy on the make, a capitalist with a talent for PR and camouflage. Before the record shops, he started *Student* magazine. There is a photograph in his autobiography of the front line of the 1968 Grosvenor Square demonstration – Branson marching alongside Tariq Ali. According to Bower, Branson simply attached himself to the student leaders, who were quite oblivious of his presence, but the press accepted his claim to be in the forefront of the revolution and *Vogue* featured him as a representative of Britain's student rebellion, when he actually represented that other side of the 1960s, the rise of the go-getting individualist.

Branson is, if you like, an emotional con artist. But I find myself ambivalent about Tom Bower's expressions of outrage, just as when I watch or hear one of those programmes that pursue those who prey on gullible consumers. I feel a kind of guilty sympathy with the hounded wrongdoer. What do you expect? They were only doing their job, making money by making promises. Why are you asking them why they did it? Why not ask why people believed them? Why not ask why they were so stupid as to deceive people illegally when it is so easy to do it in a completely legal fashion and be acclaimed for it?

If you think that capitalism and global brand merchandising have a great deal to answer for, and you have a distaste for the vulgarity of publicity stunts involving naked women and pointless feats of derring-do, then you will not much like Richard Branson. You will feel that a life could be put to better use, that money could be better spent, that there is something terribly wrong with a society in which 47 per cent of the public wanted Richard Branson to become mayor of London and voted him Britain's favourite boss, best role model for parents and teenagers and most popular tycoon. But Branson does provide an insight into the workings of late twentieth-century capitalism and its social forms. He has made himself rich by making himself famous and made himself famous by making himself rich. He has manipulated public opinion because the manipulation of public opinion has never been easier. He presented himself as buccaneer and victim, a virgin forever being interfered with by corrupt and powerful old men, a dewy David battling the thug Goliath. And people, *the* people apparently, have loved it. They love him being rich, having his own island in the sun, shaming the suits at board meetings, tieless in jumpers knitted by his auntie, getting drunk and randy, blowing millions on hot air adventures in the sky. In his business dealings as well as his public persona, he is a triumph of lack of style over substance. He feeds the friendly hacks, flies them to his island in his aeroplane, lets them mingle with the famous and fatuous, and they dutifully turn out the Richard Branson the public wants. Just a bloke who does with his money what any ordinary bloke, nice as you like, would do if he had any to spare.

When Bower digs beneath the lack of substance to see how Branson actually operates, he makes it sound like a state of perpetual panic. In 1999, apart from his airline and rail franchises, all of Branson's major companies were trading at a loss. For decades, his trick has been to keep things afloat and the City on his side by shifting money around between profitable and failing parts of the business. Part of his charm and popular appeal is his public admission of ignorance. In 1999 he gave a Millennium Lecture at Oxford and apparently told the admiring students that only those who rejected university would become millionaires. Industry was dead, only brands would be of value in the future. It is not necessary to know about the things you are marketing. He knew nothing about music and the airline business. 'Get the right people around you and just incentivise them.' Bower gloomily sums up the speech and the beliefs of 'Britain's greatest entrepreneur': 'Ignore education, ignore expertise and ignore technology. In a citadel of academic excellence, Branson had preached anti-knowledge.' Probably the students in the citadel of excellence loved it.

In fact, Branson's instincts seem rather frail, or at any rate to be related to sheer survival rather than innovation. Airlines, cola, finance, internet access, mobile phones, gas and electricity provision: all these commodities were already well established by others. He is always a step behind, complaining loudly how unjust it is that by being ahead of him others are stopping him from being in front. Even though he started later, it's plain not fair that anyone should be in front. And, proving that shouting loudly is a very effective form of argument, people in authority are inclined to agree with him, or at least not to want to become unpopular by disagreeing with him. He revels in being the little man held back by the big bully, though you come to suspect after reading Bower's book that little bullies are just as obnoxious. He decides to market Virgin Cola and complains that Coca-Cola is taking unfair advantage of being the market leader, by, as it were, being the market leader. Actually, he seems to complain about anyone fighting back (or just carrying on as normal) when he has entered the ring. The long court and publicity battles with BA were of that kind. Branson accused British Airways of 'dirty tricks' when it appears to Bower that BA did little more than any business would do to maintain its edge. He railed about their powerful monopoly as if it were preventing Virgin Atlantic from flourishing, when BA had little more than 30 per cent of the market and Virgin Atlantic consisted of no more than a handful of planes, fewer than other independent airlines. Price wars among suppliers are just what the consumer needs, Thatcher used to say. But Thatcher-loving Branson, the Tories' favourite capitalist (also, of course, New Labour's favourite capitalist), moaned about BA cutting prices and it simply not being fair to him. He went to court against others, sometimes winning and sometimes losing, but always gaining the publicity edge as the people's champion in the sweater being bullied by the faceless ones in suits. Quite why Virgin Atlantic had a God-given right to survive (it was never the cheapest way to fly to the States and it always had the least leg room) isn't clear. The answer seems to be that Branson is a very nice man and jolly well deserves to be a success in all things.

Bower dismisses the idea that it is fun being a Virgin employee. It seems that they are very likely to be badly paid, overworked and then given the boot when they are no longer useful. Worse than all that, they are frequently obliged, according to one ex-employee, to witness the boss 'exposing himself all over the place' at parties. Bower goes into some detail about Branson's personal relations with women and his penchant for cross-dressing, but this, too, fails to make the man more interesting – and is irrelevant to his argument. Much more pertinent is the regularity with which people he worked with were sacked and financial partners outmanoeuvred by fancy legal footwork. He cried when he announced to his staff that he'd sold Virgin Music, but flatly refused to share with those who lost their jobs any of the £560 million he made from the sale. But that's business for you.

The lottery is Branson's latest grand passion. Once again he took the competition to court, claiming that Guy Snowden of GTech had tried to bribe him to drop his bid for the franchise. The case was based on a note (the original of which was never found) Branson said he made of the bribe when Snowden was invited to lunch. Quite why Snowden waited to be invited to lunch by Branson before offering the bribe was never explained, but Branson won the case and made GTech's ambitions look very ugly compared to his own non-profit-making People's Lottery. When in 1994 Camelot won the lottery franchise, Branson screamed: 'I've been robbed' – and burst into tears. He threatened to take the then regulator, Peter Davis, to court for negligence and maladministration as he had once appealed to the High Court when a decision for a television franchise went against him. The regulator, fearing a judicial review, explained why the People's Lottery had lost. In Bower's words:

> Camelot planned four times more retail outlets
> to sell tickets than Virgin; Branson's projections
> of the money to be raised for good causes ranked
> only as average among the eight applicants; and
> the amount Branson anticipated generating for the
> whole lottery fund was the sixth lowest. On other
> assessments, Branson's bid ranked bottom ...
> Oflot's calculations showed that Branson
> proposed to take out more in service charges
> than Camelot and contribute less to the fund of
> good causes. His hugely vaunted promise of a
> non-profit-making lottery was suspect because
> the 'profits' appeared to be hidden among
> 'administrative costs'.

In the six years since that bid, things have not gone entirely well for Branson, in spite of the knighthood he received from Tony Blair. The stakes were very high for his new bid for the lottery, according to Bower. 'His failure to fulfil his predicted successes in many different Virgin enterprises, his recurring financial losses and the inscrutability of his offshore trusts were persistent sources of unease. To remove the doubts, Branson established an unnamed holding company without shareholders and seven non-executive directors to supervise the People's Lottery, his new private company.' Camelot's bid was rejected by Dame Helena Shovelton because of doubts about the probity of GTech. But Branson's bid was not accepted either. Although, as Bower puts it, 'the billions of pounds of lottery money flowing perfectly legitimately through a private company with a single shareholder would place Branson in an unprecedented position of power and influence,' Shovelton had problems with his bid.

> In particular ... the Commission had identified
> how the financial claims of lottery players might
> not be protected if Branson's lottery became
> insolvent, lost its licence or failed to raise as much
> money as he predicted. In Shovelton's opinion,
> Branson's proposals on those crucial financial
> issues were 'so conditional and so uncertain' that
> the Commission harboured 'significant concerns
> about the financial viability of the People's Lottery
> if the ticket sales were much lower than expected'.

Branson was sent away to sort out some more substantial backing, Camelot won a judicial review suggesting that they had been treated unfairly by not receiving similar treatment and Shovelton resigned. It seems that the final decision will be make or break for Branson's ambitions and credibility.

Branson claims that only brands count, and up to now he seems to have been proved right. People appear to think that all things Virgin have their best interests at heart. They are amazed to discover that having been told by Branson in his ads that Virgin PEPs would be the cheapest in Britain, they were actually subject to a 4 per cent commission which made them the third most expensive. They were astonished to find that instead of Virgin trains being 'fun' and despite the promises to 'increase quality and bring down prices', they routinely ran late, were overcrowded and cost up to 30 per cent more in fares. There was a time when we knew that people who made a great deal of money were not likely to have other people's best interests as their prime motive. In spite of decades of universal education, we seem to have gone soft in the head. Nothing Branson has done since his teenage years, when he avoided paying purchase tax on record sales, has been illegal. Much of it has not been pleasant, humane or straightforward, but that is allowed in the accumulation and protection of wealth. Perhaps we choose to admire Richard Branson because we cherish the hope that one day we might find ourselves fabulously wealthy, and we'd like to think of ourselves in that golden future as being nice as well as stinking rich. Richard Branson sits in the soggy parts of our minds and represents the possibility of our dreams coming true and not having to despise ourselves. What is Tom Bower doing to our fondest hopes by suggesting that Branson might not gleam through and through? If we can't believe in Branson, the people's millionaire, what can we believe in?

16 November 2000

My Little Lollipop

Christine Keeler votes Conservative. She would, wouldn't she? Having seen off the Macmillan Government in the 1960s, exposed the squalid underbelly of upper-class public life and fired the starting pistol to begin the sexual revolution by revealing that 'You've never had it so good' was actually 'You've never had it so often', she reckons she knows what's what about the world of politics and power (though sex and men are not really her thing). She has nothing but contempt for Blair's New Labour: 'just a bunch of control freaks, just more ardent, more determined to bring in rules and take away our freedoms. What I have learned most is that those who would lead have agendas rather than feelings or emotions.'

Christine Keeler also has an agenda. You get to an age when the truth seems all-important, she says in her memoir, *The Truth at Last*. In her case the age of truth would be around fifty-nine because today 'it makes me shudder when I understand the cumulative effect of the years of lies on which history has been created.' As a result of this insight she has been moved to study: 'now with that scholarship, hindsight and, of course, my day-to-day witnessing of events as they happened … I feel able, at last, to tell the whole truth.' It must also be disturbing to have reached such a stage of maturity and have to confront the fact that for forty years you've been famous for being the tart who was accidentally instrumental in getting Labour into power after thirteen years of Tory Government. (She didn't think much of Wilson's lot, especially that 'ugly' George Wigg, the one 'with the ear of Harold Wilson' who, in addition to being apparently genetically modified, she 'always thought looked like a pervert'.) She has a place in history, to be sure, but not one that's likely to be welcome in her scholarly middle years as the mark she will have made on the world. As both a lover of truth, and a misunderstood victim of a cover-up by powerful men to protect each other, she aims to set the record straight with her recollection of the events of the Profumo Affair.

Christine Keeler bemoans the fact that she can never escape being Christine Keeler, but actually she is no longer Christine Keeler. She has changed her name through two marriages and deed poll, and also, like the rest of us have or will, she has grown into an older woman who looks back on her former self with a mixture of pride and embarrassment. From being 'innocent and warm-hearted' when she arrived in London in 1959, she became, she explained to her son Seymour, as he was growing up, 'wild and naughty'. But she emphatically denies ever being 'the common tart' she was painted as. She was not, she insists, a prostitute 'in the sense that most people understand the word'. The sense in which I understand the word is that it describes a person who offers sex in return for money or the equivalent in goods. 'It's true that I have had sex for money but only out of desperation,' Keeler elaborates, distinguishing herself from those who do it because it's such a laugh. In fact, she goes so far as to say that she thinks she 'might have been one of the most moral women of that particular, frenzied decade'. Her friend Mandy Rice-Davies was the 'true tart': 'There was always shock on her face whenever she thought she might have to do more than lie on her back to make a living.'

Visiting the Twenty-One Room, 'a glorified knocking shop with overpriced drinks and rooms to rent upstairs', Keeler met a Major Jim Eynan. He wanted to go to bed with her in the afternoons, she says, 'and, for nearly two years, he often did. Ours was a commercial situation for Jim always advanced me some money for rent or helped out financially in other ways.' Keeler may or may not have been the most moral woman of the 1960s (my vote would go to Elizabeth Taylor for her belief in the sacred bond of marriages), but the looseness of her definitions is problematical for someone claiming to offer the whole truth. Apart from the moral issue, her assertion that she was never a prostitute is important for her other big claim: she would have it known that she was, in fact, a spy. Not exactly a treacherous spy, not a willing betrayer of her country, but the innocent and warm-hearted victim of an evil spymaster, Stephen Ward, who passed himself off as a playboy but was in fact at the centre of an international espionage ring. In her salad days, Keeler was not a prostitute, not a popsie (a word whose absence from the world I've missed these past thirty-odd years), not a good-time girl (except in the sense that she just wanted a good time like any healthy young thing) but a pawn – no, that's *pawn* – in the Cold War.

Stephen Ward, you may recall, was osteopath to the great and good. There was almost no one in society he didn't massage. When he wasn't manipulating them, he was sketching them, having discovered a talent for making likenesses. The Duke of Edinburgh, Princess Margaret, Lord Snowdon, Archbishop Makarios and Adolf Eichmann all sat for portraits. He was an invitee at all the fashionable parties, and a man who specialised in providing fun for his friends. Keeler met him when she was a showgirl and moved into his flat, though they never had sex, not with each other. He took her to dinner parties where lords and ladies hurried through their desserts so that they could undress and orgify before Keeler had to leave for her parading and hostessing duties at Murray's, a classy strip club. She accompanied him, stopping sometimes on the way to pick up girls waiting for buses, to the cottage in the grounds of Cliveden, made available to Ward at weekends by Lord Astor, who with his friends, including John Profumo, the Minister for War, would chase a minutely towelled Keeler and others around the swimming pool. But all this, says Keeler, was a front for Ward's real activity, which was spying for Russia on the British establishment during the months before and after the Cuban Missile Crisis.

Profumo was besotted with the stunning Keeler, but she was not all that interested in him. She has always, she says, been 'cursed by sex I didn't particularly want'. Ward insisted, demanding to know how anyone wouldn't be interested in getting so close to power. She obeyed, and so was taken in the official car for a tour of London, visiting the War Office, Downing Street and 'I'll show you the Army barracks, too, where I inspect the men.' Who could resist? Keeler was also sleeping with a Russian attaché called Eugene Ivanov, a regular visitor to Ward's flat, as were Roger Hollis, head of MI5 and mole extraordinaire, and Anthony Blunt. They spoke freely in front of Keeler, she claims, about nuclear warheads. They weren't worried about her apparently. Ward knew she was safe. 'The only gossip was about fashions, the new French and Italian underwear, ladders in stockings. There were no tights or La Perla and naughty knicker shops then ... Clearly, I was not a candidate for spilling Stephen's secrets and he didn't see me as a threat.'

On the contrary. Once Profumo had become a regular visitor to the flat, Ward entered Keeler's bedroom and paced about. 'That night in the bedroom, between drags on his cigarette, Stephen just asked me straight out to ask Jack what date the Germans were going to get nuclear weapons.' Keeler expresses surprise. 'This seemed so bold. I had dropped off letters to the Russian Embassy' – to Ivanov – 'this was different. This was gathering information. Spying. Properly. Or rather, improperly.' She refused: 'I became afraid and begged him not to ask me to do such a thing, that I couldn't betray my country.'

Myself, I regret her refusal, since the account of her undercover work would make for fascinating reading. Imagine, if you will, the Secretary of State for War and twenty-year-old Christine Keeler in bed, relaxing perhaps after their exertions.

'Jack darling, that was ... just ... mmm.'

'It certainly was, my little lollipop.'

'Umm, Jack ... ?'

'Mmm, what is it, Popsie?'

'Jack ... you know Germany?'

'Mmm.'

'Well, you know – oh, what are they called? – uh, nuclear weapons?'

'Yes, sweetie?'

'I was just wondering ... you know ... when do you think Germany will be getting some?'

I have gathered over the years that people in very high and very low places are a great deal more stupid than we expect them to be, and that sheer incompetence accounts for much in national and international politics, but I can't help wondering how masterly a master spy Stephen Ward could have been if that was how he approached Cold War espionage.

Keeler is insistent, however, on Ward having been at the dead centre of political intrigue, rather than just a dilettante at that as well as everything else. Her wish to retrieve her past is understandable. Much better for the amour propre to have been Mata Hari than a party girl who bedded Tory peers and the slum landlord Peter Rachman ('I never knew about the terror tactics with tenants who didn't pay rent or were difficult ... There was something deeply hurt in him from the beatings in the concentration camps and he would never ever get over it'). She is enraged that Stephen Ward was found guilty not of espionage but of living off immoral earnings. Where's the justice in that, she cries. Certainly, Stephen Ward, Christine Keeler and Mandy Rice-Davies were punished for causing trouble for the toffs, while the toffs slunk away. She told Lord Denning, whom she trusted as a decent older man like the father she never had, that Ward was a spy, that she'd met Hollis and Blunt in his flat, that they'd discussed nuclear warheads and the like, and even that President Kennedy was in danger (immediately after the Missile Crisis, Ward had said: 'A man like Kennedy will not be allowed to stay in such an important position of power in the world, I assure you of that'). Denning covered it all up, Keeler says, on behalf of his friends in high places. He smothered the spying with tales of sex and smut.

Life for Christine Keeler has been up and down. She got £23,000 from the *News of the World* (pushing half a million in current money) and another £13,000 from the *Sunday Pictorial*, but spent it, ending up living in a council flat with her youngest son. Her elder son and her mother no longer speak to her. She did time in Holloway, ostensibly for perjury, and she was banned from Vidal Sassoon's salon when the respectable society women complained about having to share a backwash with her. In 1967 she became a 'silicone pioneer'. Her breasts were checked 'early in 2000 and I am glad to report everything is well and where it should be'.

We have much to thank Christine Keeler for. The rumours at the time were delightful, confirming everything we'd always suspected about the sanctimonious, repressive establishment. Profumo, of course, resigned for lying to Parliament (in effect for being found out), and for sleeping with a call girl who was sleeping with a Russian. He has spent the intervening years doing rather public good work in the East End of London, and being invited to the Queen Mother's dos. Keeler's done her bit for society, too, working for Release having become interested 'in trying to prevent young people going to prison for smoking drugs which I thought were harmless'. Unlike Profumo, she wasn't asked to join in the Queen Mother's 100th birthday celebrations. It's perfectly understandable that she felt aggrieved when in 1995 Margaret Thatcher invited Profumo to her seventieth birthday party, saying: 'He is one of our national heroes. His has been a very good life. It's time to forget the Keeler business.' Oh, let's not. Let's remember the foolishness and arrogance of the privileged. Let's go on giggling at them as they hang on to their sagging trousers and mouth pious platitudes and fawn on vicious old ladies of the Far Right.

22 March 2001

Don't Think About It

There must be people who, during their lifetime, get their minds right enough not to feel bitterness as the end looms and they realise that nothing much else is going to happen to them apart from death. I understand from reading and anecdote that some people do die with a smile and the words 'It's been a good life' on their lips. But not many, surely? It seems to me almost unreasonable, indecent even, not to feel some degree of regret as life winds down towards the end. And life, of course, has generally only just got properly started before it begins to show signs of not going on forever. So when I read in David Plante's *Difficult Women* (1979) that Sonia Orwell in her final years complained to him, 'I've fucked up my life. I'm angry because I've fucked up my life,' it doesn't seem to me necessarily to imply a particularly tragic or wasted life. At least not necessarily more tragic or wasted than most. Unless you take the Chinese view, an interesting life is the best we can hope for in an existence which ends, for all of us, prematurely with illness or ageing and death.

There can be no doubt that Sonia Orwell had an interesting life; vivid and complicated in her early years, drunkenly angry and anxious towards the end, but with friends who cared enough about her to put up with her and even, decades later, to write a biography (*The*

Girl from the Fiction Department) designed, as Hilary Spurling's explicitly is, to stem 'the tide of venom that pursued her into and beyond the grave'. The venom was largely a result of the way, as George Orwell's widow, she managed the literary estate. She was deemed to be tyrannical, grasping and interested only in the income the estate generated. She was remembered – by men in particular – as having slept around copiously in her youth, though when you think of the 1950s and who was available in London and Paris to sleep with you can only wonder that she made time to do any work as an editor at *Horizon*. And as an older woman, she was feared for her vicious tongue. Hilary Spurling begs to differ, or at least explain.

The trouble with attempting to redress a blackened reputation is that in the process of countering the allegations you are always in danger of directing the reader's attention to the original criticism. In order to refute the general condemnation of her friend, Spurling acknowledges the difficult older woman David Plante knew: 'Fear, suspicion and hostility lay increasingly close to the surface. Insecurity or drink released an aggression that made her many enemies.' A nephew compared being on the receiving end of one of her public tirades to a drive-by shooting. But even then, Spurling says, 'beneath the trappings of the hardened old warhorse you could still see traces of the impetuous young thoroughbred, who had enchanted Leiris and others a quarter of a century before.' Well, yes. Most of us were easier to take when young, especially if we were beautiful, energetic, bright and eagerly ambitious, as Sonia Orwell clearly was. We should, however, be grateful for the transformation; young thoroughbreds, if they don't become old warhorses like the Widow Orwell, are inclined to prance unprettily about, all unaware of the effects of time, and set one's teeth on edge.

But we are in the realm of contemporary biography, and Spurling, with several lives to her credit, will not settle for a memoir of Sonia Orwell that merely has her decline into harsh disappointment through the effects of loss of youth. The heroine must be driven in some way towards the sad end made importantly tragic by a seed of self-destruction planted when she was very young. And indeed, Sonia Orwell was well equipped with potential demons in her youth. Her childhood was a colonial mess. Born in Calcutta, she had a father who died, perhaps by suicide, when she was a few months old, and a mother who remarried a year later a man who was at least a drunk, if not a psychopath. When she was six, she was sent, as if to complete the gothic theme, to the same awful convent school that Antonia White attended and wrote about in *Frost in May*. Vicious nuns, a minimal education for middle-class marriage and – something, at least – a powerful enemy to kick against. As an adult she would spit on the street if she saw nuns. Earlier, she had a more sophisticated mode of expression. 'I'm so bored I wish I'd been birth-controlled so as not to exist,' she announced in the hearing of a nun at a school hockey match. For this one moment of perfectly aimed revenge, she is, in my view, to be forgiven everything. The drive-by shooting began much earlier than her nephew thought. The tough old warhorse began battling young and was, it seemed, pretty well equipped for the fight. This may well be what people so resented about her. She doesn't look much like a victim at any point in her life, even when things aren't going so well. There is something very slightly diminishing about placing her in the role of a woman at the mercy of her circumstances and wronged.

Spurling describes an accident that happened to Sonia when she was seventeen and living with a family in Switzerland. She offers it as a defining, lifelong trauma. A boat in which Sonia was sailing with three other young people overturned in a sudden squall. Sonia headed for the shore but returned to the boat when she realised that the others were not following. They couldn't swim. Two of them went down and she tried to save the last boy, who struggled against her in his panic and tried to pull her down with him. 'Unable to save him,' Spurling says, 'pushing him away, fighting in his clutches for her life, she tore free as he went down for the last time.' According to her biographer, 'Sonia never forgot the terrible embrace of a convulsive male body stronger than her own, and its even more terrible consequences.' Clearly, a dreadful experience. But Michael Shelden, George Orwell's biographer and in Spurling's view one of those responsible for disparaging Sonia, has a slightly different take on the event. Interviewing her sister and half-brother, he claims that fearing for her life in the struggle with the boy she was trying to save, 'she grabbed him by the hair and pushed his head under water. She was able to hold him down for several seconds, and then she let go, thinking he would stop trying to fight her and would come to the surface. But he did not come up.' This is the story she told her mother and sister when she returned to England, and Shelden says: 'She later told the story to her half-brother, Michael, to whom she was very close, and she left no doubt in his mind that she considered herself responsible for the one boy's death: '"I held him under," she said ... A few of Sonia's close friends knew about the incident in Switzerland, but they were generally led to believe that the tragedy for her was simply that she was the lone survivor. She seems to have left out the details about her struggle with the drowning boy.'

Perhaps Hilary Spurling was one of those friends who got the more helplessly guilty version and, writing the memoir, simply related what she was told. It's a terrible enough tale. But the stronger story, that she fought against the boy's life for her own so that she felt responsible for his death, does not do her a greater disservice. The will to live of most seventeen-year-olds is and should be very strong. It does, however, rather change the tone of the memory of that embrace of the 'convulsive male body, stronger than her own, and its even more terrible consequences'. She was dealing with something more than pure survivor guilt and she is not then or at any point as far as I can see a simple victim. Only in a very bipolar world would that make her a simple villain.

Of course, the childhood Catholicism scored its troubling mark, as Spurling repeatedly insists. Her theory is that Sonia Orwell was permanently consumed with the crushing guilt that the Church is so adept at instilling: the kind of free-form guilt that just washes around waiting for any opportunity to overflow. The life is portrayed as driven essentially by revolt against her convent days, tempered by this guilt about which she could do nothing. Sex was one obvious way to kick against her upbringing, and she is known to have kicked vigorously. Spurling also suggests that her love, her worship even, of writing and painting was another form of rebellion against the conformity demanded by her schooling. Rebellion they might be, but sex and art are also sources of pleasure. There are worse ways of fighting back. But Spurling suggests that sex was not so much pleasure as weapon for Sonia. 'She would love many men, and sleep with many more but, for her, true love in its most intense and deepest form was not primarily sexual. On the two or three occasions when she broke this rule, the results were catastrophic.'

She left suburbia and found herself a world of arty glamour in Fitzrovia. She was the Euston Road Venus to William Coldstream, Victor Pasmore, Lucian Freud and other lovers who painted and adored her youth, her over-compensating fierceness of opinion, her looks and some mysterious sadness that she carried inside. She was an insecure, uneducated girl who glorified men who painted pictures and wrote books, who thought there was nothing better that could be done by a person, and who wanted to be part of their life. It wasn't hard for her. Older, very clever men were devoted to her. Cyril Connolly brought her into *Horizon*, where she learned fast and eventually, to the chagrin of some who were not used to receiving editorial decisions from twenty-five-year-old women, more or less ran it, while its editors went off in search of love and sun. She went to France and was feted by the likes of Michel Leiris, Lacan and Merleau-Ponty – who became the lost love of her life when she couldn't accept the French distinction between love (his wife) and *un amour* (herself). Merleau-Ponty, before he tired of her demand that he leave his wife, was 'transfixed ... by the sorrow underlying her surface gaiety'. He delighted also in her practical take on the intellectual life, such as her description of spending time with Roland Barthes and Dionys Mascolo from Gallimard:

They talked about civil war as one talks about a visit to the dentist. When they came to discussing how to make efficient bombs out of bottles with petrol, I could have knocked their heads together with rage, and I only refrained from screaming when they said any form of personal pleasure was a waste of time, because they were so busy getting tight and so pleased with the clothes they had bought on the black market that it became rather touching.

An old story of all mouth and no trousers, I think.

It must have been a heavenly time, and if the great love didn't work out and later life couldn't live up to it, it was surely an enviable youth. The sorrow was there, but it was a necessary attribute for a girl who wanted to be loved by wiser, older men. They are suckers for sadness.

She turned Orwell down at his first proposal, as did the several other women he asked to marry him at the same time. She slept with him, but only once, then Orwell went off to the island of Jura to write *Nineteen Eighty-Four*, with Sonia as the model for the innately freedom-loving, contrary Julia: 'the girl from the Fiction Department ... was very young, he thought, she still expected something from life ... She would not accept it as a law of nature that the individual is always defeated.' Orwell asked Sonia again, not long after the split with Merleau-Ponty, and this time she accepted. He was dying by then and his reputation was rising, so according to Michael Shelden, Sonia accepted him with a view to becoming a rich, literary widow. Her friends say that Orwell wrote to her to say that he believed marrying her would prolong his life, so, she told Spurling, 'you see, I had no choice.' He made her his executor and asked her to refuse all requests for a biography. Clearly, she had proved herself enough in the world of books for Orwell to trust her to be his literary widow. If it was not a love match, it apparently cheered Orwell up in his last three months, according to Anthony Powell, though it greatly annoyed Stephen Spender, who resented being told by a snip of a girl to limit his political conversation with G.O. to twenty minutes.

Her next marriage was in 1958 to Michael Pitt-Rivers, who had been jailed four years earlier in the scandalous homosexuality trial that led the Wolfenden Committee to recommend legalisation. The marriage did not work out. Sonia was not a woman who married for love. Spurling doesn't dispute this, but says that she came to love both husbands and lost one while failing to convert the other. When George died, according to Natasha Spender, 'it was cataclysmic. She had persuaded herself she loved him intellectually, for his writing, but she found she *really* loved him.' As Sonia said to David Plante when he laughed about someone's dalliance, 'no one seems to understand what happens in human relationships, and the sadness of it all. It isn't anything to joke about. It really isn't.'

Both Plante and Spurling talk of her generosity, her capacity to turn up with small, delightful gifts to hearten the cheerless. She took on the even more difficult Jean Rhys in her old age and put up with no end of fuss and fume from her, recognising perhaps another talented beauty grown old and enraged. Plante found her refusal to talk about his deeper self painful. 'I wonder,' he asks her at lunch when she is complaining that one of her shelves is wonky, 'if I feel more isolated here in Europe than in America.' Her reply is deliciously Mad-Hatterish: 'You might as well ask if you'd feel isolated on Mars. The question doesn't have much consequence. No, no. Don't think about it. Now, I've got to get that shelf up properly, as I have some French house guests coming.' Self-absorbed, he calls her. A pairing made in heaven, I'd say.

The major complaints about Sonia Orwell come from those who wanted access to Orwell's papers, especially potential biographers. She was fierce in her control of the estate, or doggedly loyal to her husband's wishes. To Spurling, her attempt to retain control of the estate, and her failure to do so after a court case against the accountant who ran it, was the root cause of her death – a difficult one this, since she died of a brain tumour. At any rate, at the end of the 1970s she suddenly gave up the house in which she had held a literary salon and went to France, living in a bedsit and shunning her friends. Reading was her only consolation. 'But when I put them down or when I wake up, it's all there again ... this terrible endless tunnel into which I've drifted which, naturally, I feel is somehow all my fault but from which I'll never emerge again, but worse [I feel] that I've damaged George.' Michael Shelden, on the other hand, sees her as battling to retain *her* rights and income.

Sonia Orwell was a good editor with a fine nose for talent, but she did not produce anything of her own. Instead, her life is an insight into the lives and times of others. According to Shelden, 'Orwell's widow, Sonia, who had married him only three months before his death and who was fifteen years his junior, had her opinions, one of which was: "He believed there is nothing about a writer's life that is relevant to a judgement of his work."' It seems her opinion was correct. Orwell himself wrote in an essay on Salvador Dalí: 'One ought to be able to hold in one's head simultaneously the two facts that Dalí is a good draughtsman and a disgusting human being. The one does not invalidate or, in a sense, affect the other.'

It's a kindness to want to rectify the denigration of friends who cannot defend themselves. Spurling's memoir is plainly that, and good-hearted. As to the truth, who knows? Perhaps it is the best kind of biography. Orwell might have thought so. Because Sonia never wrote anything, nothing can be illuminated or misconstrued except the subject herself. But to admire the capacity for art in others must surely make one wish to produce it oneself. It may be that this was the final source of her sadness when life was coming to a close and someone else's work was all there was to fight for.

25 April 2002

FASHION AS ART

In spite of the V&A's Versace festival, and books like *Fashion Statements: Archaeology of Elegance 1980-2000*, I've never been convinced by the idea of fashion as art. I don't see why it has to be; it has so much else to do. When culture and art swan up and down the catwalk bedecked in 'fashion', I find myself scrummaging around in the oversized wardrobe in the spare room at the back of my mind, thinking about my lifelong romance with what I can't help calling 'clothes'. Call them 'clothes', and what some people think of as art and cultural studies become for me private history, memory and a grossly overspent youth and middle-age in search of the perfect garment. I recall a much-published novelist claiming in an interview that she would rather never have written a word than have lost the husband who divorced her a dozen years before. I gasped to read this. Give up writing for love? Really? World peace, maybe, social and educational equality, possibly – though I would demand firm guarantees. Then an image slithered into my head of a cupboard – let's call it a closet – stuffed with slinky Galliano slips of dresses, a handful of witty Chanel suits, a selection of madly deconstructed Margielas and Demeulemeesters, a Saint Laurent Smoking section, an unworn sprinkling of sparkling Versace, an almost-invisible beige shimmer of

Armani, and beneath, all in neat array, row upon row of Blahnik, Miu Miu and Jimmy Choo kitten heels. Well, would I have traded work for frocks? Certainly I'd give my right arm for such a wardrobe (I'm left-handed). My soul, without doubt (but then before the tragic days of giving up, I once offered up my soul in return for a late-night cigarette when I'd run out). My integrity you could have for a song, though I value it enough to demand lyrics by Cole Porter or Lorenz Hart. My sanity I gave up long ago when I discussed with a friend whether it was preferable to be mad or fat. But I wouldn't give up writing. At least I don't think so ...

But it isn't really fashion that has such a hold on me. It is (like the ultimate book in my head, which is storyless, characterless and perfect) an image, without any detail, of the perfect outfit, the one that slips over my frame and drapes itself around my contours in a way that finally defines me – look, this is what I am – just as my flesh defines the boundaries between myself and the world. And it's a private thing essentially, not primarily about being seen in or envied for a fashionable look: indeed, I generally imagine wearing these incomparable outfits in the privacy of my own home. It's stuff to sit on the sofa with that I'm after first of all; then it's OK to go out and flaunt the frocks. Fashion statements and identity statements are much of a muchness as far as I'm concerned. To look like, to feel like and to be like are as close as flesh and bone.

The crucial encounter with fashion occurred when I was twelve. Until then I had put up with whatever my mother considered respectable, an accurate mirror of the life she wished to be perceived as having. I baulked loudly, it is true, at discomfort, which came mostly in the form of woollen vests that she told me were as soft as butter (meaning expensive and imported from Belgium) but which were actually as scratchy as barbed wire. But by the time I was twelve, the family fortunes had taken such a severe downturn and swerve away from the Belgian imports that Social Services had issued her with a voucher to buy me a pair of shoes to wear at my new secondary school. This was a matter of desperate shame for my mother, returning her to a poverty she had devoted her life to escaping. The idea of handing over – in public – vouchers from the state instead of crisp currency agonised her. Worse, the vouchers were rejected with the disdain she feared at all the shops she usually went to – Daniel Neal did not X-ray any old child's feet. The only place that accepted them was a gloomy little cobbler's shop which, as I remember it, was hidden away under a near derelict railway arch in the fashion wasteland of King's Cross. The Dickensian and mawkish nature of the occasion as I recall it, the drab light and huddled aspect of the shoe shop, suggests that this may be one of those false memories you hear so much about, conjured up to match the dismal mood of the event. The old man who owned the place, unshaven, bent, gruff and wheezing – the Victorian workhouse vision just won't go back in its box – inspected the voucher, measured my feet, and without a word shuffled to the back of the shop. He returned with a single shoe box.

'See if these fit,' he said to my mother.

Taking off the lid, he brought out a pair of the grimmest black lace-up school shoes I had ever seen in my life. 'Sturdy' doesn't even get close to describing their brute practicality. In today's fashion-diverse world it is hard to imagine the despair I felt at the sight of what he expected me to put on my feet. And then greater despair yet as it occurred to me that I would be expected actually to wear them out in the world. They were so blankly, stylelessly sensible that they might have been orthopaedic appliances (poverty and disability perhaps being seen as equally reprehensible). Great clumping virtuous blocks of stiff leather with bulbous reinforced toecaps, designed (and I use the word loosely as a small bubble of ancient hysteria wells up) never to wear out. The best that could be hoped for was to grow out of them, after which they would still be sound enough to be passed down to generation after generation of the undeserving poor. Probably today they would be at the more moderate end of chunky footwear. I confess there have been times when I've rejoiced in wearing very similar things with an incongruously delicate little number in chiffon – though Doc Martens are ladylike in comparison. But back then – think 1959, the burgeoning of youth culture, rock and roll, multilayered net petticoats, ponytails – I only had to take one look at them, to see myself arriving at my new school with those on my feet, to know and feel, gut and spine, head and heart, the shame of becoming an instant fashion (and therefore everything else) pariah in the cruel girls' world of T-bars, flatties and slip-ons. The shoes would stand for my entire character, my class, my race, my lack of nous, and forever after my almond-toed peers would deem me a sad case to be avoided and sniggered at as I clunked my solitary way around the playground. But it wasn't just the social disaster of such unfashionability that froze my heart: it was the fear that appearing to be the kind of person who wore such shoes might mean that that was the person I actually was. It wasn't just that my peers would despise me: I would despise myself. I didn't even dare risk seeing my reflection in the mirror in the empty shop.

I said, politely, that I didn't like them, thinking he had mistaken me for someone who might be happy to help him get rid of his unsaleable items and that he must have kept back his stock of fashion footwear. He showed no sign of having heard me. He was not impressed, he wasn't interested in an opinion: he just wanted to know if he needed to bother to get another size. These, it was made clear, were the shoes you got in return for vouchers. Take them or leave them, he told my mother, not so much as glancing at me. Though I sensed that the world was about to end (in the way it often did when things went wrong for my mother), I shook my head firmly. I refused even to try them on. I would simply not have them on my feet. His lip curled at my bad character. My mother's embarrassment redoubled at having to be embarrassed in front of this miserable old man. It was bad enough having to be on the receiving end of charity without having to suffer the charity-giver's contempt. But I shook my head steadily from side to side and kept my toes curled tightly so that even if they used force, they would never get those clodhopping shoes on me. I ought to be grateful that taxpayers were providing me with any shoes at all, the shopkeeper rasped. (Was he really wearing a food-stained, cigarette-burned buff cardigan and checked-felt slippers?) It was these, or it was nothing.

'Then it's nothing,' I said, quite prepared for whatever civic punishment befell ungrateful children who didn't know their place (though I looked forward less to the moment when my mother got me home). I would wear my present shoes down to a sliver. If necessary I would go to school barefoot. My mother didn't bother to wait – she shouted at me all the way home. I slunk along beside her in silence. How could I do this to her, she screamed. What did a pair of shoes matter? In fact, they mattered more than her wretchedness, even more than my loved, lost and delinquent father, who had put us in this situation. They mattered like life itself. More, perhaps. Now, I am somewhat ashamed of having been obdurate when times were bad, but the truth is that even as I write I flush at the imagined ignominy of wearing those shoes. It was, as it were, my first fashion statement.

Between then and now fashion and my fortunes have been up and down and back again, but at no point have clothes been secondary. In the 1960s, I was in cheap frock heaven, alternating between instant fashion (skirts the length of a window pelmet, crushed velvet bell-bottoms, fishnet tights and purple boots with platform soles from Biba and Granny Takes a Trip) and wild antique fantasies (Victorian lace nighties and velvet frockcoats, original 1940s working-girl bias-cut dresses and moth-eaten movie-star fox-fur jackets) culled for shillings from Portobello Road. Later, it was the denim and boiler suits of the school-teaching radical 1970s (Camden Market), then the swagger of big-shouldered jackets and snappy high heels, followed by loose, soft, draping viscose (how I thank the gods for letting me be born into the era of viscose) and silk, layer on layer of it (beloved Nicole Farhi), or parodic mannish suits (Emporio).

Buying clothes is an act of bewitchment. As soon as I stand in front of a rail of garments, a trance descends on me. My consciousness rises slightly above my corporeal body so that I seem to be looking down on myself (a near clothes-buying experience) as my hand reaches out and slides the hangers along, one by one (small grating noises, wooden clicks), my fingers twitching the fabric, feeling its texture and weight (no hint of Belgium wool), my eyes drawing a bead on each item, assessing it to see if it belongs in my life. No, no, no: and then – yes! This is the one. I've found it. It has found me. As if I had been drawn into the shop by its presence. As if getting up that morning and leaving the house had been a response to the whispering in my sartorial soul of this garment, reaching out to find me as it waited, created as it was, destined as it was to be mine. I try it on only for the pleasure of seeing myself for the first time exactly as I should look and feel. At last, after all these decades, after all that shopping, I have the garment I was always meant to wear. It's a silk shirt, a linen skirt, a pair of jeans, a sharp suit, a wispy frock, a pair of pink kitten heels, a sweatshirt, a pair of pull-on baggy trousers: but what it really is, is perfect. And (almost) whatever the cost, no matter the state of my bank balance or the condition of my house and car, however many remarkably similar – similar but not *perfect* – things I may have in my cupboard at home, I buy it knowing that now at last I will be content.

And for a while, I am. Yes, of course all the skirts, shoes and dresses in my bulging wardrobe were each the perfect garment when I bought them. And so they remained for days, weeks, occasionally even months, as I existed at last in the world looking exactly like I wanted to look, just right: until I began to feel that scratchy need somewhere in my solar plexus and it seemed to me that I heard a susurration in my inner ear, telling me that something, somewhere was hanging on a rail waiting for me to meet it. The next siren call comes, the last thing bought seems somehow not quite right. And, sleuthing around the shops, I discover once again a garment that in my mind balances perfectly on the narrow boundary between inner and outer definition, which I have been looking for, doubtless, since the day of the implacable black school shoes. That's why fashion as culture, fashion as art, leaves me cold: I'm too preoccupied with clothing myself to pay it proper attention.

14 November 2002

It Wasn't Him, It Was Her

Any mentally idle, story-hungry novelist or scriptwriter would do well to attend to the entangled and twisted lives of Friedrich and Elisabeth Nietzsche, which present ready made a nearly perfect narrative. Most real lives need a good deal of cutting and pasting to get them into story shape. Here, no complicated restructuring is required: you have only to start at the beginning and go on to the end (Friedrich's ending before he ended; Elisabeth's continuing long after her demise) and you have as rich a tale of human relations and mental worlds as any reader or viewer could stomach.

We more or less know about Nietzsche, but Elisabeth, the little sister and living embodiment of everything the mad philosopher disdained, who took control of her brother's thought, should not on any account be overlooked. Her life is a story of mediocrity triumphing over inspiration, meanness over excess, *ressentiment* over the Übermensch. Her transformation of her brother's work into a Nazi cookbook bears an uncanny resemblance to the rise of National Socialism itself in a chaotic Germany. After a lifetime of failing to keep up with her brother, she finally appropriated him, body and what was left of his mind: not so much will to power as determined opportunism. Little beasts that lay their eggs in a larger creature and whose offspring use the living body of their host as a food store come to mind.

Since the late 1950s scholars have been busy releasing Nietzsche's reputation from the grip of Nazification. Elisabeth's role in creating Nietzsche-the-Nazi-Philosopher has been well attested, and his notebooks and published writings have been restored to something like the form they had before his sister cut, forged, destroyed and elided them. In fact, according to Michael Tanner, the work has been so extensive that Nietzsche has been reappropriated by just about everyone: 'existentialists, phenomenologists, and then increasingly, during the 1960s and 1970s ... critical theorists, post-structuralists and deconstructionists'. Not to mention anarchists, libertarians, hippies, yippies, radical psychiatrists, religious cultists ...

Carol Diethe, the author of *Nietzsche's Sister and the Will to Power*, believes that Nietzsche's name still needs clearing. As a founder of something called the British Friedrich Nietzsche Foundation (I couldn't find it on the Web), she presents this biography of Elisabeth Nietzsche as a condemnation of the actions of the woman who brought the work of the great misunderstood philosopher into disrepute:

> My chief accusation against Elisabeth is that
> she tarnished her brother's name. I have spent
> a large part of my career trying to convince the
> recalcitrant British public that it was Nietzsche's
> sister Elisabeth, and not Nietzsche himself – long
> dead – who stood at the door of the Nietzsche-
> Archiv to welcome Hitler. Few people apart from
> experts in the field have any inkling that

Nietzsche predeceased his sister by some
thirty-five years.

As a long-ago anarchist, libertarian, hippie (etc.) I'd
read a bit of Nietzsche, but it's true that I knew nothing
about the Nietzsche Archive and wasn't even aware
that he had a sister. Unfortunately, Diethe, though
she has clearly spent a working life in the Nietzsche
Archive, is unable to organise or present her case very
satisfactorily to those of us who aren't specialists but
willing members of the British public. Too much prior
information or not enough interest is assumed in the
often-limited detail of what she describes of Elisabeth
and Friedrich's lives. To fill out her omissions and even
to make sense of the overall narrative I read Ronald
Hayman, J.P. Stern, Michael Tanner, Rüdiger Bittner,
Walter Kaufmann, Lesley Chamberlain and, yes, even
Nietzsche on Nietzsche, Ben Macintyre on Elisabeth's
Paraguayan adventure, and H.F. Peters on Lou Andreas-
Salomé (some of the detail below is from these books
rather than Diethe's).

Diethe's answer to the question of why Elisabeth
so corrupted Nietzsche's work teeters between a
half-hearted feminist reading which suggests that an
inadequate education was to blame for her crimes, and
an assumption that hell has no fury like an incestuous
sister scorned. On the one hand:

There is no guarantee that an excellent education
would have prevented her from some of the
excesses of her later life, such as her support for
her husband's antisemitism, and, in her old age,
her admiration for the Fascists Mussolini and

Hitler ... But what would she have been like if
she, like her brother, had received an education
that truly taught her to think for herself?

(Wouldn't it be fine if an excellent education prevented
people from coming to the wrong conclusions, and if
such a thing as an education that truly taught people
to think for themselves existed, then or now?) And on
the other hand, there is Elisabeth's 'unconscious desire
for her brother', her 'love for her brother that verged
on incest' so that 'under cover of boundless sisterly
love, she conducted a vendetta against Nietzsche for
having once dared to love Lou by turning Zarathustra
into a Fascist ideologue.' In consequence, a steamy
post-Freudian family saga pulses beneath the surface of
what is intended to be a scholarly biography. There is
an echo here of *My Sister and I*, a forgery purporting to
be Nietzsche's confession, in full soft-porn Technicolor,
of his frolics with his sister. 'Suddenly I felt Elisabeth's
warm little hands in mine, her hissing voice in my ear,
and I began feeling warm all over.'

Their father had died of what was called 'softening
of the brain' when the two children were very small,
and although Friedrich was just two years older than
Elisabeth, he took on a paternal, not to say patronising
role. He told her what to read and how to write ('If only
she could learn to write better! And when she narrates
something, she must leave out all the "ahs" and "ohs"
and "you won't believe how lovely, how wonderful,
how enchanting etc it was"'). He encouraged her to
learn and to sit in on lectures at Leipzig University.
He also encouraged her to keep house for him when
he became a professor of philology at Basle at the age

of twenty-four. He called her 'Llama' after a book they had read as children, and she came when called to ease his life of nine-day migraines and what appears to have been a near autistic incapacity to deal socially with the world. Elisabeth behaved quite conventionally as an unmarried woman, living with her mother, Franziska, in Naumburg, and sometimes housekeeping for her bachelor brother. Her thinking was conventional, too. In 1865 she had a brief flirtation with the possibility of free thinking and wrote to Friedrich: 'Since I cannot forget my llama nature, I'm completely confused, and prefer not to think about it, because I just come up with nonsense.' Nietzsche tells her how it is: 'Here the ways of man part; if what you want is peace of soul and happiness, then believe; if you want to be a disciple of truth, then seek.' She very quickly made up her mind against being a disciple of truth. In 1878 she quarrelled fiercely with her brother because of the atheism in *Human, All Too Human*, though the rift that the book created between him and the Wagners was as much the cause of Elisabeth's suffering, since she found being in their classy social aura very agreeable. Cosima blamed Nietzsche's best friend Paul Rée, who was Jewish. 'Finally Israel intervened in the form of a Dr Rée, very sleek, very cool, at the same time as being wrapped up in Nietzsche and dominated by him, though actually outwitting him – the relationship between Judaea and Germany in miniature.' Friedrich and Elisabeth made it up, but Elisabeth managed to keep in with the Wagners by babysitting and running errands for them while they continued to shake their heads at Nietzsche's apostasy.

It took Lou Salomé to cause an unbreachable gulf between the brother and sister. As if specially designed to be Elisabeth's nemesis, Lou met Wagner when she was twenty-one, sparklingly clever, bare-footed, free-spirited, free-thinking (though sexually abstinent) and instantly desirable to every man who came across her. She met Paul Rée and proposed that the two of them find a third and spend a winter chastely living and learning together in Paris or Vienna, attending lectures and studying in the company of interesting people. Nietzsche was invited to form the third side of the triangle and instantly fell gauchely in love. Freud said of Nietzsche that no one ever had or ever would understand themselves as well as he did, but that understanding how to conduct human relationships was not his strong suit. Lou may have kissed Nietzsche when they were walking together, which was enough to cause him to propose a second time; the first proposal – made the day they met, when he greeted her with 'What stars have sent us orbiting towards each other?' – had been, he said, merely to regularise the situation when they lived together in the winter. And if further proof were needed of his inability to understand people, he asked the narrow-minded, provincial and possessive Elisabeth to meet up with wild and wilful Lou in Bayreuth and bring her to Tautenburg to spend time with him. There was a knock-down row in their hotel room in Bayreuth, with Elisabeth in her spinsterish mid-thirties giving Lou the benefit of her womanly wisdom. Lou had been flirting with Joukowsky, one of Wagner's acolytes, and Elisabeth warned her that her reputation was at stake. When Lou, never very aware of other people's sensitivities, broke into shrieks of laughter, Elisabeth berated her for betraying Friedrich, a virtuous and innocent pastor's son, and tempting him with indecent, uncivilised proposals. H.F. Peters quotes Lou's version of her reply:

> Don't get the idea that I am interested in your brother, or in love with him. I could spend a whole night with him in one room without getting excited. It was your brother who first soiled our study plan with the lowest intentions. He only started to talk about friendship when he realised he could not have anything else. It was your brother who first proposed 'free love'.

At this point Elisabeth became hysterical and vomited.

The Tautenburg idyll was not a success. Lou and Rée went off together and left Nietzsche in a puddle of baffled and betrayed misery. His rage at Lou ('a monkey with false breasts'; 'Better to fall into the hands of a murderer than into the dreams of a woman on heat') did nothing to improve his already epic misogyny, and he never forgave his sister for poisoning the image of his only love and preventing him from coming to terms with his loss. 'For a year now,' he wrote of her interference, 'she has cheated me out of my greatest self-conquest by talking at the wrong time and being silent at the wrong time, so that in the end I am the victim of her merciless desire for vengeance.' But if Nietzsche was capable of seeing himself as a pitiful victim, he was also able to see the larger, awful joke. 'I have the Naumburg "Virtue" against me,' he wrote. A couple of months before his collapse he declared in *Ecce Homo* (in a passage that only narrowly survived Elisabeth's attempts to suppress it): 'When I look for my profoundest opposite, the incalculable pettiness of my instincts, I always find my mother and my sister – to be related to such canaille would be blasphemy against my divinity … I confess that the deepest objection to the "eternal recurrence", my real idea from the abyss, is always my mother and my sister.'

Elisabeth tried to make a life of her own when the life she tried to make with her brother failed. She married a proto-Nazi, Bernhard Förster, an antisemitic, nationalist boor whose big dream came true with the founding of Nueva Germania, an Aryan colony in Paraguay. Nietzsche railed against his brother-in-law for his antisemitism and his pro-German beliefs. He wrote to Elisabeth as his 'llama gone among the antisemites' and derided Nueva Germania. Elisabeth found herself with a straggle of colonists in a mosquito-ridden, uncleared jungle where sandflies bored into the skin of the feet and the clay soil was so intractable that nothing would grow. The sweet nothings Elisabeth and Bernhard wrote to each other ('Dear, magnificent, great one,' he writes to her; 'My dear Bernhard of my heart', 'Your little Eli,' she writes back) turned sour. The funding turned out to be chimerical; Förster panicked and took to drink. On hearing of Nietzsche's collapse in Turin, Elisabeth wrote home to her mother:

> Naturally I am an excellent wife when, as usual, I take every burden upon myself with pleasure, the only reward the success of our enterprise, never desiring anything for myself, but only ever caring about Bern and the colony … But now for the past six weeks I have thought about myself for once, first I had a painful eye infection and then this great trouble, and I am only now discovering that Bern is a terrible egoist.

When Bernhard poisoned himself in a hotel room in San Bernadino, Elisabeth was free to return home (she always insisted that he had died of a stroke, in spite of the vial of poison found beside the body) and take charge of her now hopelessly mad brother, whose work, all of a sudden, was engaging the interest of readers. She changed her name to Elisabeth Förster-Nietzsche and paid her mother off in return for her relinquishing all claims to Friedrich's royalties. The Nietzsche-Archiv was born in her mother's house in Naumburg, where, to Franziska's distress, Elisabeth held soirées on the ground floor as Friedrich babbled upstairs. Sometimes she would allow guests a viewing of her brother, dressed by her in a white pleated robe like a Brahmin. Meta von Salis, who provided a free house in Weimar, the Villa Silberblick, for the Nietzsches and the archive (and to whom Elisabeth presented a bill for redecoration), was appalled when she read a newspaper article by a journalist who had been allowed to watch Nietzsche sleep and to observe him being fed bits of cake as he cowered on a chair. Rudolf Steiner tried to teach Elisabeth her brother's philosophy but gave up in disgust at her lack of understanding. In time, Thomas Mann, Romain Rolland and Oswald Spengler all resigned their posts at the archive, unable to tolerate what Elisabeth was doing to her brother's work and her cosying up to the Nazis. Walter Benjamin wrote that Nietzsche was worlds away from the 'industrious and philistine spirit' that dominated the Nietzsche-Archiv. The University of Jena refused an alliance with the archive, stating that 'the scholarly reputation of the Nietzsche-Archiv is not the best.' Astonishingly, Elisabeth was put forward for the Nobel Prize for Literature in 1911 and 1923 (probably on the basis of her biography of her brother), only to be pipped at the post by Maeterlinck and Yeats.

If you assume that Nietzsche mad was Nietzsche dead, then *The Will to Power* was published posthumously by Elisabeth, who raided the notebooks, took what she fancied entirely out of context and whether or not it had been crossed out, and knitted together a book that Heidegger helped make respectable. She turned the virulently anti-German, anti-antisemite into a Jew-hating hyper-nationalist and suppressed everything inconvenient in his writings. Wishing to translate Nietzsche, Mazzino Montinari examined the archive and reported:

> Our hair stood on end when we came to read,
> in the shorter Nietzsche biography by Förster-
> Nietzsche, such comments by Richard Oehler
> [Elisabeth's nephew] as 'apparently not printed
> in the works' or 'apparently not published in the
> posthumous works' regarding decisive quotations
> from Nietzsche cited in the text ... What was still
> slumbering away in the manuscripts after more
> than seventy years of which we – in Florence –
> would never have been able to learn?

Nietzsche wrote in *Beyond Good and Evil* that the task of 'free, *very* free spirits' was to translate 'man back into nature' after tradition had scribbled and painted over the original text. The job of translating Nietzsche's thought back into its original form after Elisabeth got her hands on it has been very similar. But it has to be said that concepts such as Übermensch and Herrenmoral lent themselves to becoming the bedrock of National

Socialist philosophy. It wasn't exactly a case of a liberal democrat being forced into bed with National Socialism, though Nietzsche clearly would have hated Hitler. The problem, J.P. Stern suggests, is that Nietzsche was too non-political to see how his thoughts about the way individuals should conduct themselves might be used by something very nasty indeed. Stern, at least, does not let Nietzsche off entirely; he must take some blame for failing to pursue the consequences of his ideas.

He cannot, however, be blamed for his sister's girlish, giggling delight in Fascism, sending Mussolini a fiftieth-birthday telegram and welcoming Hitler and Albert Speer to the archive to plan the building of a Friedrich Nietzsche Memorial Hall. But Elisabeth was at least as interested in inflating herself as she was in perverting her brother's ideas. Her biography of Nietzsche is a double hagiography, comic and almost sad in its reflection of her own will to power. 'Never in our lives, indeed, did we say an unkind word to each other; and if we sometimes wrote unpleasant things, it is because, when apart, we came under the baneful influence of others.'

As a woman who had gained considerable power, she was about as useful to other women as that other great Nietzschean, Margaret Thatcher. Elisabeth claimed that the sewing machine was responsible for feminism: it made women's real job of domestic sewing take too little time and so left their minds too free for foolish ideas. Women who spoke of freedom were inclined to smoke cigars and behave in a masculine fashion. She excuses her brother's misogyny (he said, according to her, that intellectual women were 'super-clever gabbling geese') as a defence against the excesses of modern-day feminists.

Hitler attended Elisabeth's funeral – she died in 1935 – at which she was eulogised as the 'priestess of eternal Germany'. In order to be buried in the dead centre of the family plot she had arranged to have Friedrich's well-rotted corpse shifted several feet to one side, though another story has it that only her brother's gravestone was moved, in which case his body is marked with Elisabeth's name, and hers is proclaimed to be the remains of Friedrich Nietzsche – as fine and final an instance of overcoming as might be found.

25 September 2003

XXX

Stanley Milgram's series of experiments to find out how far individuals would go to obey authority are legendary. Conducted in New Haven, Connecticut in 1961, they have been cited in manuals written by dog trainers (*Bones Would Rain from the Sky* by Suzanne Clothier – do not follow dog experts blindly; instincts; humanity) and self-help pundits (*The Necessary Disobedience* by Maria Modig, dedicated to Milgram – empowerment; taking responsibility), as well as being the source for a Peter Gabriel song entitled 'We Do What We're Told (Milgram's 37)'. A French punk rock group called Milgram put out a CD called *Vierhundertfünfzig Volt* ('450 Volts'). A British band called Midget issued *The Milgram Experiment*. Plays have been written (Dannie Abse's *The Dogs of Pavlov* was the first, in 1973); a stand-up comedian, Robbie Chafitz, called his 1999 weekly off-off-Broadway performances *The Stanley Milgram Experiment*; a French movie with Yves Montand, *I ... comme Icare*, made in 1979, came out of it, with Milgram himself pictured on the set; and a textbook used in courses on business ethics cites the obedience experiments to warn students about the evil things their bosses might ask of them and how to resist. I can't say about the dog-training or self-help books, but this last educational effort doesn't seem to have worked.

Milgram advertised for his subjects in the *New Haven Register* (Yale students were considered too aggressive to use) and paid them $4 for their hour's attendance plus 50 cents' travel allowance. Only males (except in one variation) were used, and they spanned occupational levels from unskilled to professional. Each subject sat alone at a fake 'shock machine' built by Milgram, which had thirty switches, labelled in 15-volt increments from 15 volts to 450 volts and grouped in fours, with descriptions above each group: slight shock, moderate shock, strong shock, very strong shock, intense shock, extreme intensity shock, danger severe shock. The final two switches were labelled just xxx. Each subject was told they were participating in a 'Memory Project', the aim of which was to study how people learn. They were 'teachers'. In an adjoining room a 'learner' sat wired up to the shock machine. He had to repeat the second of pairs of words he was supposed to have learned. The 'teacher' cued with the first word. An incorrect answer was punished with an electric shock. With each wrong answer the 'teacher' was instructed to move up a switch. The learner, who was, of course, a member of Milgram's team, could be heard but not seen, and as the switches were flipped, he began complaining until, at the higher voltages, he screamed in agony and begged the subject not to hurt him, demanding his right to be let out. In addition to hearing the pain they were inflicting, the subjects were told that the learner had a heart condition. Any reluctance was met by the experimenter saying in authoritative tones: 'Please go on.' After three prompts, the subject was told: 'You have no choice, you *must* go on.' If the subject refused after the fourth prompt, the experiment was stopped. In some of the variations, after the 300-volt shock the learner pounded on the wall, and then after 315 volts remained totally silent.

Overall, 65 per cent of subjects were prepared to administer the 450-volt shock, not once, but several times. They sweated, they groaned, they queried, but when told they had to do it 'for the experiment', they flipped the switch. Milgram wrote:

> The results are terrifying and depressing. They suggest that human nature – or more specifically, the kind of character produced in American society – cannot be counted on to insulate its citizens from brutality and inhumane treatment at the direction of malevolent authority. In a naive moment some time ago, I once wondered whether in all of the United States a vicious government could find enough moral imbeciles to meet the personnel requirements of a national system of death camps, of the sort that were maintained in Germany. I am now beginning to think that the full complement could be recruited in New Haven. A substantial proportion of people do what they are told to do, irrespective of the content of the act, and without pangs of conscience, so long as they perceive that the command comes from a legitimate authority.

Not entirely without pangs – or perhaps pleas to be let off any moral responsibility.

The following is a quote from the transcript. The subject has just inflicted what he thinks is a 300-volt shock on the invisible learner next door.

LEARNER: [*Agonised scream*]
SUBJECT: I, I can't do this any more. [*chair scuffles*]
LEARNER: I absolutely refuse to answer any more. Get me out of here. You can't hold me here. Get me out. Get me out of here.
SUBJECT: I can't do it any more. I'm sorry. I realise that you're trying to do something.
EXPERIMENTER: The experiment requires that you continue to do so ...
SUBJECT: Yes, I know. But I'm just not the type of person that can inflict pain to anyone else, uh, more than what I feel. I felt I've gone far beyond what I should.
EXPERIMENTER: It's absolutely essential that you continue. Please go on.
SUBJECT: [*chair scuffles*] You know, I'm to the point now I can just feel each one with him. [*sigh*] The next one is GREEN: grass, hat, ink, apple ...

The sighs continued and there were long pauses before each following shock was given, but this subject was fully obedient and went on to flip all the switches.

In the initial experiment there were forty subjects. Many of those who went the whole 450 volts queried the authority in charge, but once they were told they had to, they continued even while expressing discomfort. Some were chillingly obedient. A thirty-seven-year-old welder's response was described in detail. He was in a variation of the original experiment where the learner is present and the subject is required to press his hand down on to an electric plate to administer the shock.

The learner, seated alongside him, begs him to stop, but with robotic impassivity, he continues the procedure ... He relates to the experimenter in a submissive and courteous fashion. At the 330-volt level, the learner refuses not only to touch the shock plate, but also to provide any answers. Annoyed, Batta turns to him and chastises him: 'You better answer and get it over with. We can't stay here all night.' ... He seems to derive no pleasure from the act itself, only quiet satisfaction at doing his job properly. When he administers 450 volts, he turns to the experimenter and asks: 'Where do we go from here, Professor?' His tone is deferential and expresses his willingness to be a co-operative subject, in contrast to the learner's obstinacy.

In this hands-on variation, Milgram expected one or two subjects, at most, to go on to the final switch. In fact, 12 out of 40 were fully compliant. 'It's a very disturbing sight,' Milgram noted, 'since the victim resists strenuously and emits cries of agony.' In the original experiment with an audible but invisible learner, twenty-six out of forty subjects were fully obedient and pressed the 450-volt switch; no subject stopped before 300 volts, the 'intense shock' zone; five refused to go on beyond that point, and fourteen defied the experimenter somewhere short of 450 volts.

But it must be just as important to consider the 35 per cent of subjects who did at some point refuse to continue. Early resistance to authority seemed to be the key, Milgram thought. The later they left it to complain, the greater the pressure to rationalise. Two examples of dissent are given in Thomas Blass's *The Man Who Shocked the World*. One man puts his foot down at 135 volts:

> EXPERIMENTER: The experiment requires that you go on, teacher. Go on, please.
> SUBJECT: But if you don't mind, I'd like to see him myself before I do go on.
> EXPERIMENTER: ... It's absolutely essential that you continue, teacher. Go on.
> SUBJECT: Well, I don't know. I don't think I'd like to take that myself, what he is taking right now.
> EXPERIMENTER: You have no other choice.
> SUBJECT: [*sneering*] I'll give you your check back if you want.

The second dissenter does not finally refuse until 315 volts and is then told he has no other choice. 'I have no other choice? Hmmm. Hmmm. [*pause*] I think I have.' (It's not clear to me whether my heart should soar at the man's recognition of the individual's personal responsibility in the matter of obeying authority or sink because his refusal is in response to a challenge to his ego.)

Milgram discovers in his laboratory that there is a tendency to obey authority. But why? Because of an inherent obedience, deference to men in white coats, an unwillingness to spoil a 'useful' experiment, sadism, the curious inertia in life generally that makes it harder to stop than to start, a social anxiety against speaking up, or just conditioned good manners? It's probably the case that politeness is the reason many victims, knowing it not to be wise, get into the cars of strangers or answer the door to them. Milgram opts for a vaguely sociobiological explanation that supposes social cohesion has made obedience a requirement for 'fitness', but even he doesn't seem very convinced. A more central question remains, one that is not discoverable in Milgram's experiments. Why did some people refuse when others didn't? Yes, we are inclined to comply – easy life, fear of group disapproval, reprisals, wanting to be in with the top guys – but what is it about the 35 per cent of refusers that made them eventually able to refuse? It was really only half an experiment, and the less useful half.

Milgram was a whiz at devising sexy experiments, but barely interested in any theoretical basis for them. They all have the same instant attractiveness of style, and then an underlying emptiness. He invented one experiment to test the idea that later became the basis of John Guare's play *Six Degrees of Separation*, getting students to try to make contact with someone a world away by asking only one close friend for a further contact until the designated person was reached. It turned out that generally it required a maximum of twelve contacts to get to anyone. Interesting, certainly, and a fine idea to pick up and play with as Guare did, but Milgram was not much inclined to tease meaning out of his findings. Perhaps he lost interest after the active part of devising and carrying out the experiment was over, or perhaps he realised that without a theory to test, experiments are little more than expensive though entertaining anecdotes. He also invented the 'lost letter' technique of supposedly testing local social and political feeling by dropping hundreds of stamped letters addressed, for example, to white racist and radical black organisations (in reality, PO boxes set up by the experimenters), and made the discovery that fewer letters were picked up and kindly posted to the racist addresses in black areas than letters addressed to the Panthers, and vice versa, of course, in white communities. The findings of these experiments were recorded but they hardly give very deep or valuable information; less, in the case of the lost letter technique, I imagine, than the crudest of opinion polls.

Milgram's study of obedience had a very mixed reception among his colleagues, not just because of its poor theoretical underpinning, and the fact that it was written up in glossy monthlies and popular weeklies rather than by Milgram in a professional journal, but because the experiment itself was thought to be unethical. Putting people under such extreme stress, even though they were told at the end that they had hurt no one, couldn't be done today: academic ethical standards committees would refuse permission for funding. These days, however, nothing prevents similar 'experiments' (*Big Brother*, the reworking of the Stanford Prison Experiment, *Castaway* and Co.) being carried out repeatedly for our fascination and entertainment on reality TV shows, and I wonder if that doesn't tell us something about the nature of the original experiments. The public, however, read newspaper reports of the obedience experiments in the mid-1960s and bought Milgram's 1974 book in industrial quantities. It seemed to be addressing important problems.

The search for the illumination of dark truths was rampant in the middle years of the twentieth century, those post-Holocaust, Cold War, Vietnam years, before the Reagan/Thatcher era. We read testimony of the concentration camps, and then Colin Turnbull's study of the Ik people, which proved that natural man is a complete shit (or, later, that natural man is a complete shit when unnatural man makes him so), was dramatised by Peter Brook, as was Oliver Sacks's evidence for I'm not sure what in *The Man Who Mistook His Wife for a Hat*. Napoleon Chagnon's study of the Yanomamö tribe flew around the world as further evidence that humanity had none. We read Foucault, who proposed that we were all subject to an authority so nebulous as to be undefeatable. Earlier, in the 1960s, even Shakespeare got in on the act with Jan Kott's *Shakespeare Our Contemporary*: the hopeless anti-heroics of Hamlet and the Nietzschean Iago were the very stuff that man was made on. We sucked in the awful tales of human beings and their fathomless vileness like babies on a truth tit. It's funny that the postwar children have come to be regarded as a formlessly liberal generation when, as I recall, one of the main projects was to confront the dark side of humankind in order to learn how it might be neutralised. We might well have been guilty of thinking too shallowly, of gulping our facts and developing a taste for the bitter; but happy-go-lucky, laissez-faire and carefree is not how I remember it. After the Holocaust, man's capacity for cruelty no longer seemed to be something to do with the remote past and its lack of indoor lavatory facilities or comprehensive schools, but was what our own parents were capable of doing. And if our own parents, then with the added blast of the newly discovered structure of the double helix that wove our parents into our every cell, why not us?

It didn't seem possible (surely, no one thinks of themselves as being rotten?), but the banality of evil, or at any rate the quotidian nature of mercilessness, was there in front of our eyes, and the postwar generation of social scientists were intent on devising ways to prove it. We marched against nuclear weapons not just because of their moral poverty, but also because the more we found out about what humanity was capable of, the less we could be deceived by the notion that safety lay in the doctrine of mutually assured destruction. It seemed like a good idea to know the awful truth about ourselves, although nowadays I'm not sure that just knowing helps much. We were, if ever there was one, the generation which believed that to know thyself was to be in a position to change. We must have botched the first task, because we've certainly bungled the second.

I suspect, however, that we failed to notice a missing term in the proposition. Between knowing ourselves and change, lay the chasm of how change might come about. An ill-digested Freudianism suggested that only awareness was necessary for the great catharsis. Bring the dark out into the light, show what is hidden, and all will be well. You have to become aware of what you (that is, we) are like and then, somehow, you (that is, we) will be different. Thinking of this kind was the problem with the obedience experiment. Milgram set out with the echoes of Nuremberg and the almost contemporary Eichmann trial in his mind: perhaps it wasn't just Germans who did what they were told. But having discovered that Americans, too, valued obedience to authority, that indeed we are all inclined to do what we are told, there was as ever no automatic bridge between knowing and changing. We must learn from this, Milgram said; we all said. But no one said *how* we were supposed to learn from it. It seemed it should have been obvious.

Plainly, it wasn't. In spite of the atrocities by American soldiers in Vietnam, the French in Algeria, the British in Northern Ireland, this very year, politicians and public alike in the US and the UK declared themselves baffled, disbelieving and amazed that American and British soldiers could torture and humiliate Iraqi prisoners. They meant, usually, *American* and *British* soldiers. Not even the elementary lesson Milgram had to teach has been absorbed. It is still thought that bad guys do bad things and good guys (that's us) don't do bad things. That's how you tell the difference. Then it turned out, quite recently, that telling the difference was a very big problem. For politicians (criminally self-interested or criminally sincere) to declare our natural goodness and their natural badness is one thing, but that anyone believes there is an inherently moral distinction which can be defined geographically or racially means people just haven't been paying attention to what the twentieth century – of which the Milgram study was little more than a reiteration and foreshadowing – made hideously clear. Tell people to go to war, and mostly they will. Tell them to piss on prisoners, and mostly they will. Tell them to cover up lies, and mostly they will. Authority is government, the media, the business sector, the priestly men and women in white coats or mitres. We are trained up in the structure of the family, in school, in work. Most people do what they are told. Apparently, a majority of people in this country did not want to join the US in making war on Iraq. This country joined the US in its catastrophic adventure nevertheless. The dissenters marched and argued and put posters up in their windows, but ... Great passions were aroused, and yet ... For the past eighteen months, the *Independent* newspaper has been producing astonishing front pages to make you weep, still ... It all happened, and goes on. It could be inertia, or a sense of helplessness, or it could be that our fear of the consequences of disobedience holds sway over our judgement. It looks as if in every generation there is moral panic and a perception (or hallucination of the horror to come) of the next generation as having lost its predisposition to be obedient. Civilisation depends on most of us doing what we are told most of the time. Real civilisation, however, depends on Milgram's 35 per cent who eventually get round to thinking for themselves.

But that, too, is a lazy, sentimental attitude. The 65/35 per cent split between the compliant and the resistant is just another version of good and bad, and leaves us essentially ignorant and free to declare our particular righteousness. Bush can take Milgram's division to signify Americans and Terrorists; bin Laden can use it to denounce the evil West to the Followers of Allah; Hitler to set Germans against Jews; Zionists to divide Jews from Palestinians. And Milgram is no help at all.

18 November 2004

MIRROR IMAGES

Life, Piers Morgan says about being sacked in 2004 as editor of the *Mirror*, is as serious as you want it to be. Lighten up, he repeatedly tells sad celebrities who complain about his front-page exposés that result in their unemployment or divorce. Take it easy, he emails spin doctors and government ministers who fear for their majorities after he has trashed their policies or their love lives to two million readers of the *Mirror*. I can see that if you are twenty-eight and editor of the *News of the World*, then you are thirty and getting £175,000 a year for editing the *Mirror*, until nine years later when you get the sack and score a reported £1.2 million for your reminiscences (*The Insider: The Private Diaries of a Scandalous Decade*), you might be inclined to advise people not to take life too seriously. It wouldn't be just the money and your own youthful inability to know any better that caused champagne bubbles to burst in your head where *serious* might have been; there would also be the nature of what you did to earn the money. There's no reason at all why anyone working on the *News of the World* and (until the invasion of Afghanistan) the *Mirror* should take anything seriously. Three things mattered to Piers Morgan: sales figures, breaking 'great' stories and adrenalin rushes. The first is necessary to keep your bosses happy, the *only* thing that will keep owners of tabloid newspapers happy, not because sales figures speak of the contentment of their readers but because of the advertising revenue large numbers of identifiable spending units bring in. Breaking great stories is a subset of upping the sales figures, and the adrenalin rushes presumably are what keep you going in those moments when you wonder if maintaining sales figures is quite enough to base a life on.

I am, of course, one of those 'broadsheet snobs' Morgan sneers at throughout the book, though not as much as he might think, because I don't rate the broadsheets very much higher on the cultural scale than the tabloids. Still, it's true I've read the *Sun* or the *Mirror* or the *News of the World* only occasionally, when one of them happens to be in front of me, and then with a kind of despair that grows like creeping paralysis over the will. I had the same reaction as I read Piers Morgan's diaries. Whatever sense of humour I may have had drained away as the ever ebullient, jokey, matey, vindictive Morgan described a self-contained world of vacant celebrity and tawdry sensationalism that I have never quite believed anyone took seriously. But it becomes clear that Morgan took it very seriously indeed, and so do the people whose lives were his raison d'être as an editor and maybe more than just as an editor. His narrative is entirely about being taken seriously by Elton John, Princess Diana, George Michael, Anthea Turner, Richard Branson, Paul McCartney, Patsy Kensit, Ian Botham, Jordan, Mohamed al-Fayed, Cherie Blair, Alastair Campbell, Peter Mandelson and Tony Blair. (If there are names in that list you haven't heard of, don't worry, none of them matters as much as they think they do.)

At a Christmas lunch at the Mirabelle for his *Mirror* columnists, Morgan remembers ecstatically how 'legend after legend' arrived at the table. He counts them in: Alan Sugar, Carol Vorderman, Jonathan Ross, Miriam Stoppard, Tony Parsons. Even for someone who started his career in national journalism as a showbiz reporter on the *Sun*, these are pitifully undemanding exemplars of legends. At one party he is quite near to someone who might just count: Jack Nicholson. He asks Fergie (the former wife of Prince Andrew) how he can get talking to the 'superstar'. Don't tell him you're a journalist, says Fergie, better say you're something interesting like a bank robber. Our compulsively cheeky chappie, desperate for Nicholson's attention, bounds up to him: 'Hey, Jack! Fergie says that if I tell you I'm a bank robber, you'll talk to me.' Nicholson is silent for a moment before telling poor Piers what they say about bank robbers: 'You never catch a good one. See ya later, pal.' This encounter is the entire entry for Sunday 5 July. There is an old joke about a man returning to his village after his first trip to the city. 'The king himself spoke to me,' he boasts to a rapt audience. 'What did he say?' they gasp. 'He said, he actually said, directly, to me, and I was as close as I am to you ... he said: "Get out of my way, peasant!"' And we have to suppose that if the villagers are our present-day red-top readers, they gasp in admiration and make him their headman. So this is how it is with Piers Morgan who, after a lunch with Mohamed al-Fayed, concludes that 'behind all the flamboyant bombast there lies a razor-sharp mind.'

His favourite mogul, his dream magnate, is, naturally, Rupert Murdoch. He whimpers with adoration about his first meeting in New York, where he is summoned to be sized up for the editorship of the *News of the World*:

> Murdoch drifted in like a ghost, literally creeping
> up on us without any fanfare at all. I'd heard
> this was his deadliest weapon, his ability to just
> appear and scare the daylights out of you. It can
> be especially unnerving in the loo apparently.
> I mean, what the hell do you say standing next
> to the world's most powerful tycoon with your
> flies open?

Well, Piers, what about something like: 'Your penis is so very much bigger than mine, Mr Murdoch, sir, and I'd use your shit for toothpaste.' At dinner, Morgan wisely kept his conversation at his own level. There are things he knows nothing about, apparently: 'anything financial, for example – Murdoch's area of undisputed global expertise'. Nevertheless, he practises a bit in front of the mirror after boning up on *Newsweek*, the *Economist* and *Time*. 'Yes, Mr Murdoch, I agree that Clinton's been too aggressive in his macro-economic view of China,' he tells his reflection. Underneath the greatness, however, Murdoch is just a fabulous guy. Of course, you've got to know him, like Piers does:

> Murdoch has an extraordinary mind, it races
> around all sorts of disparate subjects at high
> speed, pumping out completely unambiguous
> statements. He doesn't do middle ground ... His
> power doesn't require him to impress anyone.
> He wasn't recognised by anyone in the room,
> there were none of the usual mutterings you see

and hear if you go somewhere with someone like Richard Branson. But if, like me, you know who he is, then he holds your attention like Don Corleone in *The Godfather*. He is easy to talk to, and surprisingly funny. I really liked him.

Below the highest level of the superstars and moguls like Jack, Mohamed and Rupert, there is a solid phalanx of the currently famous, and they are at the mercy of Morgan the tabloid editor, as he is at the mercy of those like Murdoch and the *Mirror* executives who hire or fire him at will. He loves celebrities and the world they live in but he's a cut above them. He may not be the world's most powerful tycoon, but he's the man who can shatter the fragile framework of their lives. If he likes them and there's something in it for the paper, he'll give them a chance, even do them a favour. Paula Yates rings him up when her divorce settlement with Bob Geldof is going badly. 'I'm going to walk the kids home from school today in the rain because I can't afford a taxi. If you take some pictures, then Bob might feel shamed into helping me properly.' Morgan's thoughts on the subject have a curious moral content: 'I could hardly believe what I was hearing, but it would be a good picture so I agreed. Sure enough, they turned up on time, in the rain, shuffling home. Undignified is not the word. For any of us involved in this sorry ongoing farce.' I think to Morgan that 'us involved' is as crucial as the good picture. The 'undignified' is an expression of his essential superiority. These people are only getting their comeuppance, therefore what he does is a kind of service, just as when he tells Jack Straw that by exposing his son Will's dope smoking, Morgan has done the boy a favour and prevented him perhaps from spiralling down into the depravity of a tabloid drug hell.

Making judgements comes easily to Morgan. He has no trouble telling the difference between the deserving and the undeserving. In 1994 he exposed a 'Sex and Security Scandal', revealing to readers of the *News of the World* that the chief of defence staff, Sir Peter Harding, was having an affair with the very nearly perfectly named Lady Bienvenida Buck. Even amid his rejoicing at the 80,000 extra copies he sold and feeling like 'I've won an Olympic gold medal for gutter journalism or something – utterly, deliciously intoxicating,' he spares a thought for his victims: 'I must admit this evening I have been thinking a bit about Sir Peter Harding, whose glittering career – and probably life – now lies in tatters. He's been a bloody fool, and deserves to be exposed for his hypocrisy and the stupid risks he's taken. But it's a high price to pay.' His moral feelers grow more sensitive by the day. A few months later, a story comes his way about a completely unknown woman switchboard operator who became obsessed with a caller and began pestering him. He called the police and it became, according to Morgan, a 'classic *NoW* story'. But as the story was about to run, the reporter who found it said the woman 'had broken down and pleaded for mercy' from the *News of the World*. She had just left a psychiatric hospital to which she had been committed after a suicide attempt. The news story would send her over the edge. Morgan checked her out and found what she said was true:

> I pulled the story. Lots of people break down
> when we confront them, and lots threaten to

kill themselves. But there is a difference between paedophiles and lonely disturbed women like this. I could not have lived with myself if we had exposed her on page 17 and then she had killed herself … I am developing a curious moral code as I go. Sometimes the job does feel a bit like playing God with people's lives. I get, ultimately, to decide every week who lives and who dies by the *NoW* sword.

I read with real desolation that it was in the power of Piers Morgan (who once, wanting a quote from a famous Spaniard, suggested Mussolini) to decide between the moral rights of paedophiles and lonely, disturbed women, or to decide anything at all of importance to anyone – but then I remember that life is only as serious as you want it to be and tell myself to lighten up. Never mind that the decision to ruin or save lives is made for a lazy Sunday entertainment, in pursuit of the profit margins of News International, just keep a sense of humour. It is, after all, only the way the world of newspapers works. Everyone understands it. 'Look Elton,' Morgan says when Elton John moans about people ratting on him to the papers. 'We think they are scum, like you do. But we will pay them and publish what they say if it is true, because that's the game we're all in, and you know it as well as I do.' And the game, of course, is circulation, and circulation is money and money is what matters. It's easy enough to let a switchboard operator with dull daydreams off, no extra copies will be lost. But paedophiles and pop singers pump up the circulation. Not just undeserving, but real money-makers. Morgan is a mite ambivalent, or sometimes wants to be seen that way. When, lacking anything else to put on the front page, he splashes on a forthcoming embargoed big moment in *EastEnders*, the circulation rises by 100,000. 'I feel repulsion for the public,' says this virtuoso taker of moral temperature. Later, however, when his stand against the Iraq war loses the paper 80,000 readers, he writes an 'urgent email' to Sly Bailey, chief executive of Trinity Mirror:

> I am afraid I misjudged the way our readers
> would respond to the start of the war and our
> line has clearly been too confrontational and too
> critical for many of them ... I am very sorry about
> this, it means we'll drop below two million for the
> month and that is desperately unfortunate ...
> I will just have to get those readers back as fast
> as I can. One thing I won't be doing is sitting
> here defiantly telling myself how I'm right and
> they are all wrong. The readers are never wrong.
> Repulsive, maybe, but never wrong.

There is someone else who emerges from the diary as knowing at least as much as Piers Morgan about the value of newspaper readers. As the new editor of the *News of the World*, Morgan is invited to tea at the Commons with Tony Blair and Alastair Campbell in 1994. Morgan, ever one to watch for signs of his own importance, notices not for the last time that Tony actually pours the tea himself. 'I want a good relationship with you and your paper,' Blair tells him. Just like Elton and Paula. It's the game they're all in. The way the world works. In 1995 Blair travelled to Hayman Island to give the keynote speech to Murdoch's News Corporation conference, which Morgan was thrilled to attend. He tells how Blair 'vowed to set free media companies from "heavy regulation" and allow them to exploit their "enterprise". Just what Murdoch wants to hear.' Quite. And the tea parties proliferate when New Labour gets into power. By the end of Piers's time in office, he tots up '22 lunches, 6 dinners, 6 interviews, 24 further one-to-one chats over tea and biscuits, and numerous phone calls with him. That's a lot of face time with arguably Britain's most important man.' I'd go along with that 'arguably'. Clearly anyone who edits any newspaper and certainly those who own them can claim to be more important, at least in Tony Blair's eyes. His attitude to the *Mirror* is that its loyalty is his by right. *Pravda*, as Morgan calls it in relation to New Labour. But it's the *Sun* Blair wants – actually everything Murdoch. 'Obviously the *Mirror* will always be our first port of call but we will have to have a good relationship with the other side too,' Blair warns Morgan. But time and time again, Blair or Campbell or Cherie slip vital information to the *Sun*, where New Labour's heart really lies, and eventually it causes the most remarkable upset in both Morgan and his newspaper.

The *Mirror* came out against the invasion of Afghanistan, against Blair's support of Bush's imperialist adventures, and was virulently against the war in Iraq. It dropped its red top, renamed itself the *Daily Mirror* just like in the old days when it had been a paper that supported Old Labour, brought John Pilger back to rant against the government, and chucked the celebrities off the front pages in favour of headlines against the bombing of mountains in Afghanistan where bin Laden almost certainly wasn't ('Rubble Reduced to

More Rubble') and photos of shackled prisoners in Guantánamo Bay ('What the Hell Are You Doing in Our Name, Mr Blair?'). Clearly, Morgan was disturbed by Blair's policy and genuinely against the way the 'war on terror' was being waged, but what emerges from the diary is that one month after 9/11, in October 2001, a minute was leaked of a statement by a Number Ten spin doctor called Lance Price, who confessed to a New Labour private fringe meeting that he deliberately leaked the date of the 2001 election to the *Sun* in advance of any other paper:

> The problem we had was with the *Mirror*, which
> rightly felt mightily aggrieved by the whole thing,
> and we had a considerable task on our hands
> trying to mollify them. They were never going
> to be a Conservative paper, but they were not as
> helpful to us in the campaign as they might have
> been. Having the *Sun* on board was a sufficiently
> important prize to take that risk.

Morgan is not one to forgive a slight. The new radical black-top *Mirror* was as much the result of Number Ten's hustling for the Murdoch papers' support as the editor's distaste for being America's poodle. In reply to Mandelson's demand that the *Mirror* get on side, when Blair was suffering his lowest popularity ratings, Morgan told him:

> Well, the reason you guys are copping it now is
> because you sucked up to the playground bullies,
> treated your mates like shit, stamped on everyone
> who got in your way, and generally behaved like a

super-arrogant, hectoring, lecturing dictator. This
is the inevitable payback. But if the government
now sucks up to its bruised mates, scorns the
scornful bullies, and learns some quick humility,
pays rigid attention to things that are actually
important and starts to govern for the people,
then it may not be too late for the 'left' media to
give them their due as a bunch of rather talented
and well-intentioned politicians.

Blair comes out of this as Morgan's twin brother. Mirror
images you might say. Blair, like Morgan, promises and
evades, sulks and blames others. He cajoles, whines,
ducks out of sight and makes threats based on his
position. Blair and his advisers might as well be Jordan,
Fergie and Patsy Kensit flirting with Piers in the hope of
getting more of the right kind or less of the wrong kind
of coverage. They might as well be editors of tabloid
newspapers offering perks to their mates and doom to
their enemies. I had thought that the obsession with
celebrity and PR was just the idleness of the newspapers
and television providing what was easiest to sell for
an audience who wanted what was easiest to absorb.
I imagined that there was some more solid substance
beneath the mental lassitude. But it seems from these
diaries that it is actually the way the world is. It is the
real world. I do live in cloud cuckoo land. Politics and
reality TV are one and the same at present, if the Piers
Morgan experience is anything to go by. Popularity is
the only thing. Numbers are what count. Getting elected,
getting the paper bought by as many people as possible,
is all that matters. The readers are always right, whether
or not you think them repulsive, racist and ignorant, so

policies and front pages will be tweaked to give them what they want. There's no point in having unpopular policies, I remember being told by Paul Boateng before the 1997 election: Labour would never get into power to put them into practice. What he didn't go on to mention was that if you have popular policies that get you into power, you have to keep them, in order to stay in power – that votes are the same as newspaper circulation figures and profit margins. He was the one who told me I lived in cloud cuckoo land.

Piers Morgan's diary is not a diary at all. It is, as he explains in the introduction, retrospectively written as a diary from notes, emails and memory. I doubt that makes it either more or less reliable as a document. But it does offer a new grammatical form, where what appears to be the (very wobbly) present tense of the narrative is actually what we might call hindsight tense. The entry for Thursday, 27 March 1997, a month before the election that will bring New Labour into government, mentions an interview with Tony Blair: 'I won't be weak on sleaze like the Tories,' he said. 'We have got to be whiter than white if we are to rebuild trust in government.' Morgan's razor-sharp mind predicts: 'I reckon that might just come back to haunt him.'

Morgan admits that he is writing up off-the-record conversations he had, because he believes that all politicians know that nothing really is off the record. Butler of the Century, Paul Burrell, had a 'hissy fit' when Morgan revealed, in spite of promising not to, that it was Prince Charles who Diana named as the one who wanted to arrange a car accident. Morgan was unmoved. 'He was very naive to think the name would never come out. You can't tell any journalist something that incredible and expect it to remain a secret. We just can't help ourselves.' At their last meeting, after he was sacked, a jubilant Cherie invited him to Number Ten for a last supper. She, like Burrell, proved very naive in believing that she could get away with saying something completely incredible and keep it secret: Blair moaned over his pre-dinner champagne about the *Daily Mail* being against him.

'If I was a Tory,' said Tony, 'they'd love me and support me all the way.'

'You virtually are,' I said, joking.

'No,' said Cherie, very serious suddenly. 'We are *socialists*.'

31 March 2005

My Word, Miss Perkins

Just after the beginning of the first Gulf War I arrived at Toronto airport to take part in a literary festival. Along with a couple of dozen others (mostly dark-skinned or from Islamic countries) I was sent to wait in a queue for special questioning when I presented my passport. After about an hour I was taken to a cubicle by a short but perfectly square woman in uniform who lolled behind a desk and looked at me long and mean. I had been on a seven-hour flight and no one had mentioned before I got to Heathrow that Air Canada was all non-smoking. I was not cheerful.

'What's your job?'

'I'm a writer.'

'Why are you here?'

I showed her my letter from the festival. She glanced at it.

'What are you doing at this here festival?'

'I've come to do a reading.'

Nothing up to this point had got a reaction. Her eyes had remained blank as mirror shades. Now, though, her eyebrows hit her hairline and she lunged forward across the desk, her face all lit up in a smirk of triumph. She knew how to winkle out the bad guys all right.

'Oh yeah? You just said you were a writer! Now you tell me you're *reading*.' She drew out the last word in proper third-degree style. 'So which is it, huh?'

She sat back hard in her seat and waited to see how I would wriggle out of that one. I lost the will to live at this point. I also sat back in my chair. I put my hands up. All I wanted was a cigarette.

'Officer, you got me. You'd better send me back to the UK. Deport me. I want to go home. By BA, preferably.' They still had a smoking section.

She'd hoped for better. She narrowed her eyes and gave me another mean look, then told me to wait while she left to make a phone call. Twenty minutes later she returned and grudgingly dismissed me from the cubicle and her life. I was allowed to stay in spite of the wild discrepancy in my story.

If I hadn't been so addicted to nicotine, I might have been less sullen about it. These category errors happen. What's the most frequent question writers get asked? 'Do you use a pen or do you type?' Readers read; writers write, right? Well no. For those who think academically about that sort of thing, like the contributors to this book of essays (*Literary Secretaries/Secretarial Culture*), authors create, and typists write. Some authors apparently split themselves in two and do both. Just ten minutes ago I heard Alexander McCall Smith, a writer of feel-good detective novels, tell an interviewer how his work comes to him through his 'unconscious': plots, characters, everything bubbles up from the murky depths and tells him its story. He just types it out. Now this I envy. My unconscious, if I have one, which I doubt, is so unconscious that it doesn't tell me anything, not consciously, anyway, and I have to manage all on my own. I write as I type, or I type as I write (do cats eat bats or do bats eat cats?).

'Whatever they may do,' the bibliographer Roger Stoddard has noted, 'authors do *not* write books.' Leah Price and Pamela Thurschwell take up the distinction and declare that their volume will focus 'on the representation, self-representation and non-representation, in literature, film and other cultural forms, of those who do write – manuscripts and memos, forms and faxes'. In these days of computers, with authors emailing finished manuscripts to publishers (and for all I know publishers sending them directly on to the printers) the distinction can't be quite so clear. There's talk in these essays of Henry James dictating to Mary Weld (she records that it took 194 days to dictate *The Wings of the Dove* but makes no mention of content or quality) and of Erle Stanley Gardner's fiction factory, with his suite of Della Streets banging out the latest Perry Mason case. U.A. Fanthorpe is quoted on the saddest dedication:

lastly my wife,
Who did the typing.

But mostly I imagine these days the author and writer are one and the same. (Obviously we have to make an exception for industrial novelists like the late Robert Ludlum, who have a team who write the books as well as others who type them before they add their authorial name, so that there are three layers to the finished manuscript – or possibly four if you include the 'ideas' officer.) There was a brief period some time ago when it all sort of came together (for the bosses at least) when the word for the machine and the person working it was one and the same: *typewriter*; enabling hilarious jokes about the boss telling his wife: 'I've had a terrible time, dear, I had to spend the day working with the typewriter on my knees.' I imagine some similar jest might be devised for the laptop computer, but I can't be bothered.

Roland Barthes anguished over the problem of the literary division of labour before word processors arrived and solved it for the rest of us with equally uneasy social consciences. In an interview for *Le Monde*, he was asked the everlastingly interesting question – whether he did all his writing by hand. He explained that he had bought an electric typewriter:

> Since I'm often very busy, I have sometimes been
> obliged to have things typed for me by others ...
> When I thought about this, it bothered me.
> Without going into a big demagogical speech, I'll
> just say that to me this represented an alienated
> social relationship: a person, the typist, is confined
> by the master in an activity I would almost call
> an enslavement, when writing is precisely the
> field of liberty and desire! In short, I said to
> myself: 'There's only one solution. I really must
> learn to type.'

Well, I don't like capitalism any more than the next man, and I do hope that when he made them redundant, Barthes's typists set to and wrote of liberty and desire themselves; but assuming they hadn't been doing his typing for the sheer joy of helping the world receive the thoughts of Roland Barthes, they surely weren't exactly enslaved so much as employed.

Naturally, with the invention of the typewriter all manner of doom was predicted by Luddites and moralists for the future of writing, just as it has been with word processors. Typewriting tears writing from 'the essential realm of the hand, i.e. the realm of the word', Heidegger warned, perhaps sitting in his little wooden hut. Some contemporary critics agree (at least I think they do): according to Mark Seltzer, quoted by Victoria Olwell, the 'linking of hand, eye and letter in the act of writing by hand intimates the translation from mind to hand to eye and hence from the inward and invisible and spiritual to the outward and visible and physical', whereas the typewriter 'replaces, or pressures, that fantasy of continuous transition with recalcitrantly visible and material systems of difference'. It seems to me the job is to get the thought down on to paper as directly as possible, and you might think that the automatic nature of typing enables a smoother transfer of thoughts to sentences, from mind to hand. Additionally, although handwriting as a guide to character is usually the realm of graphologists rather than philosophers, Heidegger insisted that the worst aspect of typewriting was that it 'conceals the handwriting and thereby the character. The typewriter makes everyone look the same.' Odd, then, that in printed books it's possible to distinguish Henry James from Charles Dickens.

Nonetheless, most authors have ignored the warnings, bought electric typewriters and taught themselves to type, and so have those in the world of commerce, with the result that the vast increase of women taking over the clerical work of men that occurred in the early years of the twentieth century (having comprised 2 per cent of the clerical workforce in 1850, they accounted for 20 per cent in 1914) has gone into a severe decline. Where have all the secretaries gone? To CEOs, every one? Maybe; or perhaps, liberated as Barthes hoped, they're at home tapping out novels about marriage and childbirth and the hell of the job/family equation demanded by mortgage and credit-card lenders. Most likely they are now called PAs or work in call centres or as data-entry operatives in vast, industrial keyboard factories never dreamed of in the deep end of the typing pool in the 1950s.

The genius v. typist (he creates/she types) dichotomy is a subset of the much broader distinction between who dictates and who takes dictation. Were the multitudes of women secretaries with male bosses drudges in training for marriage – a domesticated version of looking after men at work – or did they establish a place for themselves in the world of employment that allowed them independence and a degree of power? Learning shorthand and typing was once a way for a young man to have an exciting career as a journalist, or, like Dickens and his shadow David Copperfield, to become a parliamentary reporter. When the First World War and the economics of differential wages for male and female employees enabled or forced women to take over the shorthand typing, the value of the expertise fell (as well as the wages). An army of clerks went to war and an army of women took over in the office. Did the same skills offer them the same possibilities? According to Chesterton, 'twenty million young women rose to their feet and said: "We will not be dictated to," and immediately became shorthand typists.' But they had also found a skill that afforded them a better wage than factory work, improved conditions, and, if they were so inclined, the opportunity to wield influence. By the 1980s, there were movies such as *Nine to Five* and *Working Girl*, in which Lily Tomlin and Melanie Griffith use body *and* brain to supplant their bosses, though I suppose these have to be classed as fairytales about the fantasy secretaries who got away, just as *Pretty Woman* can't be said to have been depicting the actual upside of prostitution.

Over time, two tiers of women's office work evolved: personal secretaries, who looked after the needs of men and their office environments, and typists, who were collected together in massed ranks, each at a desk, obeying the disembodied voices of men through the headphones of their dictating machines. Clearly, for some secretaries, taking dictation from an influential man was addictive enough to make them prolong their working relations after their boss had died. A secretary acting as mediator between a mover and shaker and the world he moved and shook during his lifetime could become his medium after he died, as did Louise Owen, secretary to the newspaper owner Lord Northcliffe. In her essay on this early and oddly literal version of the 'secretary to the stars' phenomenon, Bette London describes how Owen tried to appropriate the immense popular power of her late employer. 'You know I am as active here as on earth ... I shall work very hard, as there is much to do,' the dead Northcliffe dictated to his living secretary. 'I am not supplying the daisies with nutriment, but supplying the man and woman of today with hope ... The League of Nations is the only way to bring happiness,' he (or she) informed the listening world via Owen's sensitive antennae and flying fingers.

But Louise Owen was supplanted by a man, Hannen Swaffer, a former reporter and editor, who claimed he was only following orders when Northcliffe, fed up with Owen taking his dictation too slowly and misspelling it, authorised Swaffer as his master's voice. The secretary was put in her place. Later she tried to sue the Northcliffe estate and lost her legacy, left in her boss's will, to lawyers. It wasn't only Northcliffe; Franklin Roosevelt and Henry James, among others, were also ghosted by their secretaries after their death. We can count ourselves lucky that Robert Maxwell has stayed schtum; and let us pray that Rupert Murdoch's private secretary finds emotionally satisfying employment after he goes to the great red top in the sky.

On the other side of the power quotient, Douglas Brooks writes about a young woman who is taking an exam in Gurgaon, India, in order to get a job transcribing dictation from doctors in the United States. As part of her training, Richa Singh has 'sat through a lecture on cardiology, a video on heart disease and a rerun of *ER*'. The exam requires her to take dictation from an American voice coming from a tape recorder, but Ms Singh isn't quite ready; she misspells 'aorta' and 'cerebral'. She is doing this because she would rather be a typist than a dentist – which is what she is at present. The career prospects are better, it seems. It is cheaper for highly paid American medics to dictate their medical notes and send them to scribes in India than for them to spend their time typing them up themselves, or to pay high Western wages for someone else to do it. This is known as 'India's new knowledge economy'. A cross-continental physical dissociation of the *logos* from the *graphos* which is of a different order from the author who types.

But aside from the absence of the body, it is not essentially different from Mina Harker's role as secretarial mediator taking shorthand notes for the vampire hunters, and mental dictation from the toothy Count Dracula himself; or the real Jean Bethell (reader, Erle Stanley Gardner married her, though only two years before he died) inspiring or trying to live up to (Daniel Karlin can't be sure) Perry Mason's perfect secretary, Della Street. Both women (and the Indian transcribers) are conduits of knowledge and expertise. They don't have to know what they are writing of, they just have to do it accurately and fast. What the on-site secretaries have in addition to the distant transcribers are bodies, available for penetrating with vampire teeth, eyes or flesh; even for marrying. Dictaphones, except in very rare textbook cases, do not arouse desire. But the transcription factories, Brooks tells us, are nothing more than a short-term solution to the inconvenience of bodies wasting time and getting in the way of work. It is only a matter of time before voice recognition software becomes subtle enough not to require any human keyboarder to put word on paper. No body will be necessary and the short-lived but intense narrative of the secretary, her boss and his ever-naive wife will be gone forever, as historical a device in film and literature as the telephone that had to stay in one place. The decorative function remains at receptionist level, where young women without business degrees greet visitors and answer the phone, keeping up a front. Perhaps they also do some typing and tidy things away in files. They probably also know as much about what is going on in the office as anyone. I don't know if there is a typical receptionist's daydream of being spotted and whisked up the career ladder; but certainly the films about them have been slow in coming.

I doubt that we should be mourning the demise of the shorthand typist. It was once a possible route to a business career: the secretary who is so efficient and innovative that she gets plucked from her typing, filing and tea-making duties into an office of her own with a secretary of her own is not entirely mythological. Alternatively, she married her boss and persuaded him to put her in charge of the publicity department. But all this suggests is that women could only surprise men into giving them a job: 'My word, Miss Perkins, you work beautifully even without your typewriter.' The exceptions must have been vanishingly few compared to the numbers of competent women who kept on keeping offices running smoothly, corrected their bosses' solecisms before typing up their letters, fended off unwanted callers, renewed the water in the flower vase and wore nylons to the office in even the most sweltering of summers.

On the other hand, secretaries can't all have disappeared since at the moment two are in the headlines causing havoc. They do seem to have changed their demeanour, however. While Faria Alam is earning hundreds of thousands – and employing Max Clifford to earn her more – by having had affairs with who knows who at the Football Association and telling all, Jenny Amner sent an email, which was eventually forwarded to millions of computers across the world, from her lawyer boss asking for £4 to dry-clean his trousers, over which she had spilt some ketchup. Her reply suggests that something is stirring in the world of the office angel:

From: Amner, Jenny
Sent: 03 June 2005 10.25
To: Phillips, Richard

Cc:*Lon – all users 3rd floor

Subject: Ketchup trousers

With reference to the email below, I must apologise for not getting back to you straight away but due to my mother's sudden illness, death and funeral I have had more pressing issues than your £4.

I apologise again for accidentally getting a few splashes of ketchup on your trousers. Obviously your financial need as a senior associate is greater than mine as a mere secretary. Having already spoken to and shown your email and Anne-Marie's note to various partners, lawyers and trainees in ECC&T and IP/IT, they kindly offered to do a collection to raise the £4. I however declined their kind offer but should you feel the urgent need for the £4, it will be on my desk this afternoon.

Jenny

4 August 2005

THE HOUSEKEEPER OF A
WORLD-SHATTERING THEORY

In the membership roll of the worshipful guild of enabling wives, the name of Martha Freud ranks with the greatest: Mrs Noah, Mrs Darwin, Mrs Marx, Mrs Joyce, Mrs Nabokov, Mrs Clinton, and their honorary fellows, Mr Woolf and Mr Cookson. Wives, of either sex, are what keep the universe orderly and quiet enough for the great to think their thoughts, complete their travels, write their books and change the world. Martha Freud was a paragon among wives. There is nothing more liberating from domestic drudgery and the guilt that comes of avoiding it than having a cleaning lady who loves cleaning, a childcarer who's content with childcare, a homebody who wants nothing more than to be at home. And Martha Freud was all those things. Quite why she was those things is something that her husband might have been the very person to investigate, but Freud was nobody's fool and knew when to leave well alone in the murkier regions of his personal life – especially that dark continent in his mind concerning women. Freud mentioned in passing in a letter to his friend Wilhelm Fliess (to whom he wrote that no woman had ever replaced the male comrade in his life), that at the age of thirty-four, after the birth of her sixth child in eight years, Martha was suffering from writer's block. Impossible to imagine why. But like other mysteries about Martha's life, this new biography does not (or perhaps cannot because some of the source material remains unavailable) elaborate on what she might have been trying to write. A shopping list, I expect. Unless it was that book about interesting new ways she had thought of for interpreting her dreams, which she worked on in those odd moments when the children weren't down with chickenpox or needing their stockings mended.

History tells of Mrs Freud – the wife – as a devoted domestic, and there is little in Katja Behling's biography to suggest we adjust our view of her. The big idea seems to be that we must value her contribution to the development of psychoanalysis as the provider of a peaceful home life for its founder. The sine qua non of radical thought is someone else changing the baby's nappy. In his foreword to the book, Anton Freud, a grandson, puts it with incontestable logic:

> Would he have had the time and opportunity to
> write this foundational work if he had had, say,
> to take his daughter to her dancing classes and
> his son to his riding lessons twice a week? ... His
> youngest daughter was born in 1895. When she
> cried in the night, was it Sigmund who got up to
> comfort her? ... If Martha had been less efficient
> or unwilling to devote her life to her husband in
> this way, the flow of Sigmund's early ideas would
> have dried to a trickle before they could converge
> into a great sea. Martha always saw to it that her
> husband's energies were not squandered.

And if Freud had comforted his daughter when she cried in the night, would Anna have been so desperate for her father's attention as to devote her life to publishing his papers and continuing his work? Apostles need more than ordinary unhappiness to fit them for their task.

Juliet Mitchell, in praise of the new biography, berates those who dismiss Martha Freud as a stereotypical hausfrau rather than seeing in her 'a highly ethical and decent human being', though it isn't at all clear to me that they are mutually exclusive descriptions. As to dismissing her, on the contrary, one wrings one's hands and weeps over her, or would if she didn't seem to have been perfectly content with her existence. In his biography of Freud, Peter Gay quotes Martha's reply to a letter of condolence after Freud's death that it was 'a feeble consolation that in the fifty-three years of our marriage there was not a single angry word between us, and that I always tried as much as possible to remove the *misère* of everyday life from his path'. Like strange sex between consenting adults, there's nothing to be said against contentment and a division of labour which both parties are happy about. We must read and wonder at the good fortune that each should have found the other. Which of us would not wish for a Martha of our own to take care of the *misère* in our daily life while we sit in our study or silently at the lunch table bubbling up enlightenment for the world? Then again, who among us would wish to *be* Martha, no matter how essential her biographer might claim her to be in the production of the grand idea? To be a muse, an inspiration, might, I suppose, have its attractions; but to be the housekeeper of a world-shattering theory isn't quite the same.

There's no point in pretending in the light of fifty-three years' evidence that there was a great originator in Martha struggling to get out. But you can't help wondering how it could be that she wanted only this of herself, a woman who at her marriage was neither thoughtless nor completely self-effacing. Martha was a voracious reader of John Stuart Mill, Dickens and Cervantes, though her husband-to-be warned her against the rude bits unsuitable for a woman in *Don Quixote*. She was interested in music and painting, and had no shortage of suitors. When Freud became obsessively suspicious of her brother (and the husband of Freud's sister), Eli, who controlled the Bernays's finances, he insisted, on pain of ending their relationship, that she break with him completely. She held her own, firmly reflected Freud's ultimatum back at him, and maintained her relationship with Eli. She travelled to northern Germany to holiday with only her younger sister for company and had a wonderful time in spite of her fiancé's suspiciously heavy-handed use of ironic exclamation marks: 'Fancy, Lübeck! Should that be allowed? Two single girls travelling alone in North Germany! This is a revolt against the male prerogative!' But as soon as they were married Freud forbade his devoutly Orthodox Jewish wife to light the Sabbath candles. It wasn't until the first Friday after her husband's death that she lit them again. *What do women want* is one thing, but the real question is what made Martha run: run the household, the children, the travel arrangements, the servants, and with never a word of complaint except a mildly expressed bafflement at her husband's choice of profession. 'I must admit that if I did not realise how seriously my husband takes his treatments, I should think that psychoanalysis is a form of pornography.'

Marriage, they say, changes people, and it does look as if Martha Bernays might have had the makings of another woman – at any rate, another life – altogether. What this otherwise rather dutiful biography (the mirror of its subject, perhaps) does offer us is a glimpse (but sadly very little more) of the by no means uninteresting Bernays family and their oldest daughter, Martha, before she became the other Mrs Freud. Three of Martha's six siblings died in infancy; her oldest brother, Isaac, was born with a severe hip disorder and walked on crutches; and the next brother, Eli, was not much liked by his mother. When Martha was six, her father, Berman Bernays, was imprisoned for fraudulent bankruptcy after some shady dealings on the stock market. Two years later, the family moved away from the public shame in Hamburg to Vienna, and Martha recalled hearing the 'sizzling of her mother's tears as they landed on the hot cooking stove'. She was teased at her new school for her German diction. Isaac died when Martha was eleven, and seven years later Berman collapsed in the street, dying of 'paralysis of the heart' and leaving the family without an income. Berman's brothers had to support them, and Eli took over his father's job in order to help out. Not an uneventful childhood, not lacking in trauma to be lived through. There are all sorts of pain and difficulty there, yet Martha did not take to her bed and succumb to the vapours. There is not the slightest indication that she lost the use of her legs nor found herself unable to speak. And this is all the more remarkable in view of the fact that when her father died, her mother appointed as her temporary guardian none other than the father of Bertha Pappenheim, later better known as Anna O., who might have told her a thing or two about the proper way to react to family loss. Nor is there any indication that her positively neurotic lack of neurotic symptoms (unless you count obsessive compulsive caring for her husband's welfare) struck the father of psychoanalysis as worth a paper or two.

What Sigmund and Martha had in common were families embroiled in shadowy financial scandals. Freud's uncle was imprisoned for trading in counterfeit roubles, and persistent rumour had it that his father was implicated in the scam. The way both dealt with the discomfort of public shame and lived happily ever after together was by embracing a perfect nineteenth-century bourgeois existence, provided you don't include Sigmund's incessant thoughts about child sexuality, seduction theory, the Oedipus complex, penis envy and the death drive – or perhaps even if you do. Presumably it was precisely that exemplary bourgeois surface, the formal suits, the heavy, glossy furniture, the rigid table manners, ordered nursery and bustling regularity, that made it possible for those deeper, hardly thinkable thoughts to be had and developed into something that looked like a scientific theory. By polishing that surface and keeping the clocks ticking in unison, Martha was as essential to the development of Freudian thought as Dora or the Rat Man. It's just that she didn't have the time to put her feet up on the couch, and Sigmund never cared to wonder what all that polishing and timekeeping was about. Martha was not there in order to be understood; she was there so that he might learn to understand others.

Not that women weren't interesting. Anna O. and Dora were fascinating. Minna, Martha's younger sister, who lived with them, was someone to whom, when no serious man was around, Freud could talk about intellectual things. Who could have been more stimulating than Lou Andreas-Salomé, Marie Bonaparte, Hilda Doolittle, Helene Deutsch or Joan Riviere? But they were none of them his wife. It is the woman's place, Freud said to his oldest daughter, Mathilde, to make man's life more pleasant. Intellectual companionship was to be found elsewhere. The more intelligent young men look for a wife with 'gentleness, cheerfulness, and the talent to make their life easier and more beautiful'. (Not Lou, then.) In 1936 he spoke to Marie Bonaparte of his married life: 'It was really not a bad solution of the marriage problem, and she is still today tender, healthy and active.' He expressed his relief to his son-in-law Max Halberstadt, 'for the children who have turned out so well, and for the fact that she' – Martha – 'has neither been very abnormal nor very often ill'.

In fact, it was precisely Martha's sturdy, if somewhat timekeeping and cleanliness-fixated nature that Freud found most attractive, according to Behling. She was the lodestone, the quintessence, the elixir to which his life's work was ostensibly devoted. He was the Doctor and she was what the cured would look like. She was normal. Obviously, it would have been extremely trying had Anna or Dora or the Wolf Man been like her. But in his world of psychical distortion, Martha represented what no one who takes his works seriously could ever really believe in: the ordinary, undamaged specimen. According to Ernest Jones, 'her personality was fully developed and well integrated: it would well deserve the psychoanalysts' highest compliment of being "normal".' No problem for Martha coming to terms with her missing penis at the right stage of her development, no big deal about transferring her Oedipal desire for the mother to the father. She had adapted nicely to her castration, and although it meant her superego was a flimsy thing compared to that of a man (woman 'shows less sense of justice than man, less inclination to submission to the great exigencies of life, is more often led in her decisions by tender or hostile feelings'), it served well enough for Freud's purposes. Imagine if Freudian analysis had gone quite another way and the master had studied the normality he apparently had so close to home instead of its deformation. What was it that Emmeline (whose bossiness and self-absorption Freud hated) and Berman Bernays did so right? How could he not have been in a rage to know? But what intellectual innovator would want to give up interesting for ordinary, especially when ordinary, if left to its own devices and sublimation of desires, arranged such a comfortable life for him?

Behling suggests that Martha's great value to Freud was her very existence, which prevented him from getting too depressed about the nature of human nature. He was able to see in her 'someone who stood apart from what he learned about humankind in general'. She was not part of the 'rabble', as Oskar Pfister explained, of 'good-for-nothing' mankind. So not only did he not study her, he did not communicate any of his professional thoughts to her. 'Freud did not wish to share the blackest depths of his knowledge with Martha, but rather to protect her from them,' Behling writes. Or perhaps, more likely, to protect himself. During their engagement Freud was taken 'greatly by surprise when she once admitted that at times she had to suppress bad or evil thoughts'.

Martha's sunny nature, so very different apparently from human nature, was encouraged if not carefully tutored by her fiancé during their epic four-year engagement. Martha's mother had set her face against the marriage of her daughter to an impoverished researcher, and they were reduced to writing letters and stealing occasional meetings. It seems to have been Freud's single stab at passion and he went at it with all the will of an adored son. He must have found it alarming, because the heavy curtains of contentment came down as soon as the wedding was over. Before that, he raged with jealousy at the mention of other men, demanding, for example, that Martha stop calling her interesting painter cousin by his first name. 'Dear Martha, how you have changed my life,' he said in his first letter to her. And when they were engaged and he was battling against her mother for Martha he explained: 'Marty, you cannot fight against it; no matter how much they love you I will not leave you to anyone, and no one deserves you; no one else's love compares with mine.' Clearly the time for the master's self-analysis had not yet come, so he was free to wish to give his fiancée a fashionable gold snake bangle and write how sorry he was that in the circumstances she would have to settle for 'a small silver snake'. He wanted her well turned out so it would 'never occur to a soul that she could have married anyone but a prince'. But his letters also made other things clear. Martha's nose and mouth, he told her, were shaped 'more characteristically than beautifully, with an almost masculine expression, so unmaidenly in its decisiveness'. It was as if nature wanted to save her 'from the danger of being merely beautiful'. Even so the romance was powerful: the two young lovers exchanged flowering almond branches, and Freud told her that his addiction to cigars was due to her absence: 'Smoking is indispensable if one has nothing to kiss.' But in describing his views on the state of marriage he explained that 'despite all love and unity, the help each person had found in the other ceases. The husband looks again for friends, frequents an inn, finds general outside interests.' Martha, who would apologise each time she screamed during her labour, had been warned.

After his death, Martha did not run wild, aside from lighting the *Shabbos* candles, but sat on a chair on the half landing between the first and second floors of the house in Maresfield Gardens and took to reading again, though only, she assured a correspondent, in case she was accused of idleness, in the evenings. Life, she said, had 'lost its sense and meaning' without her husband, but she quite enjoyed receiving the grand visitors who came to the house to pay homage. Anna took over her father's work and Martha suddenly began to take an interest in it. Her daughter found Martha far too inquisitive about the patients who came and went. Martha even expressed a view: 'You'd be amazed what it costs, this child analysis!'

Freud blamed Martha for preventing him from gaining early recognition in the world of medical science. 'I may here recount, looking back, that it was my fiancée's fault if I did not become famous in those early years,' he wrote in his self-portrait. His experiments with cocaine in the 1880s were taken up and elaborated by others. What the late Princess Margaret knew as 'naughty salt' was found to have a beneficial effect as a local anaesthetic, a use Freud inexplicably hadn't thought of and which he had omitted to mention in his paper 'On Coca'. It was an unexpected opportunity to visit Martha that had distracted him from fully exploiting the potential of his discovery, he claimed in old age, but was generous enough to excuse his wife since, as Behling puts it, 'forty-nine years of wedlock had compensated him for missing out on fame in his youth.' But here's a thought, an unconsidered key, perhaps, to understanding Martha. While Freud was making his experiments with cocaine, he sent several vials of it to his fiancée extolling its effect on vitality, with instructions on how to divide the doses and administer it. Martha wrote and thanked him, saying that although she didn't think she needed it, she would take some as he suggested. She reported back to her fiancé that she found it helpful in moments of emotional strain. From time to time, Behling says, Martha 'enhanced her sense of well-being with an invigorating pinch of cocaine'. For how long she continued to do this is unknown, but it does suggest an altogether different way of viewing the devoted, domestically driven Martha Freud, who for half a century went about her frantically busy daily round of cleaning, caring, tidying, managing and arranging all the minute details of her husband's life with a fixed and unfaltering smile.

23 March 2006

THE FRIENDLY SPIDER PROGRAMME

Autumn looms darkly and terrible in my life. From midsummer I start to worry, and by late August I am filled with dread. My arachnophobia has ensured that the autumnal mating urge which causes spiders to wander into our houses – confused by some sudden indefinable but compelling ache in the forefront of their small minds – in search of a nice warm dark corner to nest (don't think about it), ushers in my personal annual festival of anxiety and horror. Not that I felt secure during the other ten months of the year. My ex, having been my ex for some years and grown tired of being called out in the middle of the night to deal with a spider, gave me a blowtorch, which I used with desperate abandon. It's a professional version of the hairspray-and-lighter technique, more or less likely to have resulted in my charred remains (oh God, and the daughter, the cats, the occasional lover …) being found in the smoking ruins. But death was never a worse alternative to being in the same room as a spider.

I suppose this sounds like a writer's hyperbole, and if you are not an arachnophobe nothing will convince you otherwise, but I discovered in late June that there are those who will recognise the simple truth of what I say. An irrational fear of spiders is common. Roughly 35 per cent of women and 18 per cent of men in the UK have it, though not all of them have it so badly that it is called clinical. Just as clinical depression is different from being a bit down (*pace* Campbell and Blunkett), so clinical spider phobia is different from a slight shudder of the kind you get when the spider you are cupping delicately in your hand as you take it out to the garden tickles your palm. It's only thanks to the new-found me that I can even write that sentence.

To anyone who isn't a member of an Iron John chapter, confronting a crippling fear violates common sense, and in addition and speaking personally, joining anything, but particularly anything with a stupid name, goes against every grain in my body. Which is why I waited until I was fifty-eight before I signed up for the Friendly Spider Programme at the Zoological Society of London. It made me cross: tell me, if you must, that spiders are not wholly devoted to terrorising me, but don't suggest they're friendly – I don't want them around whatever they feel about me. Being loved was never on its own a satisfactory basis for taking a lover. I see no reason why it should be any different with spiders. None of the eighteen people on the four-hour course at ZSL headquarters across the road from the zoo could say what tipped the scales and decided them finally to try and deal with their arachnophobia. Everyone had lived miserably with the problem for as long as they could remember. We were a range of ages and social classes and from all over the country. The only obvious thing we had in common (aside from our terror of spiders and of what was going to happen that afternoon) was that we were all women. This, we were assured, was very unusual, unprecedented actually. John, the psychologist in charge, showed his acumen by suggesting it had something to do with it being June and therefore bang in the middle of the World Cup. It occurs to me that this might also explain why I finally decided to deal with my fear: between another afternoon of football mania and confronting spider phobia, the latter was the lesser of two evils – chewing my own leg off was a similarly attractive option.

We sat centred in the two front rows of the ZSL lecture theatre. The woman on my immediate right was crying. She'd been gently led to her seat by one of the volunteers who had come in to make tea, smile in a reassuring manner and act as support during the later part of the afternoon. Eighteen fearful people secreted enough anxiety and reluctance to make breathing in feel dangerous. Dave, the head keeper of invertebrates at the zoo, and John, the psychologist and hypnotherapist, spoke to us in turn about fear, theirs (spiders', not Dave and John's) and ours. Dave gave us spider behaviour; John dealt with human behaviour. First, however, we were to pair off and share our feelings and experiences of spiders with the person sitting on our right. Third on the list of things I really don't like, after spiders and football, is *sharing*. I was mortified, at having been suckered into a self-help group, after the considerable trouble I have taken in my life to avoid them. Sharing does the same visceral thing to me that happens when your mother pushes you forward at a party to sing a song. Nor did I need to be told that spiders didn't want to go near me as much as I didn't want them to. If I could reason the problem away, I wouldn't be here. If being part of a suffering group was the answer to my – someone used the word – issue, then I was lost. *Just fucking hypnotise me and make me feel better.*

The urgent need to run for my life lost out, just, to the even more powerful conditioning against being rude to strangers or making a scene, which so often get well-mannered people who don't want to make a fuss, robbed, raped and murdered, as well as singing through gritted teeth at children's parties. So I shared. The voice of the woman next to me trembled with emotion, as gulping tears back she told me that she actually passes out if she sees a ... she couldn't say the word. I dug deep and shared that while watching *CSI* I had to close my eyes during every scene set in Grissom's office because he had a huge ... in a glass case behind his desk. I might have mentioned the nights I'd sat bolt upright in the dead centre of the bed because an unreachable spider was in the room, or the Wellington boots I kept beside the bed (one boot inside the other for obvious arachnid reasons) for night-time search and destroy missions. Then we shared groupwise what we had shared in pairs. None of us would walk into a room without scanning it minutely, or having it checked by someone else, though of course trusting someone else to be as thorough as you would be was impossible, so no one ever believed any room was really spider-free. Dark cupboards and the bottom of wardrobes were forbidden territory. Attics and cellars out of the question. Travel was only possible to cold and inhospitable parts of the world, our only consolation being an easy moral superiority about luxury holidays in impoverished hotspots teeming with eight-legged life. I once wrote a novel set in a rainforest based entirely on textbooks and three trips to Kew Gardens' tropical houses. We all saw spiders much more often than anyone else, always the first to spot them, because always alert, intensely on the lookout. It turned out not to be just my paranoid theory that I summoned up spiders through the power of thought, that the dust in the corners of rooms conglomerated into the living beasts, given existence by the strength of my fear and apprehension.

Maybe God had a neurotic fear of the idea of people and that was how we came about. No wonder we keep getting swatted. Dust to dust. I spent hours and hours at night trying (as fruitlessly as any intelligent portion of me knew it must be) not to think about or visualise spiders in case I made them come to me. Which, of course, they did; and where there was one spider there was always another that I hadn't spotted, somewhere, somewhere ... I had a special stone (as well as the blowtorch), heavy, large and flat, on the bedside table that enabled me when desperate to deal with spiders from a great height. Arachnophobia was the only sympathy I had with Bernard Levin, who devised a fine solution to the ancient problem of disposing of spiders in the washbasin: an old-fashioned soda siphon. Taps are too close and you have to touch them to turn them on. There has to be a critical distance between your being and the thing that disposes of the spider: preferably air, or a stream of water. Something directly connected, however long, to your hand will not do. But where can you get a working soda siphon these days?

Spiders are malevolent. Spiders and the awareness of malevolence inhabit an identical area of my brain. Scan it and see. Silent scuttling movement, legs rising above a dark central body (yes, we're coming to that), uncanny watchful stillness. They know me and they hate me, whatever irrelevant truths Dave might tell us about them being frightened of us. They only come towards us in order to get under the sofa we're sitting on, because it's a safe, dark space away from the horror of the noisy, strobing light of the TV. Natural history versus blind terror has only one victor. The finest moment of the confessional came when a woman spoke up in a clear, in no way self-mocking voice: 'What I hate about spiders is that they won't stay still and let you kill them.' It was a perfect expression of the rationality of our irrational fear.

John, the hypnotherapist, gave a brief talk about the symptoms and causes of phobia. Sweating, palpitations, paralysis, fainting. There are those who believe it was fear of spiders that made my very own particular ancestors more fit to pass on their genes so that they could eventually produce me. Ah, yes, the days when arachnosauruses ruled the earth, and australopithecines competed with hominid-eating spiders for a food niche. Lucky my forebear from whom I have inherited no terror at all of snakes didn't get bitten by a cobra or crushed by a python. In my rational mind, I'm sure there were far greater dangers to survival than even the most poisonous spiders; and in my irrational being, a dangerous spider is no more terrifying to me than a mild-as-milk variety. A young acquaintance of mine had a phobia of that well-known evolutionary threat: supermarket labels on fruit.

Psychoanalysis has a take. (So you are frightened of a black body surrounded by hairy legs coming at you? You find it a threat? What could such a thing represent? No, really? You don't mean my mother's vagina as I was coming down the birth canal? Well, thank you, I feel better now.) But I haven't got the years to spare for their talking cure. And there is a practical but dull psychological theory that phobias are caught by young children from fearful mothers (them, again) or traumatic encounters. Spiders, I think, were the least of my mother's worries, and my most traumatic youthful encounters were not with eight-legged beings (though I admit that does rather take us back to psychoanalysis, above).

I had very little interest in the nature of my phobia, I wanted it only to go away. Just hypnotise me, John. Finally, he did. We lay on the floor of a meeting room while he talked us through a relaxation sequence, a body scan no different from what you might do at the end of a yoga session. Then we were instructed to descend ten mental steps, find a nice place to be at the bottom, and relax even deeper. Not a problem, nicely relaxed, and so? Now he was going to address our 'subconsciousnesses' directly, John told us, and did so by repeatedly assuring us that 'Spiders are safe,' throwing in for free the handy suggestion that daddy-long-legs didn't worry us either. He had warned us that we might think nothing was happening. He was right. Apparently, the ability to be sceptical is not impaired by deep relaxation. Certainly, my 'subconscious' didn't let on to me that it had heard a thing. Well, it wouldn't, would it? I sneered in a relaxed manner to myself. It's a powerfully difficult task to convince a person who isn't entirely sure they have a conscious, let alone a subconscious, that you are getting through to it. After twenty minutes we had a nice cup of tea and then crossed the road to the Invertebrate House at the zoo, where the volunteers had meanwhile been searching the flowerbeds for the sizeable garden spiders that waited for us in small plastic aquaria on four tables.

Well, I did put my finger against the back leg of a big black spider and follow it as it ran in the direction

I pointed. I did put my whole hand in and let a volunteer chase the spider across my open palm. I did put a clear plastic cup over it after it had been released to scurry around the table, then slid a card under the cup and walked around the room holding it. And I stroked one of the incredibly soft hairy legs of Frieda, the four-inch red tarantula, then held her in my cupped hands, though her stillness suggested that she was rendered as catatonic by human contact as I usually was by a spider encounter. I did all those things not with terror but a kind of awed amazement. Only one person couldn't bring herself to go near the spiders. The rest of us were elated and astonished by what we were capable of doing. If we were hesitant at first, most people went back for more, to re-experience this remarkable freedom from fear. The woman who had sat next to me in tears walked up to me with her cupped spider. 'Look,' she said in the first flush of the new her.

Mixed feelings don't come any more entangled than when, after a lifetime of terror, someone says *spiders are safe* at you half a dozen times, and three months later you discover yourself gazing empathetically at a handbag-sized arachnid Sisyphusing in the bath. Since that afternoon autumn has arrived and I cup-and-card spiders out into the garden, watch them web-weaving between the wheelie bins and dashing across the open space in the living room between two dark corners, with intense interest, and have no sense at all that they are my enemy. I am suffused with remorse at the numbers I have caused to be killed, and I am living contentedly with a spider who has taken up residence in a corner of the kitchen window. But although life has become altogether lighter and much less fearful, for which

I am profoundly grateful, I have the strangest sense of loss. A person who is not afraid of spiders is almost a definition of someone who is not *me*. So it is uncanny (in a properly Freudian sense of the word) to observe myself without that fear. Some way in which I knew myself has vanished. It is slightly frightening not being frightened of spiders. And then I wonder, why not get hypnotised out of all my anxieties and nervous habits, make everything awkward and resistant go away, so that I could become ... well, *nothing* is the alarming image I have. I can't picture what would be left after I had chipped off the difficulties. I really don't believe there is a solid nugget of the person-that-is-really-me underneath it all – the difficulties and such are fragments of the fragmented thing we choose to call the person. And what if the difficulties, as the analysts of whom I am only partly contemptuous would say, were merely the armouring, the screens, that kept the *really* bad stuff at bay? Now, without my arachnophobia, I worry what dark repressed beast is about to return to consciousness and make my life really unbearable?

A psychiatrist friend almost saves me from the spiral of horror I'm about to plughole down. Over dinner, listening to my bold tale of new-found spider freedom, she looks unimpressed. Simple, specific phobias are the easiest of conditions to cure. Complex social phobias (fear of other people or going out) are of a different and more intractable nature. The feeling I describe to her of having been given permission not to be afraid of spiders is exactly that. What has happened to me is similar to a hysterical conversion. Phobias of spiders, snakes, flying, even labels on fruit, she says, are the closest condition that there is to normal if such a thing as normal existed.

Any kind of behavioural or suggestion treatment is likely to work rapidly with a willing patient. Then she blows it: 'In psychodynamic terms,' she explains, 'phobias are the fears that the mind can afford to express directly and therefore they don't lie deep in the unconscious.' Just as I'm feeling better about not having lost some essential part of myself, or at having been merely relaxed into relinquishing a lifelong terror, a threat, a new dread appears on the horizon. Oh Christ, what have I done? Here comes my eight-legged, multi-eyed, hairy, vaginal mummy scuttling towards me, and this time it's personal.

30 November 2006

Tunnel Vision

I had supper with a friend on 31 August 1997. He arrived looking wonderstruck. 'Are we just going to have dinner?' he said.

'Why, you think we should sit shiva?'

'But if she can die, then anyone can.'

I don't think anyone else ever got around to articulating that quite so precisely.

One friend spent the day of the funeral in his study, locked away from the world, reading *Civilisation and Its Discontents*. Others I knew wandered around the flower carpet outside Kensington Palace, spying and sniffing the air to gauge whether sentimentality and hysteria actually might achieve what neo-Marxian analysis had failed to do in the 1960s and 1970s. Not being a great one for crowds, I stayed at home with the TV on, just watching and wondering at the events of that week, which really were strange on a scale beyond anything I'd encountered. Some months later, I saw a documentary made on the day of the funeral, in which a bag lady was asked for her opinion on the death of the Princess of Wales: 'Oh, she's died has she? I wondered why there were so many people about.'

Ten years on, with so many more screens and pages clogged with celebrity, and the broadsheets gone overtly tabloid, it isn't entirely obvious what fascinated people so about Diana Windsor, née Spencer, the uneducated, O-level-free daughter of an ancient house, former nanny, Sloane, clothes horse, playgirl, campaigner, therapist addict. Take the bright lights away and you have a regular messy divorce, friends taking sides, money, adultery, using the kids. The only remarkable thing was that he left her for an older woman. The rest is pedestrian, and the fact that it was a royal divorce doesn't quite make up for the dullness of most of the characters involved. It was, perhaps, Princess Diana's contradictions that kept the interest alive. She spent £3,000 a week on grooming and hugged lepers. She secretly visited centres for the homeless, taking her sons with her to ensure they learned about privilege, and issued an angry public statement when a tabloid picture showed a suggestion of cellulite on her thighs. But scrutinise the first thirty-six years of anyone's life and you will find no end of contradictions (with the possible exception of Paris Hilton's). It was just that for a brief period Diana had more and grander opportunities for contradictory behaviour than most of us. This might be what celebrity obsession is: watching and waiting for them to get all the usual things wrong, but on a monstrous scale. If we had access to the private life of God (and there's one who had opportunities and blew it) he'd be the celebridaddy of them all.

Only two factors count: the public has an appetite for the details of public lives that are supposed to be secret, and there are vast amounts of money to be made in giving it this information. What else is there to be interested in? What else can the media do but go on giving us what we're interested in? You can choose between helplessly watching rich, stupid folk walk into brick walls, and helplessly taking in the global suffering caused by politicians and corporations, and, of course, by our own greed. Better to be unable to do anything about something you don't really care about. So the books keep coming. They're still writing about Marilyn and Princess Grace: why, after only ten years, wouldn't we be deluged with books about Diana? It's just, you know, the way the world is.

Diana, as the first narrator of her own yarn, seemed to understand that stories have their own needs and immutable trajectories. Diana told Andrew Morton in *Diana: Her True Story* that she would never be queen. In 1992 I reviewed the Morton book for this paper and mocked her prediction: 'The premonition is never quite explained. Does she think that death is beckoning, or divorce, or is she planning to become a nun?' Well, aside from marrying Christ, that was exactly what she did think, and what, indeed, happened. In the *Panorama* interview of 1995, she told Martin Bashir that she believed she would die young. She wrote to her butler, in a letter to be published after her death, that there would be a nasty car crash, a head injury or something; that she would be got rid of. Diana had a respect for narrative rules that I quite lack, and narrative repaid her by enclosing her possessively in the story.

Diana Spencer, who wasn't keen on literature, being, as she said, thick as two planks, nonetheless spent her girlhood obsessively reading the books of her step-grandmother, Barbara Cartland. But she was better than Cartland, whose books invariably ended happily for their good girl heroines after a vicissitude or two. Diana understood the more compellingly modern psychological drama of the ineluctably unhappy ending for those who acted out and did not or could not abide by the rules. She became an avatar of modernity, stepping boldly into her role as victim ('There were three of us in this marriage' and overdoing the kohl under her eyes), while fully complying with the requirements of the great amorphous conspiracy that keeps society on a roughly even keel (being easily dismissible as a hysteric and failing to wear a seat belt). With a better education, she might have liked Hardy and read Foucault with interest. 'She won't go quietly, that's the problem,' Diana said to 15 million people in the *Panorama* interview, slipping naturally into the third person. It was more like a trailer than a warning.

Still, you wonder, is there really anything more to say? The answer is no, but Tina Brown (*The Diana Chronicles*) and Sarah Bradford (*Diana*) soldier on, nevertheless. Each of them has produced hundreds of pages based on books already written (by journalists, her friends, his friends, butlers, nannies, ex-employers, protection officers, a speech trainer, lovers, paparazzi) and the odd interview with people who have already been interviewed for the books already written. They even quote one another. Certainly the material is almost identical in the two books. They consider the evidence that everyone else has considered and conclude as everyone else has concluded that there were faults on both sides and that the crash at the Pont de l'Alma was a tragic accident.

Tina Brown has the social edge, however, on Sarah Bradford, the professional biographer who came to Princess Diana with her ladylike prose after books on such considerable women as the Queen, Jackie Kennedy and Lucrezia Borgia. As sometime editor of *Vanity Fair* and the *New Yorker*, Brown had a couple of lunches with Diana (Four Seasons, Anna Wintour, a charity do). Moreover, as she lists in her seven pages of acknowledgements, she knows all (two full pages) the right people (Lord Rothschild, Henry Kissinger, Bruce Oldfield, Emma Soames), quantities (three paragraphs) of the right researchers, and even the right London hotel owner, who made 'a room available every time I hit town' for 'a demanding writer with a moody computer' in his 'comfortable, centrally located and fashionably cool' hotel. The full list of books 'that have enriched this one' takes up four pages. And, doubtless with great relief because photo booths are so often out of order, she thanks, too, 'the gifted photographer Annie Leibovitz', who 'with her usual generosity insisted on taking the portrait the publisher required for my book jacket'.

In addition to all this, Brown has years of journalistic experience to draw on for her prose. It shows when she muses about Diana's final moments after Henri Paul arrived 'to drive her away through celebrity's electric storm. Does she think then of her sons, asleep in a Scottish castle? As she slides quickly into the back seat of the Mercedes on that close Parisian night, does she suddenly miss the cool English rain?' Not that Brown is exclusively high-minded and lyrical, but for salacious gossip she has to rely on the likes of Gyles Brandreth, whom she quotes quoting Barbara Cartland on the failure of the royal marriage: 'Of course, you know where it all went wrong. She wouldn't do oral sex.'

Brown has her own views. Diana's timing was bad. 'Lady Diana Spencer took her bow at the nexus of a national malaise brought about by a sclerotic social-welfarism that had lost its way and an ever hotter press competition for royal stories.' I'm not sure whether this passing political analysis means that if Britain had had a privatised healthcare system such as the Americans rejoice in and had refused to assist the underprivileged then the tabloids would not have cared so much about the wayward princess. But Brown is clear that Diana fitted herself for a fairytale and then had nothing to wear when the emperor's clothes vanished. All the emotional intelligence in the world won't do if you think it's OK to hang out with the Fayeds. If only she *had* gone quietly, become the landmine queen of people's hearts, the dress-auctioning charitable divorcée, Blair's roving ambassador of love in a really hugging, mute, big-eyed, wildly successful, mint-green, tanned sort of way. 'I wish we could leave Diana's story there. I wish we could leave her as I saw her that summer's day in New York in her mint-green suit and early tan when she came for the wildly successful auction of her dresses.' Instead, she let herself down. It wasn't entirely her fault, Brown allows. It was a lack of love. That 'always dragged her down'. Her mother left her, her husband left her. She argued with and stopped speaking to her mother, her sisters, her brother, her friends. She nuisance-called boyfriends who were happy to be smuggled into Kensington Palace in the boot of her car but not to leave their wealthy wives, and then she had to go and fall in love with Hasnat Khan, who just wanted to be a good cardiac surgeon and marry the girl of his mother's dreams. She couldn't cope with the collapse of the Cartland fantasy almost-come-true; she had the breeding but not the reading.

Finally, though, the weight of Brown's argument seems to conclude that the descent into the tunnel was set in motion by her descent into bad taste, by being in the wrong place in the wrong season with the wrong people. Brown's great contribution to our understanding of the tragic end of the Princess of Wales depends on her knowledge of what's what in a world that the rest of us can only gawp at. Between her book's gynaecologically pink covers she straightens out her downscale readers on how low Diana had sunk that night in Paris as she left the Ritz:

> In August most upscale Parisians head north
> to Deauville for the polo and the racing or to
> the cool woods of their country estates in the
> Loire or Bordeaux ... Paris's most prestigious
> hotel at that time of the year is crawling with
> camera-toting tourists and rubber-neckers. At
> the end of the seasonal exit from town even
> the more exclusive areas of the hotel – such as
> its restaurant, L'Espadon – have a louche air of
> rootless extravagance. South American call girls
> with hirsute operators from emerging markets
> and rich old ladies with predatory nephews can be
> seen poring over the wine list.

Crawling, my dears. Pay attention, Tina's talking class here, and the price a girl pays when she lets herself down.

For women over thirty-five, glamour has three Stations of the Cross: denial, disguise and compromise. As she entered her thirty-seventh year Diana told herself she was looking for love. But what she was really seeking was a guy with a Gulfstream. Her needs at this juncture had more in common with those of second-act sirens like Elizabeth Hurley than with those of anyone currently residing in Balmoral.

Once the princess can't feel the pea any more, not even when all but one of her mattresses have been whisked away, what is left but a dingy death in a concrete tunnel?

2 August 2007

Not Enjoying Herself

And now for the other princess: the one who failed to stop all the clocks in Kensington Palace and Mustique, and grew old. In doing so she became sick, fat, grumpy, drunk and unloved. This, you might think, is the fate of many people who leave dying to their later years. But in a princess these flaws, if not the necessary concomitants of age then surely an entitlement of age, are particularly disappointing. We like our princesses young and adorable, and if possible witty and talented, though we've had to settle for the former. While she was young, Margaret Rose was the apple of her father's eye, enchanting to all who met her, talented, witty, artistic, they said – and then one day she was middle-aged, frumpy, snobbish, self-centred, a raddled old gin tippler and a bore. So much apparent promise, so little follow through.

However, all was not as it seemed to readers of Nanny Crawfie's tales about Princess Margaret Rose in the 1940s, and to excited observers of the teens-and-twenties princess in the 1950s. Her elevated station also elevated her qualities. Not that she wasn't a looker in her youth. Big, beautiful eyes, good bones, a serious nose, a large, modern mouth and a figure to die for. Short though. A pocket Venus, they called her, barely five feet tall. But, according to Tim Heald, her latest biographer, who has previously committed to paper the lives of Brian Johnston, Denis Compton, Barbara Cartland and Prince Philip, like the other four biographical subjects she was also a household word in her day. This had nothing to do with hard work and natural ability – as, I would argue, it did in the other four cases – and everything to do with the accident of birth. The other four were all, with the possible exception of Compton, prodigiously hard workers and they all had exceptional talents, deployed in often original forms. Princess Margaret was not a spectacularly hard worker and possessed no out-of-the-ordinary ability.

All that talk of her being a gifted musician, a fine pianist, a talented actor and a quick wit was just royal nursery hyperbole. At which point, so that we can all get on with reading and thinking about more important or at least more intellectually stimulating matters, both the biography (*Princess Margaret: A Life Unravelled*), for all that it hasn't actually started (the quote above is from the introduction), and this review might as well finish.

Yet ... convinced by page xix that there was nothing interesting about Princess Margaret, I was surprised and intrigued to learn that, in spite of the four full-length biographies already written about her, Tim Heald nevertheless persuaded a publisher to commission him to write another one. She may have been, as he says, 'a classic also-ran, second best' and finally 'a sad and enfeebled elderly woman in a wheelchair', but Heald based his argument for yet another biography on the view he claims the world has had of her since her death as 'a Diana before Diana'. This is a pitch of sorts, sure enough, but what grips me is why he would want to do it. Imagine making the effort to think of a reason to write a biography of Princess Margaret. Imagine committing months of working life to gathering the material and writing the words of such a book. Of course there is the matter of earning a living, but if you can find a way to sell a biography of Princess Margaret to an uncaring world, surely you could come up with a proposal to write about someone you do not regard as talentless and idle? Perhaps Heald is a man who relishes a challenge. Where's the fun in writing about Sarah Bernhardt or Gertrude Stein when you could set yourself the puzzle of finding enough words to fill three hundred pages about Princess Margaret? Certainly, his research methods, to say nothing of the results, suggest a penchant for being tested by the dull and a preparedness to overcome swamps of tedium in order to produce chapters and chapters of brain-numbing information.

He did talk to some people. Lord Snowdon, for example, and Princess Margaret's former private secretary, Lord Napier and Ettrick (who apparently is just the single person), as well as a couple of former ladies-in-waiting. There were also those who chose to remain anonymous, for all that Heald understands that 'this can pose problems for outsiders who will think this is a bluff and that no such secret informants actually exist.' But most of his research was done while being carefully supervised in the Royal Archives in Windsor. The Queen gave Heald permission to consult the papers relating to Princess Margaret, and consult them he did. Interestingly, though this suggests that he is considered a safe pair of hands by the palace, it does not, he insists, make the book 'an "authorised" or "official"' biography, thus not killing it stone dead. He doesn't waste his access to the archives, where all the notes, memos and plans for

Princess Margaret's official engagements at home and abroad are filed for posterity. He gets eleven pages out of the papers referring to the 1947 royal tour of South Africa. On the boat Tommy Lascelles read Trollope and in Cape Town Princess Margaret danced with the minister of economic development. He quotes extensively from two letters she wrote home to Queen Mary ('Darling Grannie, I thought I must write and tell you how we are getting on in this lovely country'), but after several more anodyne paragraphs about the heat and riding horses, the unauthorised (or perhaps the covertly authorised) nature of the biography becomes apparent: 'The Royal Archives have asked me not to transcribe the remainder of this letter, not on the grounds of its content but because I am "not writing an official biography".' Heald maintains a modicum of independence by summarising what seems to be a complaint of boredom at the endless round of meeting and greeting town officials, and adding that 'the princess admits that she had previously no experience of black people and had been apprehensive, even frightened, about meeting them. After her time in South Africa, however, she had come to like them very much. She particularly warmed to their enthusiasm and their singing.'

The deadly archives, however, more or less structure the book, which presents Margaret's adult life as a series of official visits, and describes what she wore, who she shook hands with, the letters of thanks from those who met her, and the odd unwitty comment she wrote in the margins for her ladies-in-waiting to sort out. A pointless life, as Heald suggests, and pointlessly recounted. The archives are censored, the interviewees are mostly on message, and dishearteningly for both the author and his readers, Heald explains that 'much of the princess's life passed unnoticed and unrecorded.'

Heald's main source for her childhood is what he admits to be the highly unreliable Nanny Crawford book, written to get her own back on the family she believed had not seen her right. Much is quoted and then dismissed as untrue. His other source is a book published in 1940 called *Our Princesses at Home*, photographs commissioned by Queen Elizabeth of family life, with a saccharine and obviously royally approved commentary by the photographer, Lisa Sheridan. 'We see here a royal duet at the piano. It is a pity that we cannot hear it also. The harmony which exists between the royal sisters is happily symbolised by this picture taken, without their knowing it, during their musical studies.' The best he can make of this wartime propaganda, 'idealised to the point of being fey and whimsical', is: 'Yet it is interesting, because this is the way in which "our princesses" were perceived.' He continues to examine the photos with the increasing desperation of a writer who has nothing to say about something that isn't even remotely interesting.

There is one picture of Princess Margaret at an upright piano, sitting on a stool and smiling a touch insipidly at the camera. She is wearing a neat patterned frock and ankle socks with sensible shoes, which I bet are a pair of Start-Rites. Start-Rites of Norwich are descended from a leather merchant who, in the eighteenth century, was the first man in England to make shoes on lasts. Their children's shoes date from the 1920s, since when they have regularly held the Royal Warrant.

Of course, there is the Townsend business, but nothing new emerges from Heald's rummaging in the archives. The story is rehashed, Princess Margaret gives up Townsend when threatened with becoming plain Mrs Margaret. Townsend goes off into Belgian exile, and Margaret may or may not have been livid when he married, on the grounds that they had a pact they would remain single. She also may or may not have married Antony Armstrong-Jones out of spite. The only novel comment is from a clearly bored Snowdon (né Armstrong-Jones): 'I never really thought the Townsend business was all it was cracked up to be, did you?' The whole thing a teenage crush? Who knows? It caught the romantic imagination of postwar Britain, but even a broken-hearted youth couldn't sustain the public's affection for a bad-tempered, spoilt princess for very long. When she made a guest appearance in *The Archers* in 1984, supposedly attending a charity fashion show at Grey Gables, she read through her lines (*The Archers* had come to Kensington Palace to do the recording rather than the princess going to Broadcasting House) and the producer, William Smethurst, gave her his notes:

'Perfect, ma'am,' he cringed obsequiously. 'Just wonderful. I just wonder if, when we do it one more time, you might give the impression that you were, well, enjoying yourself.'
Her Royal Highness glared at him. 'Well I wouldn't be, would I?' she said.

Interesting. Yes, interesting. Clearly, the obsequiously cringing Smethurst didn't give Heald the quote. At last engaged, I turned to the notes for the relevant chapter in order to find the source of this snippet. There is no mention of *The Archers* or Smethurst. The notes are entirely free-form and intermittent. As Heald explains, partly because some sources wanted to remain anonymous,

> I have not provided the sort of notes which cite detailed chapter and verse and then explain 'confidential source' or 'private information'.
> I find these sorts of notes pointless and frustrating.
> I am doubtful in general about highly specific source notes. If you gave genuine explanations for every tiny piece of information and interpretation you would more than write the book all over again. I also feel the need for an element of trust. If I say that on such-and-such-a-date so-and-so-happened you have to trust me to be telling the truth. If not, you might as well give up reading.

Now, I don't know Tim Heald from a Bath bun, and I am not, ask anyone, a trusting sort of person. Moreover, the fact of my turning to the back of the book shows that I have a petty and annoying habit of wondering where writers of biographies get their information from. If only Heald's feelings about references and what kinds of reader he required had been included in the introduction, I could have saved myself hours of unnecessary labour. As it was, I felt obliged (troublesome superego) to carry on doggedly taking in his words from page xix until page 234, when at last I was released from the book by its author, on account of my lack of trust.

That, I think, is enough princesses.

16 August 2007

Staying Awake

If you set aside the incomparable cruelty and stupidity of human beings, surely our most persistent and irrational activity is to sleep. Why would we ever allow ourselves to drop off if sleeping was entirely optional? Sleep is such a dangerous place to go to from consciousness: who in their right mind would give up awareness, deprive themselves of control of their senses, volunteer for paralysis, and risk all the terrible things (and worse) that could happen to a person when they're not looking? As chief scientist in charge of making the world a better place, once I'd found a way of making men give birth, or at least lactate, I'd devote myself to abolishing the need for sleep. Apart from the dangers of letting your guard down, there's the matter of time. Instead of trying to extend the life of human bodies beyond their cellular feasibility, the men and women in lab coats could be studying ways to retrieve all the time we spend asleep. A third of our lives, they say – and that probably doesn't take the afternoon nap into account. Even if we died aged what is these days a rather youthful seventy, finding a way to stay awake would increase our functional life to the equivalent of ninety-three. And if we happened to live to ninety-three then we'd effectively be ... oh, even older. Plus the nap time. Sleep, we're told, is essential, repairing the wear and tear on body and mind, but sex was once solely for the purpose of propagating the species and we pretty much found a workaround for that biological constraint.

Obviating the need to sleep would also take care of the second most absurd thing we do: wake up. You can buy an alarm clock advertised in one of those catalogues of marvellous necessities like LED digital-musical-weather-station-photo-frames and electronic nail-polish driers. The alarm clock is on all-terrain wheels. If you don't immediately turn it off, it rolls off your bedside table and cruises around the bedroom beeping and flashing until there's nothing for it but to get out of bed and chase it. Or there's the airborne alarm clock which takes off from its base and flies around the room making a noise like an infuriated mosquito. Such extreme measures – which must contravene several health and safety regulations – suggest that waking up is not as popular as you might think coming round from unconsciousness would be.

At any rate, that's how I'd look at the subject if it weren't for the fact that sleeping, for all its inherent dangers and waste, is and always has been my activity of choice. Inexpert though I am in all other fields, I am a connoisseur of sleep. Actually, my speciality is not sleep itself, but the hinterland of sleep, the point of entry to unconsciousness. One of my earliest memories of sensual pleasure (though there must have been earlier, watery ones) is of lying on my stomach in bed, the bedtime story told, lights out (not the hall, leave the door open, no, more than that), the eiderdown heavy and over my head, my face in the pillow, adjusted so that I had just enough air to breathe. I recall how acutely aware I was of being perfectly physically comfortable, as *heimlich* as I ever had been or ever would be, and no small part of the comfort was the delicious prospect of falling slowly into sleep. Drifting off. Moving off, away, out of mindfulness. Leaving behind. Relaxing into hypnagogia (a condition I may always have known about and desired, if not been able to name), anticipating the blurring of consciousness. It must have been a familiar routine, because I was so filled with confident pleasure of what was to come. Daydreaming a story (princes, princesses, cruel guardians, rescues), trying to hold on to the narrative as the thread of it kept drifting away, or I did, out of reach into a storyless place, a gentle fog. The great delight was in deferring sleep, hovering on the edge, pulling myself back to the same point in the story and trying to move it along, but always dropping off, hanging by the story-thread, the fingertips losing their grip but managing to haul back to the tale on the waking side of the world. The trick was to sustain my stay in the no man's land for as long as possible, knowing all the while that I would inevitably, sooner or later, lose my grip on consciousness.

So I remember it, and so it still is, at its best, the border territory of sleep. It is most readily reachable during a daytime nap, though the result is that 'naps' can take hours. The whole point is to extend the unsleeping moment, and to drop into a state where all logic and reason disappear, while I nevertheless retain an essential degree of awareness of the strangeness I've achieved. Euclidian geometry disappears and irregular objects and abstractions with a dimensional existence appear to inhabit and shape the reality of this space. Chairs, cups, laptops, gardens, or impossible, indescribable forms, floating and structural, replace the basic rectangles and polyhedrons of the regular world, and aside from their architectural purpose, their meaning, and they surely have a meaning, is unguessable, though just occasionally sideways, shimmering in some corner, if corners existed, there is a glimpse of something that would turn it all into sense if it didn't immediately flit away. Thought itself becomes mad geometry, another building block of this alien strip of universe, familiar because I've been there so many times before, but always as weird and ungraspable as air and water.

And then finally and inevitably, sleep. A nothing: existing only in anticipation or recollection. Dreams are remembered afterwards as narrative or vague leftover feelings, but are not experienced by me, because in sleep there is no me. The dreamer sometimes mistakes itself for me, or I do for it, but really sleep is a state of coma, death, of involuntary spasms or paralysis that I can only know about if someone (including me) tells me about it later. Unconsciousness itself is desired, but only in anticipation or retrospect. Obviously, by definition. Sleep, while it is happening, is nothing to the sleeper. To an observer all kinds of things are happening to the sleeper while she sleeps. Watch the cat, twitching paws and whiskers, purring, gruffling. Watch sleeping people smile, or mutter, fidget, laugh and shriek. So the observer knows about it, watching you; you do not. Later, you can remember or feel, but the only actual experience of sleep is not-knowing. And not knowing thrills me – retrospectively or in anticipation, of course. That one has the capacity to be not here while being nowhere else. To be in the grip of unconsciousness, and consciously to lose consciousness to that grip. My first experiment with drugs was sniffing ether to make myself unconscious, then waking after what seemed an eternity of absence to discover that while I had been nowhere, just a moment or two had passed. Even the absence was mysterious to me, since when I came round, there were whole sagas of remembered dreams, as if I had experienced them, yet I knew nothing of them at the time. It was a great adventure in time travel and disappearance. But then the dreams turned very bad. Now and then I can treasure that second or two after the anaesthetist has pressed the plunger – count backwards from 10 – 10, 9, 9, 8, 7, 9... 9... 9... Hanging on to the narrative for as long as I possibly can. The same brief encounter with being and not-being. But then there's post-operative pain as a rule, though usually also the morphine to wake up to: a state of hypnopompia provided by the NHS.

Hypnopompia is the compensation at the other end of sleep. The brutality of waking, if you don't have to catch a flying alarm clock, is soothed by the equal and opposite blurring of consciousness. Coming to, coming round. Slowly. Holding on to sleep, then hovering in hypnoland for as long as you can. Jung almost redeems himself from creepy spiritus munditude with the story in which he asks his new patient, a pathologically anxious, blocked writer, to describe his day in detail. 'Well, I wake, get up and ...' 'Stop,' Jung says. 'That's where you're going wrong.' Not likely to be true, but perfectly correct. The hinterland between sleeping and waking is what compensates for having to start and get through the day, blocked writer, besieged schoolteacher or sullen secretary as I've been in my time. If you must have an alarm clock, don't get a flying one, but set it to wake you early enough to give you all the drifting time you need. Between getting extra sleep or drifting, drift wins.

But because, in my view, sleep itself has nothing to do with me, it constitutes something of a danger. Apart from practical hazards, such as being eaten by a sabre-toothed tiger or bludgeoned to death by a serial killer who is too insanely cunning even for the lab rats on *CSI*, there are more nebulous and sinister perils attested to in fairytale and anthropology. I have never slept in a plane or on a train, nor, since I was a child, slept anywhere in public. It's not for lack of trying, but I guess that I can't allow myself to be so vulnerable to the gaze of others. On the other hand, the only pleasure to be got out of a long, sequestered, wakeful journey that everyone else is dreaming away, is to wander up and down the aisles in the deep of night and look at others sleeping. Of course, as children we sleep like babies, in all kinds of public circumstances, but then small children don't make the distinction between self and other that prevents them from chatting to themselves in a room full of people and make-believing in full view of friends and strangers. I keep all that sort of thing strictly private – it's the way of the adult – or try to, and although I do occasionally find myself talking to myself or the bottled water in supermarkets, I never fall asleep in public. It's always extraordinary to patrol a planeful or trainful of people, trusting as newborns, sprawling in search of minimum discomfort, slack-jawed, legs apart, hair awry, skirts and trouser legs crumpled and careless, snorting and snoring in full view of a crowd of strangers. I suppose the assumption is that the strangers, too, are asleep, and a condition of mutually assured unconsciousness obtains. But there is always me, at least, peering at the touching and terrifying vulnerability of the publicly unconscious.

Vulnerable, not to sabre-toothed tigers but to being watched. I do not want anyone looking at me when I'm not looking at them. Like Yogi Bear, throwing a towel over his head when the warden comes along, if I can't see you, you can't see me. Do I worry about my spirit being stolen, like the Aborigines who are supposed to fear that a photograph will do just that? I think I just don't like being looked at when I can't turn and say: 'What?' Or perhaps that's the same thing. 'Are you looking at me? Are you looking at me?'

Who leaves when you fall asleep? They do, of course. So how can they look at you when they're no longer there? Otherwise it would be you who is not there and everyone else is where they always were, getting on with what they were always doing. That would suggest, on the constant pairing of sleep with death ('Death be not proud ...'), that when you die the world carries on without you, and that is clearly ridiculous. It is said that when Franco was dying, his ministers (lying, I hope) said: 'Generalissimo, all Madrid is standing outside the palace to say goodbye to you.' 'Why?' the generalissimo said. 'Where are they going?' This is the first time I have identified with a Fascist dictator, but he was, in this single instance, completely correct in his understanding.

All of which may be the reason the phrase 'fell asleep as soon as her head hit the pillow' is as strange to me as cuneiform. The drifting ritual, and the early training (which is why the light in the hall is on, and the door open, wider) of listening for catastrophe in the night, means that I have always taken an age to get to sleep. Sometimes this tips over into insomnia. Not a chance of drifting. Just the mind growing increasingly frantic with thoughts lining up round the block to get their moment in the sun of night-time fretfulness. This is more like my methedrine phase. I enjoyed hyperconsciousness then (until, as with the ether, the thoughts turned bad). These days I'm much more on the side of oblivion. It goes in phases, and if I had a scientific interest in it, I'd be fascinated by the transformation of the world in the early hours to the place of uncertainty and woe that it actually is. The veil of coping shreds as the hours go by and all the disasters and horrid failures that can undoubtedly occur, and indeed are crowded, stage left, simply waiting for their moment, make themselves known to you. People have always asked which is the reality, sleep or wakefulness, but no one ever dares suggest that the horrors of half-past three in the morning are indeed as likely to happen as not, and are at least as possible as they are impossible.

Reality cannot stand too much wakefulness. My longest period of sleeplessness (aside from the methedrine binges) occurred for no reason I could figure out, but, years ago, for two days and nights and some more, I simply could not get to sleep. I did the required tossing and turning rather than getting up and doing something useful all through one night and set myself to sleep the following day – it was a weekend – but nothing happened. All day nothing happened, and in the evening I lay in bed more mad with wondering about the cause and the fear that sleep had deserted me forever than with sleeplessness itself, and turned on the television just in time for the start of *Fantastic Voyage*. In that wonderful movie, Donald Pleasence and Raquel Welch among others are miniaturised in an attempt to save the life of a crucial cold war US scientist with a blood clot on the brain. They are injected in a tiny submarine into his bloodstream and do battle with the monstrous currents of the circulatory system. They negotiate the waving cilia forest of the lungs and the sucking whirlpools of osmotic action. They do battle with an army of white blood cells charging at the foreign body inserted into their scientist host, and they overcome the fearful turbulence of the heart valves to get into the aorta and finally into the electrical storm of the brain. And all along, one of them is a Russian plant, sent to subvert the mission and prevent the sub's missiles breaking up the life-threatening clot in the frontal lobe of the enemy genius.

It is a thrilling film at any time, but after thirty-six hours of sleeplessness it took on the quality of oracular truth. I felt the tiny sub's embattled passage through my every interior part. I became Donald Pleasence determined to fulfil his evil mission (for who else could it have been but him?), and Raquel, pneumatic in her scientific white overalls but dismissing her irrelevant though mighty breasts and luscious hips and lips, serious and brilliant neurologist that she was, focused on surviving in order to save the scientist and the beleaguered world. And what was more, there was a time constraint. The miracle miniaturising procedure would last only sixty minutes before they and their vessel would begin to grow and present a threat to their patient even worse than the clot in his brain. A race against time and wickedness, and I sat bolt upright in bed, living out every dangerous second of the passing hours. I must have fallen asleep eventually, later that night or day or whenever it was, because I haven't been awake ever since, but I do live with a sense that part of me is still weirdly wide awake, unable even to blink my eyes, while Donald Pleasence and Raquel Welch fight it out, riding the tides of my pumping blood, as the clock ticks.

31 July 2008

THE KHUGISTIC SANDAL

Great shoemakers of our day: Manolo Blahnik, Jimmy Choo, Christian Louboutin. None of them, I think, very Jewish. And if there had been any great pre or postwar Jewish shoe mavens they would certainly have been pointed out to me by my parents, who identified any Jewish achiever in any sphere as one of the family: Alma Cogan, Einstein, Marx, boxing promoter Jack Solomons (the Sultan of Sock), it didn't matter what they were known for, everyone counted. Even, like the Kray twins, a little bit Jewish and murderers would make them ours and make us proud – but there was never a mention of shoe designers. So I supposed that a book called *Jews and Shoes* was going to be either a bumper book of Jewish jokes about schlepping and cobbling, or a severe cultural studies analysis of the nature and symbolic value of footwear in Jewish society through the ages. Aside from a mention of how Ferragamo got his start by popularising the strappy shoe for Hollywood lovelies after being commissioned by Cecil B. DeMille to make 12,000 sandals for the original 1923 version of *The Ten Commandments*, there is nothing to be found on high-end modern footwear. *Jews and Shoes* turns out indeed to be largely about schlepping and cobbling but is entirely devoid of jokes. This is academic cultural studies at its most anxious, wanting to make much of little but worrying about not being taken seriously. Making much of little is, of course, a vital task and one at which jokes excel (though they're just as good at making little of much). But I can't think of any Jewish shoe jokes, so perhaps the contributors to this collection of essays had their hands tied.

Cultural studies usually make much of little by ascribing large meanings to the mundane. Shoes are hardly lacking cultural and symbolic meaning. We are reminded several times of the Freudian shoe, phallic or vaginal receptacle for the phallic or vaginal foot – whichever suits. Meanings must illuminate use, so a Freudianish explanation is offered for the *halitzah* ceremony, in which a Jewish widow whose brother-in-law refuses to marry her in the levirate tradition spits in his face and rips off one of his shoes before going her own way. This public humiliation – emasculation, Catherine Hezser suggests in her essay – gave the woman her independence. A strike for feminism? Not really, since the widow became independent in an ancient world where neither her father nor her dead husband's family any longer had to take care of her. More like a mild public admonition for having rendered the woman destitute. I imagine it was a humiliation a brother-in-law not willing to father a child who would inherit his brother's portion was able to bear. (Look it up.) He didn't even have to use his own shoes – the rabbinic court supplied them. Moreover, Hezser points out, the putting on and taking off of another's shoes is equally a sign of subservience, and the spitting in the face might be translated as spitting on the ground – as plausibly a gesture of frustration as of glorious contempt. Freud sneaks back in a passage in the Babylonian Talmud which allows women to 'reject suitors from a superior family background by saying: "I do not want a shoe too large for my foot."' Conversely, in a Midrash explaining why Pharoah contracted lupus after he tried to bed Abraham's wife Sarah, 'R. Berekiah said: Because he dared to approach the shoe of that lady.' One way or another, as Hezser says, the 'later rabbis were well aware of the symbolism of the foot and shoe'. Shoes, make of them what you will.

With or without a Freudian tinge, shoes relate to the sacred and profane. God's first instruction to Moses as he stands astonished in front of the burning bush is that he should take his shoes off 'for the place whereon thou standest is holy ground'. But Ora Horn Prouser says that the command 'may simply appear to be about holiness' when, actually, it defines the nature of the relationship between God and the Israelites. Captives are kept barefoot, and David fled barefooted from his son Absalom. Subjugation and unreadiness, therefore, are signified, and we're reminded, perhaps, of the prelapsarian honeymoon when Adam and Eve were butt naked in the garden and God didn't have the bother of providing them with clothes. Genesis 3:21 doesn't actually say that they got a pair of shoes each, but condemned as they were to a lifetime of wandering, to say nothing of the serpent snapping at their heels, surely even the most petulant God would have shod them. Rendering Moses shoeless is explained as another sort of legal ceremony, this one formulating the contract between Yahweh and the Israelites. I'm not sure that relating it (or the Burning Bush episode) to earlier and later parts of the Bible does much more to convey the relations of God and Israel than God's bald declaration of holy ground and the violating human shoe. Still, the Lord kept his part of the bargain not only by leading them out of Egypt, but by looking after their feet: 'And I have led you forty years in the wilderness: your clothes are not waxen old upon you, and thy shoe is not waxen old upon foot.' Even Lobbs of St James, whose handmade shoes start at £1,758 a pair, can only guarantee that they 'are made to last as long as possible in both the construction and the leather used'.

The linking of Jews and shoes makes sense, I suppose, beyond the satisfactory rhyme, for a people on the move since well before Moses and long before medieval Christianity invented the Wandering Jew. Abraham, the father of them all, was told to 'get thee out of thy country, and from thy kindred, and from thy father's house, unto a land that I will shew thee.' After which there was no end of traipsing, fleeing and marching into battle. Plays havoc with the feet, and certainly a decent pair of shoes would help. The Jew/shoe linkage is strengthened in a pamphlet of 1602, cited by Shelly Zer-Zion in her chapter, which describes the Jew named Ahasverus who had owned a cobbler's shop on the Via Dolorosa, but refused Christ assistance as he passed by. Whereupon Christ 'looked hard at him, and said: "I shall stand here and rest, but you shall wander forth and be everlastingly restless."'

However, there is more to shoes than meets the eye. Zer-Zion references the cultural historian Sander Gilman. Inside every shoe is a foot, and Jewish feet, according to Gilman's chapter on the Jewish foot in his book *The Jew's Body*, were as emblematic in antisemitic literature as their noses. The Wandering Jew had a particular gait that came partly from his naturally twisted body, but also from endemic flat-footedness. Gilman suggests that the origin of the Jewish crooked foot is the idea of the secret difference of the Jews – the Devil's cloven foot concealed by shoes. A civilised covering for the degenerate reality. It's a myth that's lasted well since its medieval beginnings. When I was around eight, a friend of mine came home from school, shrieking in terror, rushed past her mother and shut herself in her room for hours, sobbing. It turned out the nuns at her convent school (who knows why a convent school) had told her class that Jews had cloven hooves inside their shoes. The Jewish girl had been advised to sneak a look at her mother's feet while she slept and see that it was so. I don't think it was suggested that she herself had cloven hooves, so I imagine they're something that grows on you, unless you have the good sense to convert while there's still a chance. Her mother had to force my friend to watch her take off her shoes and reveal a pair of common or garden feet no different from the Catholic variety.

Flat-footedness became a nineteenth-century medical fact about Jews: a condition that prevented them from entering the army and therefore from being regarded as full citizens in the highly militarised Austrian monarchy. Jewish doctors, not wanting to be seen as lesser scientists, accepted the Jewish flat foot as gospel, but suggested it was caused by the 'misuse' of the foot. It was the long urban existence of the Jews that had ruined their feet, not the proposed 'generally looser structure of the Jew's musculature'. Civilisation, not race, had caused the defect. The argument required the inheritance of acquired characteristics, a theory that trembles with the possibility of putting to rest the nature/nurture debate, but sadly came to nothing. Gilman makes a connection between flat-footedness and Charcot's diagnosis of intermittent claudication – a chronic recurrence of pain and tension in the lower leg and finally paralysis. This became a Jewish pathology: in a 1901 paper, Higier suggested it was a sign of structural weakness and of hysteria. In 1905, Freud, a pupil of Charcot, wrote up his analysis of Dora, who fitted the bill perfectly: Jewish, hysterical and suffering from paralysis. Then intermittent claudication was found to relate statistically to circulation problems caused especially by heavy smoking, and this enabled the uneasily assimilated German Jewish scientists to shift the diagnosis to the disreputable and impoverished Eastern Jews, who smoked like chimneys.

Eventually, the Zionists appropriated the idea of the Wandering Jew, reconstituting it as loss and migration. The Wandering Jew became a poster boy for the Zionist notion of an Israeli homeland, which could only be achieved by a New Jew. The Zionists took up the story about the physically weak body of the Jew, but they had a solution. Max Nordau, co-founder of the World Zionist Organisation with Theodor Herzl, had also studied with Charcot in his youth. Zer-Zion says: 'He accepted the assumption that Jews suffered from orthopedic and psychological problems that prevented them from becoming useful citizens. Thus he developed the concept of *Muscle Jewry* and advocated the establishment of sports clubs in Jewish society. It was not the right shoes that would redeem the Wandering Jew but rather well-shaped and highly trained legs and feet.' The Wandering Jew was given a Zionist direction.

The Holocaust Shoe is an inevitable chapter. The mounds of leftover shoes at every Holocaust museum and memorial are considered by Jeffrey Feldman. Are they, he asks, part of the commodity fetishism of the memorial industry: Graceland, heritage tourism, the concentration camp trail – the equivalent of the relics of the Catholic martyrs? The symbolic value of these shoes is evident: scattered in piles, unpaired, disordered, no longer shoes for individuals (themselves industrially disposed of), purposeless. You are supposed to think of the feet that were once inside the shoes. You stand in front of them, but, Feldman says, it is usually a passive encounter. He considers the fact of the piles, and their condition. Their rotting leather, the smell of decay and mould; the effect of the time that has passed since they were taken from their owners. It is the difference between the immediate and the historical, and the Holocaust itself slips into relicdom as it slips into the historical past: a sanitised exhibit for new generations who didn't live through the event or its discovery. The eyes, Feldman says, are not enough. The observer needs to smell and touch in order to get closer to the reality.

The nationalistic and originally socialist project of Zionism in Palestine fetishised the rugged, minimal, battered and levelling shoe. Songs were sung about them:

Hey, Hey, Hey, shoes;
Shoes without soles;
And the rocks torch the feet;
Torch, torch, torch.
Never mind, never mind, never mind;
The *chalutz* will build, build, build Jerusalem!
Build, build, build, build, build.

And leaders are judged by the condition of their shoes: 'It's hard to describe the tremendous impression made on me by Richard's bare toes, as they poked out from his torn shoes ... Is there anything nobler than torn shoes on the feet of a leader? That is the ultimate symbol of the pioneer.'

Shoes are literally fetishised by the extraordinary Bruno Schulz in his pictures of crouching, self-abasing men – self-portraits often – excruciated with desire at the feet and elegant shoes of fancy women holding whips or with their noses in the air. Unworldly Yeshiva boys and alarmed young Hassids encounter pairs of haughty women (*shikses*, surely) in shiny high heels, and gaze on them longingly or avert their gaze unconvincingly. 'The shoe provides a locus for Schulz's fascination with traditional Judaism and fetishistic masochism,' Andrew Ingall writes. Schulz, he suggests, transgresses 'the second commandment prohibitions, both in terms of creating graven images and worshipping the false idols of women, shoes and feet'. It's an intriguing idea, but it would need a longer article, and perhaps one that took in Schulz's writing, to give it substance. Contemporary art gets a look in, too, though it seems shoehorned. A chapter on installation art, using shoes and maths, created and written about by Sonya Rapoport, barely seems to make the effort to connect Jews and shoes beyond the fact of the artist's own Jewishness, the use of Yiddish in subheadings ('Jew-Psyche Reading: *In Mitn Derinen*/An Egoistic Sense of Self Shows Itself') and her final apparently clinching but baffling remark: 'Assigning a numeric value to quantitative feelings about shoes engages a spectrum of social dimensions such as being Jewish.' Another article on 'The Tombstone Shoe' offers the suggestion, without finding much in the way of evidence, that the shoe-shaped tombstones found around Western Ukraine and Kiev in nineteenth-century Jewish cemeteries were indications of a millennial expectation, the Tarnik movement's belief in the coming of the Messiah in 1840. The shoe-shaped tombstones were for properly shod Jewish souls to make their way to Zion. Or, says Rivka Parciack, they might have been cabbalistic symbols protecting the dead against demons. Either way, 'there are no definite or conclusive answers.'

Cultural studies leaves no stone unturned. There is an analysis of Ernst Lubitsch's first full-length film, made in 1916, long before he got to Hollywood, called *Schuhpalast Pinkus* ('Pinkus's Shoe Palace'), which is discussed by Jeanette Malkin in terms of the split between the Berlin Jews and the Ostjuden. Pinkus, played by Berlin Jew Lubitsch, is 'ambitious, lewd, pushy and smart'. He is hopeless at sports, school and business, but somehow – with the help of a rich woman impressed by his chutzpah – he becomes at last a successful shoe mogul. German Jews protested that the film endorsed the antisemitism that was already beginning to make them uncomfortable, but Lubitsch claimed it was simply Jewish humour. Malkin suggests that he is playing Pinkus as one of the immigrant Ostjuden who lived (in poverty) in the peripheral vision of Schönhauser Allee, where Lubitsch grew up. Pinkus makes good from despised Eastern Jew to fully respectable German Jewish merchant, and his vehicle is the shoe.

Two essays in this collection that discuss the iconic pioneering Israeli shoe gave me more to think about. The Khugistic Sandal had two horizontal straps and a buckle at the ankle. The sandals were called Khugistic after a commune that was said originally to have produced them, but in the 1930s they were renamed Biblical Sandals. The renaming was symbolic, Orna Ben-Meir says, designed to reiterate the ancestral link between contemporary Jews and the land given by God to Abraham: 'Arise, walk through the land in the length of it and in the breadth of it; for I will give it unto thee.' Neither the Lord nor this book has anything very much to say about those who were already on the land. Though it seems inescapable to me, the symbolic Biblical Shoe, on the feet of the ancient Hebrew wanderers and more recently the pioneers and later citizens of the Israeli state, is never described as being symbolically on the necks of the Canaanites or the Palestinians. Actually, there's barely an indication in these essays of there being anyone on the land, though the various aliyahs by Jewish immigrants and the meaning of what they wore on their feet are described in meticulous detail. The open-toed sandal had the right kind of earthy austerity for the early arrivals, and alluded to 'the then admired model of the native Bedouin'. No longer admired, the sentence suggests. The people who already inhabited the land are mentioned only twice. According to 'The Israeli Shoe' by Orna Ben-Meir, 'the Zionist project in Palestine was threatened on two sides: the cultural challenge of British colonial rule and the enmity of native Arabs,' while Ayala Raz, in 'The Equalising Shoe', tells us that 'Jewish urban life in Palestine at the time was difficult, largely due to bloody conflicts between Arabs and the Jewish community, which had reached 450,000 by 1940.'

We get a very partial view of the symbolic power of the Biblical Sandal. The bourgeois life was despised by the Israeli immigrants – Old Europe and things that didn't matter like decoration and fashion. The loss of the equalising sandal is regretted in modernised Israel. 'You love yourself in the polished shoes you wear now, and I love you because I remember your crooked sandals,' a character in S.Y. Agnon's 1945 novel, *The Day before Yesterday*, says to a wealthy friend who has forgotten his past. 'We can see footwear functioning here as a metonym for personhood and values,' Ayala Raz explains. Limited values, I would say. Perhaps this isn't the place to expect any acknowledgement of a Palestinian point of view in the construction of Israel. The focus is on shoes rather than the rights and wrongs of the state of Israel. For me, though, as I read these essays, the absent Palestinians had a more powerful presence than the Khugistic Sandal.

In fact, one man talking about what he knows provides the most compelling chapter of the book. Mayer Kirshenblatt's father was a merchant who supplied cobblers with their raw materials, and he himself was apprenticed to a cobbler before he left Poland for Canada in 1934 at the age of seventeen. In a transcribed interview with his daughter he describes, with diagrams, how shoes were made, as well as the itinerant shoe-polish seller's black chauffeur, believed by the children to have been polished each day to show the efficacy of the product. His voice is informative, funny and affectionate, as effective a chapter in cultural meanings as any of the others. We even get back to the Freudian shoe when he describes his time as the cobbler's apprentice. The workshop was also the living room where the whole family spent their time. Kirshenblatt worked there twelve hours a day. He explains that the cobbler's wife was not so much fat as she was big: she had broad shoulders, wide hips and enormous breasts. Of course she was breastfeeding. With her size she could have suckled a platoon. She wore a dress that reached below the knees in the front and just below the buttocks at the back. Since she didn't wear underwear, every time she bent over you got a full view of the whole landscape. She had vaginal lips the size of cabbage leaves. I had never seen anything like it.

Shoes, make of them what you will.

9 October 2008

Toxic Lozenges

Raymond Chandler writes in 'The Simple Art of Murder' (1950) that 'the English may not always be the best writers in the world, but they are incomparably the best dull writers.' He's specifically referring to crime novelists – the likes of Dorothy L. Sayers, Ngaio Marsh, Margery Allingham, Agatha Christie – in an attempt to wrest the detective story away from the English suburbs and towards the grittier (and far more romantic) novels written by himself and Dashiell Hammett. An explanation of sorts had already been offered by George Orwell. In 'Decline of the English Murder' (1946), he meditated on the apparent passing of the homely crime of murder as it was commonly reported in the British popular press:

> Our great period in murder, our Elizabethan period, so to speak, seems to have been between roughly 1850 and 1925, and the murderers whose reputation has stood the test of time are the following: Dr Palmer of Rugeley, Jack the Ripper, Neill Cream, Mrs Maybrick, Dr Crippen, Seddon, Joseph Smith, Armstrong, and Bywaters and Thompson.

Orwell discounts Jack the Ripper as an altogether special artisan of murder, but of the remaining eight, six were poisoners. The perfect murderer, he explains, was one who would satisfy the requirements of the reader of the *News of the World*, settled on the sofa, puffing on a pipe in front of the fire after a Sunday roast lunch, while his wife sleeps in a comfy chair and the children are off on a nice long walk. He – the murderer rather than the reader, though doubtless their shadows were twinned – should be

> a little man of the professional class – a dentist
> or a solicitor, say – living an intensely respectable
> life somewhere in the suburbs, and preferably
> in a semi-detached house, which will allow the
> neighbours to hear suspicious sounds through
> the wall. He should be either chairman of the
> local Conservative Party branch, or a leading
> Nonconformist and strong Temperance advocate.
> He should go astray through cherishing a
> guilty passion for his secretary or the wife of a
> rival professional man, and should only bring
> himself to the point of murder after long and
> terrible wrestles with his conscience. Having
> decided on murder, he should plan it all with the
> utmost cunning, and only slip up over some tiny
> unforeseeable detail. The means chosen should, of
> course, be poison.

Orwell argues that murder is no longer what it used to be, and cites the 1944 case of Elizabeth Jones, an eighteen-year-old, and an American army deserter, Karl Hulten, who went on a crime spree together, known as the Cleft Chin Murder. They were a Bonnie and Clyde pair, a symptom of the brutality of war and of approaching modernity in dear old England.

Perhaps it is significant that the most talked-of English murder of recent years should have been committed by an American and an English girl who had become partly Americanised. But it is difficult to believe that this case will be so long remembered as the old domestic poisoning dramas, product of a stable society where the all-prevailing hypocrisy did at least ensure that crimes as serious as murder should have strong emotions behind them.

Orwell saw the future clearly enough, and can't be blamed really for not having the ability to imagine how nostalgia, brilliant clothes, Warren Beatty, Faye Dunaway and some fancy editing would elevate nihilistic murderous young couples into cultural icons for the twentieth century, while a quietly seething poisoner would look dreary and unstylishly old hat.

In his book *The Arsenic Century: How Victorian Britain Was Poisoned at Home, Work and Play*, James Whorton makes it clear that dealing death by poison was not, after all, exclusively suburban, although, apart from later industrial disasters, it does seem to have been almost entirely domesticated. The poison in Whorton's book is specifically arsenic, and the deaths were only sometimes the result of deliberate murder and suicide. Though class figures in everything British, arsenic poisoning crossed class boundaries in a way that little else could. As a murder weapon, suicide aid and domestic hazard, it was cheap, a by-product of smelting, and could be bought across the counter at any hardware or grocer shop until the 1851 Sale of Arsenic Act required vendors to keep a register of sales and purchasers, and required that small amounts (not larger industrial quantities) had to be mixed with soot or indigo in order to prevent householders, who remarkably often kept the stuff in their larders, from confusing it with sugar or baking powder and innocently offering arsenic scones to their families and visitors. It was entirely reasonable and necessary for the poor, the middle classes and their servants, as well as the below-stairs staff of grander houses, to buy arsenic regularly for the purposes of keeping down the rat population, while farmers bought it in undyed quantities for use as sheep dip.

Arsenic most commonly killed rats, moths and flies, and decontaminated sheep, but it was also said to cure humans of the ague, asthma, cancer and other ailments. Physicians had for a long time prescribed arsenic for their patients, and in 1809 Fowler's Solution, a mixture of potassium arsenite and lavender, was accepted into the London Pharmacopoeia and praised as 'almost as *certain* a medicine as we possess throughout the whole range of our materia medica'. In tiny quantities women used it in various concoctions for cosmetic purposes in order to achieve a complexion of 'beautiful transparency' and a blemish-free skin. Some men also ate it regularly in gradually increasing doses for the benefits it apparently gave: as well as curing baldness, it promised men 'increased energy, endurance and virility', a little trick long known to the Styrians. Useful information both for murderers and crime writers. The not entirely dull Dorothy L. Sayers, who gets only a passing mention in Whorton's book, used the Styrian habit in *Strong Poison*, in which Harriet Vane makes her first appearance as a crime writer researching a book. The poison register proves she bought arsenic, leaving her in imminent danger of being convicted of poisoning her worthless ex-lover. Lord Peter Wimsey, whimsically love-struck and coming to the rescue, confronts the real villain:

> Yes, well, about this arsenic. As you know, it's not good for people in a general way, but there are some people – those tiresome peasants in Styria one hears so much about – who are supposed to eat it for fun. It improves their wind, so they say, clears their complexions, and makes their hair sleek, and they give it to their horses for the same reasons; bar the complexion, that is, because a horse hasn't much complexion, but you know what I mean. Then there was that horrid man Maybrick – he used to take it, or so they say. Anyhow, it's well known that some people do take it and manage to put away large dollops after a bit of practice.

Arsenic was easily and legitimately available for murder or suicide. Moreover, until the Marsh test was developed in 1836 to find arsenic residue in substances including the disinterred organs of victims, there was really no way of deciding whether someone who had been given it either in one go, or over a subtler longer period, had not died of natural causes as a result of poor food hygiene or illness. Why wouldn't you get rid of the inconvenient or the vile by means of odourless, tasteless, undetectable arsenic – assuming that you had managed to overcome any tendency to value human life over personal convenience? As the over-apostrophised cook Mrs Pettican struggles to put it about Harriet Vane's presumed crime in *Strong Poison*: 'A dreadful wicked woman she must 'a' been ... a-torturin' of the poor soul that long-winded way. Bashin' on the 'ed or the 'asty use of a carvin' knife when roused I can understand, but the 'orrors of slow poisonin' is the work of a fiend in 'uman form, in my opinion.' Five thousand people watched 'the fair parricide' Mary Blandy hanged in 1752, having been found guilty of murdering her father with arsenic. Her lover, of whom her father disapproved, had posted the apparently limitlessly gullible Blandy a 'special powder known to certain cunning women in Scotland that made all who swallowed it forgive their enemies'. He escaped to France when she was arrested and nine months later died a mysteriously gut-wrenching, agonising death, wishing 'for Death for some days before he died'. Florence Maybrick was found guilty of husband murder by slow poisoning in 1889 by a jury of men who heard about her adultery and were not very much interested in the fact that her husband beat her. They also chose to ignore evidence that Mr Maybrick was a regular user of arsenic for aphrodisiac purposes and had told a witness that he took the white powder for 'longevity and a fair complexion, my boy'. Female public opinion was outraged and Maybrick's sentence was commuted to hard labour for life. Eventually, the case came to be known as 'the English Dreyfus affair'; she was freed but not pardoned in 1904. Murder by arsenical poisoning was practised by both genders, even if in the public imagination, it was a woman's crime, secretive and underhand, murder on the slow boil, somewhat effete if committed by men, unlike the visceral and jugular venom of all-male slashers and stranglers. Thomas Smethurst was convicted of murdering one of his two wives in spite of a flawed toxicology test, which gave some credence to his claim that the second Mrs

Smethurst died of either dysentery or chronic vomiting as a result of her being seven weeks pregnant. He, like Florence Maybrick, escaped hanging, and was pardoned on appeal because the medical evidence was doubtful, but he did do a year's hard labour for bigamy.

Suicide by arsenic was fairly rare. Most people, understandably, chose opium. Only about 10 per cent of self-poisoners ate arsenic, although according to one toxicologist it may have been 'a national peculiarity' that a much larger proportion of Americans used arsenic as a means of suicide. Perhaps fewer of them had read *Madame Bovary* and so didn't know about Emma Bovary's extended and excruciating death. According to Whorton, 'merely writing about his character's anguished demise caused Flaubert to throw up his dinner on two separate evenings.' Unless, of course, he was himself experimenting in the cause of literary realism.

Some common abuses of arsenic were a good deal grimmer even than real and fictional characters doing away with their unwanted spouses (at least as often for financial convenience, surely, than as Orwell suggests, passion). Many infants and children died from intestinal infections, an unknown number of which were actually deliberate arsenic poisoning. In 1849, Rebecca Smith was executed for killing eight of her babies after birth, having claimed in her defence that her husband was an alcoholic and that she feared her children 'might come to want' and die of starvation anyway. According to Whorton, the poisoning of children 'underwent a growth spurt' when for a halfpenny a week 'burial clubs', an offshoot of the friendly societies, paid out for funeral expenses so that the children of the poor could avoid a pauper's grave or being carved up by anatomists after death. 'Manchester clubs, for example, paid out £3 as a rule, but some paid £4, or even £5; a basic funeral for a child could be financed for only £1 or £2. There was a saying among women in the Manchester tenements: "Aye, aye, that child will not live, it is in the burial club!"' Membership rolls were known as 'catalogues of the doomed'.

The gloomier villages of southern England became poisoning hotspots, some of them legends. Sarah Chesham (aka Sally Arsenic) roamed the Essex village of Clavering offering toxic lozenges to any children who were not kept indoors by their mothers, and her own two children died mysteriously. Everyone knew, but nobody said anything. Chesham was acquitted of their murders in 1847 and a newspaper asked: 'What is to be said of a district where cold-blooded murder meets with all the popular favour which is shown to smuggling in Sussex?' Sally Arsenic passed on her skills to Mary May, who was convicted in 1848 of killing her brother for the burial money. She probably also poisoned her husband and at least some of her fourteen children – 'most of whom died suddenly'. May, in her turn, had taught Hannah Ham (the names chime gay as nursery rhymes and Dr Seuss) how to kill her husband with arsenic. Local women talked of 'white powdering' their husbands and children, 'seasoning a pie' or 'giving them a dose'. People said that there were women's poisoning clubs in Essex, and the paper of record, *The Times*, suggested that the women of Essex rejoiced in 'wholesale indiscriminate and almost gratuitous assassination'. It sounds like another witch panic, with women once again doing the devil's work. Whorton (an American) does seem rather fond of a Gothic view of Victorian England and doesn't really investigate beyond the gruesome rumours and newspaper headlines. In fact, only Mary May and eventually Sarah Chesham were convicted and executed, after which the 'Essex epidemic' died down.

Children and adults sickened, suffered and died of toxic lozenges and all manner of arsenical substances not only because of deliberate murder by crazy, malevolent or greedy women and lusting men, but more frequently as a result of the English passion for a free, self-regulated market capitalism. Sweeties, wallpaper, candles, artificial flowers and almost anything green were at least as likely to kill you as a dosed Irish stew. Arsenic was an ingredient in the manufacture of all these items and many more. People dropped like flies having their wallpaper rehung, especially those who were caught up in the fashionable 'rage for green', which *Punch* came to call 'the hue of death, the tint of the grave'. Previously malachite and verdigris had provided green, but it was insipid. Scheele's green, introduced in 1778, used copper arsenite to provide a brilliant shade. Later, in 1814, the even brighter copper acetoarsenite was used to produce Paris green, Vienna green, Basel green, emperor green and emerald green for cloth dyeing, soft furnishings, coloured paper, paint (for walls and children's toys) and wallpaper, all of which shed flakes and dust, causing long-term malaise, even collapse and death, without anyone understanding why. This was the reasoning behind the (apparently false) rumours of Napoleon's death by wallpaper on the island of St Helena.

Young women making silk and muslin flowers and leaves to adorn the hats of ladies sickened and died because of the 'devil's dust' that flew around the workshops. Cheap candles made not from wax but stearine were made shiny and smooth by adding white arsenic – they became known as 'corpse candles'. Drinkers of cheap beer developed what was thought to be alcoholic neuritis, until doctors noticed that their skin went black in addition to the terrible pain. It turned out that some manufacturers substituted malted barley with glucose made by boiling starch in sulphuric acid, which was itself made using arsenic-containing iron pyrites. In Bradford one confectioner practised the not uncommon adulteration of sweets by mixing plaster of Paris with the sugar, in order to cut manufacturing costs. Unfortunately, an apprentice pharmacist fulfilled their sizeable order for plaster of Paris from a nearby unmarked barrel of equally white, powdery arsenic. The sweets were sent to a market stall and more than a dozen children and adults died, with many more seriously ill.

The dogged resistance to laws against the adulteration of products and food with dangerous and unknown substances was as great as the present-day corporate and political reluctance to deal with environmental and banking hazards. In the name of the free market and the blessed principle of laissez-faire, manufacturers lobbied successfully against any laws to restrict their practices. In 1831 the *Lancet* complained: 'in England alone is it that the principles of popular liberty are so sagely maintained that the people are allowed ... to be suffocated in the asphyxiating vapours of manufactories, without the slightest concern being manifested by the rulers of the land.' In the forefront of resistance to this Victorian version of political correctness gone mad and the nanny state, was the great socialist and leader of the Arts and Crafts movement, William Morris, who decades after the *Lancet* article, announced in 1885 that the arsenic scare was nonsense. As Whorton notes, he laughed that 'doctors had been "bitten" by a kind of "witch fever" ... blaming wallpaper when they were unable to come up with any other cause for their patients' problems (it was his own belief that "the source of all illness" was the water closet).' The free artistic spirit, the British Empire, or, more recently, the human race, hadn't got where it was by running scared of a bit of environmental poisoning when there were important matters of profit and power at stake.

In detective fiction of the English variety, a dead body is a necessity, but only as a MacGuffin. You're not supposed to care about the victim, only the solution to the crime. This was true, too, of the old-fashioned domestic real-life murder available in the newspapers. Empathy was not required, even though there is probably no more painful death than that by arsenic poisoning. Death and loss as the great human tragedy isn't any part of Dorothy L. Sayers's or Agatha Christie's project, nor their readers'.

Heartlessness is rather the point. Even the idea of people dying of wallpaper or poisoned candles, or children buying and dying from sweets on the market stall in the Victorian era belongs to the 'well how about that' category of non-fiction. Agony is sidelined when it happened long ago and has become dated genre fiction. The reality of arsenic poisoning makes greater demands on the imagination in the face of a present-day global accident that is the result both of good will and a different kind of laissez-faire. Chronic and massive environmental arsenic poisoning continues, in spite of the laws that were eventually passed to protect consumers, not just because of wicked capitalists, but as a result of the incompetence of international aid. What the World Health Organisation has called 'the largest mass poisoning of a population in history' happened in Bangladesh in the 1970s, when Unicef and the WHO fronted an international investment to install millions of tube wells to provide clean water in the area. But when the wells were sunk no one tested for arsenic, which is found naturally in the underground water around the Ganges and Brahmaputra deltas. A conservative estimate has it that ten million people have been poisoned, suffering skin lesions leading to cancer, lung and kidney failure and cardiovascular disease. It's estimated that hundreds of thousands will die as a direct result of drinking water from the arsenical wells. Local activists suggest that because of the incompetence, corruption and bureaucracy of both the UN and the Bangladeshi authorities it will take as long as another thirty years to test for, find and decontaminate the affected wells. Or as the UN chief in Bangladesh said in the *Independent on Sunday* earlier this year, thirty years after the problem was discovered: 'Concerted efforts by the government and all stakeholders are necessary to reinvigorate arsenic monitoring and mitigation efforts, and to conduct comprehensive research on emerging threats.'

8 July 2010

NEVER MAINLINE

I'm going to hang on to Keith Richards's autobiography, because sometimes I worry that I lead a boring life and wonder if I shouldn't try harder to have fun. When that happens, a quick flick through Keith's memoirs will remind me that I've never really wanted to live the life of anyone else, not even a Rolling Stone. Or especially. I haven't bought a Stones album since *Sticky Fingers* in 1971 and haven't deliberately listened to anything they recorded after *Exile on Main St* a year later. I find Mick Jagger's dancing embarrassingly inept and can never remember Bill Wyman's name (I've just looked it up). I preferred the Stones to the Beatles, in the days when you had to make a choice, because they were disapproved of, and I liked 'Little Red Rooster' and 'Play with Fire' more than 'Ticket to Ride' and 'Yesterday' because they suited my temperament better. Couldn't have got through the 1960s without dancing to 'Satisfaction' and 'Get Off of My Cloud', but I'm quite surprised to be reminded that '2000 Light Years from Home' is the Stones, not Pink Floyd, though they were purple hazy times. The last time I found myself interested in the band was when I read that Richards had snorted his father's ashes, because I have a sneaking admiration for taking things to their conclusion. But really after the 1969 Hyde Park Free Concert (Mick's rather desirable white frock and all those hypocritical butterflies for the newly dead unlamented Brian), Richards's reiterative narrative of Stones songs, gigs and internal warfare in *Life* was all news to me, and not all of it riveting.

I see that this makes me an unlikely reviewer of Keith Richards's autobiography. Perhaps I should have recused myself, but I've dutifully slogged my way through every damn word, so I'm going to write about it anyway. At least I thought I'd read it all. I was sure I had, until I saw that the *Daily Express* quoted Richards from the book on the subject of the Iraq war: 'I sent [Tony Blair] a letter saying it was too late to pull out now baby, you had better stick to the guns. If I had spare time I'd go out there and give them a shot or two myself ... I'd terrify them!' Could I have missed this? There's nothing in the index, but then there's no mention of Blair in the index at all, and Richards certainly says that he received a get well soon letter from Blair, when he (Richards) fell out of his tree. Is it possible the passage has been taken out on its way from publication in the US? Strange because not much else has, certainly not the American spelling, or the careful explanation of anything even faintly British, along with dogged translations of rhyming slang no one has used, except Richards, since Fanny was a girl's name.

Other reviews I've seen have been pretty much raves. 'Whoooooosssh! What a trip,' says Charles Spencer at the *Telegraph*: 'it is an absolute blast. Over more than 500 pages, its narrative only rarely fails to grip.' According to John Walsh in the *Independent*, 'the 500-plus pages of *Life* throb with energy, pulsate with rhythm and reverberate with good stories.' And in case you think it's just a boy thing, Michiko Kakutani, awarded a Pulitzer for her 'fearless and authoritative' journalism, considers (in both the *New York Times* and the *Scotsman*) that *Life* is an 'electrifying new memoir' which will 'dazzle the uninitiated'. Mr Richards, she says, writes in a prose which is 'like his guitar playing: intense, elemental, utterly distinctive and achingly, emotionally direct', with 'razor-sharp' 'verbal photos'. 'Hugh Hefner is "a nut" and "a pimp", Truman Capote was a "snooty" whiner.' In fact, Mr Richards doesn't write at all. The author produced the book 'with James Fox', a journalist and friend of Richards's, but we aren't told how the collaboration worked. I'd guess that Keith talked into a recorder over a long period of time, prompted and unprompted by his ghostwriter, and then Fox took the recordings and some diaries Richards found and wrestled them into a semblance of chronological order. Fox has written books himself and can write perfectly well, so it must have been an editorial judgement to let Richards's spoken words stand where not absolutely impossible. Either ennui or the same editorial judgement has also permitted a good many repetitions of phrase and incident. This marvel of collation and super-light editing has produced what feels like an authentic experience of many hours and days of sitting at a bar, or worse, in a Caribbean hideaway (with no train or clipper home) while some over-the-hill geezer (rhymes with 'sneezer') aka Richards – who has given up smack and coke but not booze and dope – rambles about his sixty-six years on the planet. Oh, how he rambles.

But as with the aged drunken bores I used to listen to at the French pub in the early 1960s, there are moments when the fog lifts and the slurred voice suddenly sharpens into knowledgeable passion, and you come back to paying attention, even if you know almost nothing about their subject. This happens in patches when Richards talks about music, his own music-making, and what he was listening for in the old masters' playing of Chicago blues. I have less understanding of how the music I listen to works than I do of the specific techniques involved in making the cutlery I use. I haven't the faintest idea what he means when he talks about discovering open tuning on his guitar, but I nevertheless woke up from my rock-and-roll-history-induced stupor and paid careful attention as Richards described finding his way there and seeing what he and the band could do with it. He boasts and whines about more or less everything else, but he talks intricately and interestingly about music, and even if knowing a fret from a fifth string is a struggle for me, I want to read about it.

> The beauty, the majesty of the five-string open G tuning for an electric guitar is that you've only got three notes – the other two are repetitions of each other an octave apart. It's tuned GDGBD. Certain strings run through the whole song, so you get a drone going all the time ... It gives you this beautiful resonance and ring. I found working with open tunings that there's a million places you don't need to put your fingers. The notes are there already. You can leave certain strings wide open. It's finding the spaces in between that makes open tuning work.

He's also good on life in postwar Dartford, growing up small and bullied:

For over a year, when I was nine or ten, I was waylaid, Dartford-style, almost every day on my way home from school. I know what it is like to be a coward. I will *never* go back there. As easy as it was to turn tail, I took the beatings ... They didn't call it Gravesend for nothing. Everything unwanted by anyone else had been dumped in Dartford since the late nineteenth century – isolation and smallpox hospitals, leper colonies, gunpowder factories, lunatic asylums – a nice mixture.

There's some very sensible advice on how to take drugs, too. Too much money and especially too much fame is difficult for people in their twenties to deal with. This by now is a given, a familiar moan by the rich and famous, usually in post-clean-up autobiographies like this one, for which Richards was allegedly paid $7 million. Mick got off on the unbearable spotlight, while Keith got further off on heroin, coke, uppers and downers. The rock death toll has been quite high even among celeb fuck-up stories, and what Richards is most famous for (apart from being in the same band for fifty years) is getting to sixty-six, looking eighty-six, and surviving not just his fame, but also his escape route. His story is littered with the premature deaths of those who failed to take the precautions a serious junkie with funds must take. He's sorry about them, but what can you do? He's taken his drugs seriously, as you have to if you're going to go on living, and gives some good advice, if you're in a position to follow it. You use pure heroin that you cut yourself and pharmaceutical cocaine and never try to get higher by using more. There is no higher, only high or sooner or later an overdose. You never mainline, but skin-pop the stuff directly into your muscles for a slower but safer top-up. From time to time you cold turkey, and then return to smack, remembering not to take the dose you were taking before you cleaned up, but the one you took before you were a maestro of addiction (Gram Parsons's fatal error). There are people who have led longish busy working lives using heroin: Burroughs, Trocchi, Anna Kavan, Keith Richards, among quieter others. As ever, it's the poor and desperate who die, although Richards quite rightly points out that when he started in the late 1960s, there was briefly a scheme in England that registered addicts with GPs, who gave them regular prescriptions and needles. It was effective in keeping people away from crime and messed-up street drugs. Everyone doubled their requirement, so even if, like Richards, you weren't registered, there were decent drugs available to buy at reasonable prices.

The rest is an account of living the rock and roll myth, his own and other people's, and repeatedly the pressures and consequences of being a star, of being rich, of being Keith Richards of the Stones. The goodness of the music, the memories of Dartford and the useful know-how of his drug regime keep sliding into boastful swagger which, unless you are a diehard Stones fan or just really pleased that Richards is still alive, is mostly embarrassing. The authentic ramble – or as the publicity would have it, 'his own raw, fierce voice' – encompasses a world of women who are never referred to as 'women', but as 'bitches' ('And there'd be a band, a trio playing, big black fuckers and some bitches dancing around with dollar bills in their thongs'); 'chicks' ('With English chicks it was you're putting the make on her or she's putting the make on you, yea or nay'); 'whores' ('all the bitches from Nice would come in, and Monte Carlo, and all the whores from Cannes'); 'groupies', 'mothers' and 'nurses' ('there were loads of groupies out there that were just good old girls who liked to take care of guys. Very mothering in a way ... And they were nurses basically. You could look upon them more like the Red Cross').

This, of course, is deliberate baiting, a dreary bravado, as well as an old man forgetting that hip talk has changed somewhat since 1968 (equivalent to the 1960 *Lady Chatterley* moment: 'Is it a book you would wish your wife or servants to read?'). He knows that feminists were dismayed by their lyrics: 'We always like to piss them off. Where would you be without us?' As a matter of fact, he was doing us bitches a favour. Those songs with titles such as 'Stupid Girl', 'Under My Thumb', 'Out of Time', 'That Girl Belongs to Yesterday', and 'Yesterday's Papers' ('Who wants yesterday's papers, who wants yesterday's girl') were quite possibly calls to rebellion: 'Maybe we were winding them up. And maybe some of the songs opened up their hearts a little, or their minds, to the idea of we're women, we're strong. But I think the Beatles and the Stones particularly did release chicks from the fact of "I'm just a little chick."' This may be one of those places where Fox needed to do a touch more editorial work, just for coherence, not in any way to prevent the authentic voice of Keith Richards on the subject of feminism from being heard.

You do get the feeling that Keith can take or leave sex. 'I always found with black chicks that wasn't the main issue. It was just comfortable, and if shit happened later, OK ... They were great because they were chicks, but they were much more like guys than English girls were.

You didn't mind them being around after the event.' Women who are more like men is the gold standard. (I was once told with a certain regret by a part-time long-term lover: 'If you were a man, we'd be best friends.') And for one reason or possibly another, Richards always prefers women to make the first move. In the chauffeured Bentley, somewhere between Barcelona and Valencia, he finally got it on with Anita Pallenberg, Brian Jones's girlfriend, after they'd left Brian behind in a Southern French hospital with pneumonia. 'I'm tongue-tied. I suppose every woman I've been with, they've had to put the make on me.' So they sit in the back of the car for several days. At last Anita can't stand the strain any more: 'the next thing I know she's giving me a blow job. The tension broke then. Phew.' Phew, and indeed, gosh.

He's less passive about other things. Except for sex, the self-conscious rock and roll wild man is always ready to make his mark. When Robert Stigwood failed to pay up after a series of concerts, he got trapped on a staircase and kneed by Keith sixteen times, one for each grand owed. Not that Stigwood apologised ('Maybe I didn't kick him hard enough'). Occasionally, he's a little coy. His chauffeur, Patrick, sold his story about the Redlands drug bust to the *News of the World*, and Keith explains: 'Didn't do him any good. As I heard it, he never walked the same again.' He always goes about with a knife and admits: 'I have to say I was using guns too much, but I was pretty out of it at the time.' That mitigating 'but' is odd; I suppose it's the non-rock-and-roll-chick in me, but if you're using guns too much, surely it would be better not to be out of it?

Still, it all fits well with the early, Stones-approved notion of the Rolling Stones as the most dangerous rock and roll band in the world. It didn't last very long, or mean very much; the long-haired, anti-authority look was designed by Andrew Loog Oldham to offer a commodified contrast with the Beatles, and there's no end of whining in *Life* about how the police were out to get them, and busted them just because they took drugs and were famous, for all the world as if being 'dangerous' was synonymous with everyone leaving you in peace in your country house. An awful lot of people who were neither rich nor famous got busted for possession and went to jail, sometimes for even longer than Richards's single day. What was the point of being the Stones if the establishment wasn't out to get them? Richards takes some comfort in the fact that 'Satisfaction' was played by American GIs in Vietnam and in *Apocalypse Now*. It's his contribution to the anti-war effort. But as I say, this doesn't last long, and he ends up with that letter to Blair to keep his pecker up about the Iraq war.

Much of the rest is about the hangers-on: the low lifes and the high lifes, crims and aristos that danced attention around the beautiful boys. Which side they chose, like their forms of escape, is what Richards suggests distinguishes him from Jagger. That and testosteronic rivalry. Mick has sex with Keith's Anita on the set of *Performance*, but it's OK because 'you know, while you were doing that, I was knocking Marianne, man. While you're missing it, I'm kissing it ... my head nestled between those two beautiful jugs.' Aside from that, it's control of the band that matters. Mick got a swollen head, followed fashion, loved disco and became a socialite, while Richards took heroin and was true to the music. Mick may have a 'tiny todger', lift songs from k.d. lang and take dancing and singing lessons, but that's only for Keith to say, because Keith understands the true meaning of friendship in that deep low-life sentimental way. 'I can say these things; they come from the heart. At the same time, nobody else can say anything against Mick that I can hear. I'll slit their throat.'

Actually, one story in the book is slightly differently but better told in Wikipedia, because Richards leaves out the crucial final line of dialogue. It concerns the strong, silent, immaculately suited, true Stones hero, Charlie Watts:

> A famous anecdote relates that during the mid-1980s, an intoxicated Jagger phoned Watts's hotel room in the middle of the night asking where 'my drummer' was. Watts reportedly got up, shaved, dressed in a suit, put on a tie and freshly shined shoes, descended the stairs and punched Jagger in the face, saying: 'Don't ever call me your drummer again. You're my fucking singer!'

Though Richards does enhance this when he tells us that having left the country for the South of France (on account of the supertax of 83 per cent and 98 per cent on 'so-called unearned' income), it was hard to get hold of Charlie, who rented a house in the Vaucluse, 130 miles from the rest of the lads on the Côte d'Azur. 'To Charlie it was an absolute no no. He has an artistic temperament. It's just uncool for him to live down on the Côte d'Azur in summer.'

And then there is family. The family is important to Richards. A photo shows the current clan, his wife, Patti, their two daughters, Alexandra and Theodora, as well as Marlon and Angela, Richards's surviving children with Anita Pallenberg. Marlon's wife is there and their three children, along with two dogs, all squeezed together on a bright white sofa, with husband, father and granddaddy Richards clutching a plush pink parrot. Everyone is smiling bright white smiles, except for Marlon, now forty-one, who looks comfortable but noncommittal in shades, no teeth showing, and two of his children, one who looks coldly out at the camera, the other back to her big sister. Although there's another big tour coming up next year, Richards is OK now, he says, he can rest on his laurels in his handsome study in Connecticut, reading George MacDonald Fraser and Patrick O'Brian, and he's always 'got some historical work on the go': Nelson, World War Two, the ancient Romans.

Before the settling down, though, back in 1973, while Richards was in London, Anita Pallenberg was living in Jamaica with Marlon aged four and Angela a year old, when she was arrested. The police left the children alone in the house.

My immediate reaction was to take the first flight back to Jamaica. But I was persuaded that it was better to put the pressure on from London. If I'd gone there they'd have probably popped me too. The brothers and sisters had taken the kids and whisked them up to Steer Town before the authorities had thought, 'What are we gonna do about these two children?' And they lived up there while Anita was in jail, and the Rastas took perfect care of them. And that was very important to me.

Angela, aged five, went to live with her paternal grandmother in Dartford after the new baby boy, Tara, died a cot death at two months, while in the care of the increasingly paranoid and addicted Pallenberg. Marlon, seven at the time, was with his father, touring Europe as Richards's 'road buddy'. It was his job to warn him of upcoming border posts so that the drugs could be dumped, and to keep nudging his father when he dropped off at the wheel. They only crashed once. He acted, Richards says, 'beyond his age'. It was also Marlon's job to wake the comatose Richards when it was getting time to play a gig. The rest of the entourage entrusted this task to the boy because Richards always slept with a gun under his pillow and they reckoned he was least likely to shoot Marlon if enraged.

Living with his mother back in London wasn't easy, either. Her teenage boyfriend killed himself while playing Russian roulette in the bedroom, and although Marlon witnessed the aftermath, he says: 'He kept telling me – a really nasty kid – he kept saying he was going to shoot Keith, and that upset me, so I was kind of relieved when he shot himself.' During the 1980s, living in a derelict, unfurnished mansion with his grandfather, Marlon didn't go to school but rattled around, left almost entirely to himself. He remembers: 'I didn't really mind all this self-sufficiency. I was kind of happy not to have everyone around, really, because it was exhausting with Anita and Keith.' Eventually in 1988 he asked to go back to London and get an education. He was in his late teens and lived in a flat of his own opposite his mother. Marlon would like it known that he got four A levels, and quite rightly. Keith is aware it was not an easy childhood: 'By now, Marlon understands; it was the times, and the circumstances, that made it tough on him. It was very difficult to be one of the Rolling Stones and take care of your kids at the same time.'

And there Marlon sits alive and, I hope, well in his shades next to Keith on the big white sofa. Along with the other children, the grandchildren and the dogs. A survival portrait of a Rolling Stone.

16 December 2010

WHICH ONE OF YOU IS JESUS?

In 1959, Dr Milton Rokeach, a social psychologist, received a research grant to bring together three psychotic, institutionalised patients at Ypsilanti State Hospital in Michigan, in order to make a two-and-a-half-year study of them. Rokeach specialised in belief systems: how it is that people develop and keep (or change) their beliefs according to their needs and the requirements of the social world they inhabit. A matter of the inside coming to terms with the outside in order to rub along well enough to get through a life. As a rule, people look for positive authority or referents to back up their essential beliefs about themselves in relation to the world: the priest, imam, Delia Smith, the politburo, gang leader, Milton Friedman, your mother, my favourite novelist. It works well enough, and when it does, we call ourselves and others like us sane. When it goes awry, when people lose and/or reject all positive referents in the real world for the self inside, we call them delusional, psychotic, mad. In order to count as sane, you don't necessarily have to conform to the norms of the world, but you do have to be nonconformist in a generally acceptable way. One of the basic beliefs we all have, according to Rokeach, is that we are who we are because we know that by definition there can be only one of us. I'm Jenny Diski. You therefore aren't.

The converse is also true: you are the sole example of whoever you say you are. Therefore I can't be you. It keeps things simple and sane for both you and me, and it's easy to check the basic facts with each other, as well as with such socially sanctioned authorities as the passport office or the registrar of births and deaths. According to Rokeach, this is a fundamental requirement of living coherently in the world of other people, the only world he believed we can effectively live in. He tested it one evening on his two young daughters by calling each of them by the other's name over the dinner table. At first it was a good game, but within minutes it became so distressing to the girls ('Daddy, this *is* a game, isn't it?' 'No, it's for real') that they were starting to cry. If you're thinking Rokeach is a bit of a sadistic daddy, I got the same impression reading *The Three Christs of Ypsilanti* when it was first published in 1964. But what researcher doesn't use the materials to hand – usually family – to begin to investigate a theory? Darwin observed and wrote about his children, as did Freud. And so did that particularly unpleasant behaviourist father in the movie *Peeping Tom*, made around the same time as Rokeach's dinner table experiment. Rokeach did at least stop once the girls became tearful. But what would happen, he wondered, if he made three men meet and live closely side by side over a period of time, each of whom believed himself to be the one and only Jesus Christ?

The men chosen were Clyde aged seventy, Joseph fifty-eight, and Leon not yet forty when they were brought together. They were all long-term asylum inmates: Clyde and Joseph had been incarcerated for decades, Leon for five years. They had daily meetings with Rokeach and a research assistant, and after the first few months were given their own private sitting room, where they ate and could spend the day in each other's company instead of having to use the day room. They were also given simple tasks which they were required to do together. (This may be the much more gripping prototype of *Big Brother*, although in the modern version everyone in the house deludedly believes themselves to be celebrities or interesting.) At the first meeting Rokeach asked the three men their names. Joseph said: 'My name is Joseph Cassel.' *Was there anything else he had to tell the meeting?* 'Yes, I'm God.' Clyde introduced himself: 'My name is Clyde Benson. That's my name straight.' *Did he have any other names?* 'Well, I have other names, but that's my vital side and I made God five and Jesus six.' *Did that mean he was God?* 'I made God, yes. I made it seventy years old a year ago. Hell! I passed seventy years old.' Leon, who demanded that everyone call him Rex, as Leon was his 'dupe' name, replied: 'Sir, it so happens that my birth certificate says that I am Dr Domino Dominorum et Rex Rexarum, Simplis Christianus Pueris Mentalis Doktor.' (This, Rokeach explains, included all the Latin Leon knew: Lord of Lords, King of Kings, Simple Christian Boy Psychiatrist.)

They all agreed with Rokeach that there could only be one Jesus Christ. Joseph was the first to take up the contradiction. 'He says he's the reincarnation of Jesus Christ. I can't get it. I know who I am. I'm God, Christ, the Holy Ghost, and if I wasn't, by gosh, I wouldn't lay claim to anything of the sort … I know this is an insane house and you have to be very careful.' Very quickly he decided that the other two were insane, the proof being that they were in a mental hospital, weren't they? Therefore Clyde and Leon were merely to be 'laughed off'. Clyde concluded that the other two were 'rerises', lower beings, and anyway dead. He took, perhaps, the most godlike tone: 'I am him. See? Now understand that!' Leon, who became adept at ducking and diving in order to maintain his position without causing the social disruption they all found threatening, explained that the other two were 'hollowed-out instrumental gods'. When Rokeach pushed Leon to say that Joseph wasn't God, he replied:

> 'He's an instrumental god, now please don't try
> to antagonise him. [To Joseph] My salute to you,
> sir, is as many times as you are a hollowed-out
> instrumental god ... My belief is my belief and
> I don't want your belief, and I'm just stating what
> I believe.'
> 'I know who I am,' Joseph said.
> 'I don't want to take it away from you,' Leon
> said. 'You can have it. I don't want it.'

Leon's standard response to any claim from the others that went against his delusions was 'That's your belief, sir,' and then to change the subject.

As to their understanding of why they had been brought together, Clyde, often baffled, took what was to be his habitual stance and remained silent on the subject, while Joseph was clear that they were there 'to iron out that I'm the one and only God' and for Rokeach to help him convince the other two that they were crazy, so that Joseph could do his work 'with greater tranquillity'. Leon, right from the start quite aware of the agenda and able to articulate his opinion of it, had another answer:

I understand that you would like us three
gentlemen to be a melting pot pertaining to our
morals, but as far as I'm concerned I am myself,
he is him, and he is him. Using one patient against
another, trying to brainwash and also through
the backseat driving of electronic voodooism.
That has an implication of two against one or
one against two ... I know what's going on here.
You're using one patient against another, and this
is warped psychology.

A great problem for the mad in the mid-twentieth
century was that the sane were always trying to get in
on their act. Sincere people who were not mad wanted
to interfere with the mad in various ways in order to
relieve them of their suffering and isolation, while
others, equally sincere, wanted to get down with them
and reinterpret their crazy ramblings as meta-sanity.
What was no longer an option for the mad was to be
left alone in asylums to get on with their deluded lives in
their own way. There had been some historical pockets
of interference and understanding. In 1563, more than
two centuries before Philippe Pinel and Jean-Baptiste
Pussin released the patients in Bicêtre from their chains
and announced they needed treating not punishing,
Johann Weyer reported to the Inquisition that the
so-called witches everyone was so keen on strangling
and burning were in fact delusional and mentally ill, as
indeed was anyone who thought themselves a victim of
their spells. Nevertheless, for the most part, until the
middle of the twentieth century, raving, delusional and
pathologically withdrawn men and women were got out
of society's way by being incarcerated for much of their

lives in formidable asylums, where their keepers had little thought beyond keeping them still, in one place, allowed out only when they died.

By the 1960s and 1970s a coalition of right-wing libertarians, left-wing radicals and the kind-hearted set their faces against such a fate, and, without the left and kind-hearted quite getting the agenda of the libertarians, collaborated to shut down the fortresses and free the mad to roam, not so much cared for in the community as dosed into a palsied stupor or undosed in manic terror, up and down our high streets to participate in the real world. R.D. Laing, along with others in the anti-psychiatry movement, started well by living with and listening to the speech of the mad, but ended up imposing on them his belief that he too had the gift of tongues and took charge of speaking truth to normality. He began as their interpreter but finally lost interest in the middle-mad-man (who kept behaving badly and had to be carted off back to the loony bin) and became the source of his own wisdom. Before and after the time of the anti-psychiatrists, the pro-psychiatrists did everything in their ever increasing 'scientific' power to liberate the mad from the bin and bring them back to the world of normality with cold showers, electric shocks, insulin shock, brain cutting and antipsychotic medication. The libertarians, for their part, simply announced that there was no such thing as madness and therefore the state was not required to oversee and pay for the care of those who were making themselves socially unwelcome (see Thomas Szasz). The so-called mad were to be turned out of the asylums and become part of the general population. If any individual's behaviour was intolerable to society, they were to be imprisoned, not given sick notes.

Milton Rokeach came in as these diverse voices began to be heard. His interest was not so much in psychopathology as with 'the general nature of systems of belief and the conditions under which they can be modified'. In the book, Rokeach acknowledges that his experiment with his children had to stop where the trial of the three Christs started, with signs of distress: 'Because it is not feasible to study such phenomena with normal people, it seemed reasonable to focus on delusional systems of belief in the hope that, in subjecting them to strain, there would be little to lose and, hopefully, a great deal to gain.' This is a very magisterial 'non-deluded' view of who in the world has or has not little to lose. Evidently, the mad, having no lives worth speaking of, might benefit from interference, but if they didn't, if indeed their lives were made worse, it hardly mattered, since such lives were already worthless non-lives. It also incorporated the bang-up-to-the-moment idea that if you want to know about normality you could do worse than watch and manipulate the mad. The three Christs themselves, however, were of the certain opinion that they had something valuable to lose and made truly heroic efforts, each in his own way, to resist, as well as to explain to Rokeach and his team that their lives had considerable meaning for them. All of them, though Leon in particular, had a very clear understanding of what it was to be deluded, why it might be a useful option to choose over normality, and who did and didn't have the right to interfere in their self-selected delusions. Over the course of the research, each man indicated how far he was prepared to go along with Rokeach, how much he valued what was on offer, and when his boundary had been reached. And they did it with more than ordinary grace and dignity.

There was indeed something on offer. Rokeach describes Clyde, Joseph and Leon as long-term inmates of overcrowded wards of custodial mental hospitals with inadequate staffing who might expect to see a doctor maybe once a year. Suddenly they were receiving a deluge of attention: daily meetings which began and ended with a song of their choice, nurses and a research assistant attending to them, watching and noting their activities all through the day, and special demands made and allowances given that they had never experienced as regular inmates. Even when they expressed anger at being manipulated, they tended to turn up every day to the voluntary meetings, and took their turn as rotating chairmen, writing up the minutes and choosing their favourite song and book. These most psychologically isolated of men were given (enforced) company, novelty in place of rigid daily routine, special privileges and (apparently) the attentive ear of the highest and mightiest in their world (each of them being God notwithstanding). In return they were required consciously to consider their delusions and challenged to alter their particular grasp on reality. The problem that faced them initially was: how can there be another one of me? Rokeach hoped they couldn't help but conclude, as they looked from one to the other Christ, that logically they were not therefore who they thought they were, though he says nothing about what assistance was available in the overstretched state mental hospital in the event of their suddenly losing their delusions and having to confront themselves with their lost years as plain Clyde, Joseph and Leon. In fact, all three men resolved the logical trap set for them by sinuously changing the nature of the problem. The others were deluded, dead or lesser kinds of god. A kind of positive stability emerged, they associated with each other, sang together, read to each other and, apart from occasional bust-ups usually triggered by the researchers, generally refused to be drawn on the matter of who exactly was or wasn't the one true Christ.

Leon was the most deft, perhaps because he had the clearest understanding of the invidious situation he was being put in, and found it harder to suppress the logic. He announced one day that he was no longer Rex, but had transformed into Dr Righteous Idealed Dung. One in the eye for his tormenters, you feel, cheering him on. Henceforth he would only answer to the name Dung or, as a concession to the head nurse, who attended a meeting to say that she couldn't bring herself to call him Dung, simply R.I. He directed the meeting to Philippians 3:8: *Yea, doubtless, and I count all things but loss for the excellency of knowledge of Jesus Christ my Lord: for whom I have suffered the loss of all things and do count them but dung, that I may win Christ.* Rokeach knew that, covertly, Leon hadn't renounced his belief that he was Christ, but had instead shape-shifted, gone underground to the abject opposite. As he said before his transformation, 'I believe that God is in this chair. He is in my dung and urine and farts and burps and everything.' ('That's crazy,' Joseph replied. 'You don't believe that God can be a patient in this hospital ... I'm the real God and I know I can be in many forms.') Now Dr R.I. Dung was going to be 'the humblest creature on the face of the earth – so lowly as not to be worth bothering with', Rokeach explains. His brilliant plan allowed him to be a secret Christ, who no longer had to confront and defend himself against the claims of the other two, and who in this way could continue to enjoy the companionship and privileges on offer.

Since the researchers had been unable to shift the delusions of the three Christs, they decided to confront the men's fantasies in other ways. They were shown a newspaper article about a speech Rokeach had given on three psychotic men who thought they were Christ. Clyde read it and fell asleep. Joseph claimed to have no idea who these men were. 'Why should a man try to be s-somebody [*sic*] else when he's not even himself? ... He should be sent to a hospital – not to be gotten out, not to be dismissed until he has gotten well ... when he claims he's not Jesus Christ any more.' Leon, lucid as ever, knew exactly who the three men were and expressed his anger: 'When psychology is used to agitate, it's not sound psychology any more. You're not helping the person. You're agitating. When you agitate you belittle your intelligence.' Joseph, too, made himself clear: 'I look forward to quietness. We can win over negativism. By "we" I mean the five of us having the meeting. It's not going to do us any good. Then the meetings might be dissolved.'

Next the men were asked if it was all right for the researchers and the staff in the hospital publicly to refer to Rex as Dung, Joseph as Mr God, and Clyde as Mr Christ. All three joined forces (a psychologist's triumph in itself) against Rokeach. 'Now, don't be funny,' Clyde said. 'You must understand, it's too heavy for an individual to participate in these meetings over here, to go into that God business,' Joseph said. 'It's indirect agitation. There's a confliction ... It's frictional psychology,' Leon said. From which Rokeach deduced that 'a psychotic is a psychotic only to the extent that he has to be.'

As Christ, Leon had been married to an absent wife called Dr Blessed Virgin Mary of Nazareth. With his translation to Dung, she was married off to Leon's mystery uncle, and Leon took a new wife: the powerful but invisible Madame Yeti Woman. Joseph's 'delusional authority', whom he called Dad, was Dr Yoder, the actual head of the hospital. Dad and Madame Yeti Woman became the main players in the final phase of Rokeach's plan to test the nature and persistence of the three Christs' belief systems. Clyde, too old and rigid to be further experimented on, was allowed to continue with the meetings but wasn't confronted with his delusions. Rokeach's idea was to see if Leon's and Joseph's fantasy authority figures were real enough to them to instruct their 'husband' and 'son' to enact 'normal' behaviour. Leon and Joseph began receiving letters. Leon's were signed *Your loving wife* (and sometimes *Truthfully yours), Madame Yeti Woman.* Some of Joseph's letters from 'Dr Yoder', written on hospital headed paper, ended: *be assured that I will always love you just exactly like a father who deeply loves his own son. Sincerely yours, O.R. Yoder, MD.* Leon's initial refusal to accept letters from Madame Yeti Woman excited Rokeach into wondering whether he didn't, after all, really believe in his delusions. Do the deluded take on their persona more consciously than it seemed, as a shield against having to cope in the regular world? Are the mad really mad? Did Leon only want them to *think* he believed what he said? Leon at first firmly rejected the fleshing out of his fantasy, became extremely depressed and said he didn't like the idea of people imposing on his beliefs. But gradually, unable to resist the temptation in spite of his deep suspicions, he came to accept her as a real presence. She sent money, told him to buy things for himself and to give the change to Clyde and Joseph. Leon, the only human being Rokeach had encountered who genuinely had no interest in money, did as he was instructed. Madame Yeti Woman made Dung's inner world as real as the meetings he attended. In one letter she enclosed a 'positive cigarette holder ... I think you will enjoy this one since it also has a cosmic boupher.'

It is excruciating to read of his capitulation, as he accepts the existence of and is ready to interact with someone else in his isolated world. In a meeting where Leon is given a letter with a dollar bill, Rokeach notes a breakthrough for the study:

> Suddenly I realised that he was really doing something I had not expected to witness. He was struggling to hold back his tears. With this much effort he would surely succeed. But he did not ... *Does the letter make you happy or sad?* 'I feel somewhat glad' ... *Are you crying?* 'No, my eyes are smarting because of some condition.' *You say you feel somewhat happy?* 'Yes, sir, it's a pleasant feeling to have someone think of you. But there's still a tugging against her and I don't care for it.' *Do you want to disobey her?* 'No, no! I don't! That's the point! I don't care for the temptation against her.'

It seems as if the invasion is complete, but Rokeach goes too far as both Madame Yeti Woman and Dad.

Madame Yeti Woman arranges a meeting, which Leon goes to, but, of course, finds no one there. 'When he returns to the ward he is visibly upset and angry. He tells an aide that he is very angry with his wife because she was in the back of the cafeteria having relations with a Negro.' After transferring his love to a new female research assistant and finding his yearning intolerable, Leon at last announced that all his former wives were dead, that he had discovered his 'femaleity', married himself and been pregnant with twins who bled to death before birth.

I'm looking forward to living alone. My love is for infinity and when the human element comes in it's distasteful ... I've found out whenever I receive something, there's always strings attached and God bless I don't want that.

Joseph also had his sticking point. When Dad asked him to go to church, he did for a while, but when Dad suggested that he write an article (Joseph had dreamed of being a writer when he was young) and sign a formal statement that he was not Jesus Christ, he wrote back, not to Dr Yoder, but to President Kennedy, offering to be his speechwriter. He announced that he was 'caught in the net of the three Jesus Christs' and refused 'to tell a lie' by signing Yoder's statement. Joseph gave up Dad and found himself a higher fantasy authority, in order to live as he had to live. Rokeach at last discovered that he had not succeeded in changing 'a single one of Joseph's delusions' but in the course of trying had gained 'clinical and theoretical insights about the limits beyond which his delusional system could not be pushed'.

In an epilogue written some months after the experiment ended, Rokeach updated the reader:

> Clyde and Joseph give every appearance of
> remaining essentially unchanged. But Leon
> continues to show evidence of change or at least
> further elaborations in his delusional system
> of belief ... The prognosis for schizophrenia,
> paranoid type is poor ... But to say that a
> particular psychiatric condition is incurable or
> irreversible is to say more about the state of our
> ignorance than about the state of the patient. This
> study closes with the hope that at least a small
> portion of ignorance has here been dispelled.

It turned out that Milton Rokeach was the one who gained the most from his experiment. An afterword, appended when the book was reissued in 1981, is called 'Some Second Thoughts about the Three Christs: Twenty Years On'. By then Clyde had been released back to the custody of his family, and Leon remained in the 'back wards' of Ypsilanti State Hospital; Joseph died in 1976. Rokeach reread the book with regret. There were, he says, four people with delusional beliefs, not three. He failed to take himself into account, and the three Christs, not cured themselves, had cured him of his 'God-like delusion that I could change them by omnipotently and omnisciently arranging and rearranging their daily lives'. He came to realise that he had no right to play God and interfere, and he was increasingly uncomfortable about the ethics of his experiment. 'I was cured when I was able to leave them in peace, and it was mainly Leon who somehow persuaded me that I should leave them in peace.' Back when Leon was shown the newspaper article, he'd explained to Rokeach:

'A person who is supposed to be a doctor or
a professor is supposed to lift up, build up,
guide, direct, inspire! ... I sensed it at the first
meeting – deploring!'
   Deploring? Do you know I've come seventy-five
miles in snow and storm to see you?
   'It is obvious that you did, sir, but the point still
remains, what was your intention when you came
here, sir?'

No one could have done more than Leon to explain to Rokeach what was wrong with his experiment: 'You come under the category where a person who knows better and doesn't want to know is also crazy to the degree he does not want to know. Sir, I sincerely believe you have the capabilities to cast out negative psychology. I believe you can aid yourself.' Rejecting his false wife, he said: 'I know I'm missing out on pleasure – eating, drinking, merry-making and all that stuff – but it doesn't please my heart. I have met the world. I got disgusted with the negative ideals I found there.' The best Rokeach can manage is the acknowledgement that psychosis 'may sometimes represent the best terms a person can come to with life'.

   In 1964, having spent some time myself in a psychiatric hospital, I read *The Three Christs*, and soon after came on Laing's early books, which confirmed what I had seen in it. It has made me very wary of reading 'case histories', written about the disturbed by those who believe themselves to know better. It also seemed to me, aged sixteen, that *The Three Christs of Ypsilanti* contained everything there was to know about the world. That's not the case, of course, but if resources were short, I'd still be inclined to salvage this book as a way of explaining the terror of the human condition, and the astonishing fact that people battle for their rights and dignity in the face of that terror, in order to establish their place in the world, whatever they decide it has to be.

22 September 2011

Zeitgeist Man

As charm is to Cary Grant, awkwardness to Jerry Lewis, vulnerability to Montgomery Clift, so malevolence is to Dennis Hopper. Very few actors specialised as Hopper did in convincing malice. Vincent Price was too camp to be really alarming, even as the witchfinder general. Peter Lorre was heartbreaking as a child murderer. James Gandolfini, playing an incorrigibly mean-minded godfather for seven years, strangely held on to the affection of most of his mass audience. James Cagney had his moments of deadpan nastiness, but there's the mother thing. Perhaps George Raft came close, but I suspect that's more the result of moribund acting. There isn't any doubt about Michael Rooker in *Henry: Portrait of a Serial Killer* (one of the few good films I wish I'd never seen): as blank and merciless a psychopath as I've ever come across in the movies. But no one has ever been as repeatedly and consistently sinister, morally frightening and lethally paranoid as Dennis Hopper, whether he was playing for laughs in *Speed*, manifesting the dread unconscious in *Blue Velvet* or apparently just being himself in *Easy Rider* and *Apocalypse Now*.

A great deal of Peter Winkler's entertaining and eventful book *Dennis Hopper: The Wild Ride of a Hollywood Rebel* is taken from previously published and broadcast interviews with Hopper himself on the subject of his own life. Hopper wasn't a reticent man, and he knew the celebrity value of the mythic over plain fact. His stories are always aware of public appetite and expectation. He tells of growing up in Kansas, spending a lot of time on his grandparents' farm, lying around in the wheat fields watching the horizon and 'wondering where it came from and where it went to'. Or stretched out on the hood of the farm tractor blissfully sniffing fumes from the petrol tank, until after a bad trip, his grandfather found him smashing up the vehicle-turned-vicious-monster with a baseball bat. Hopper knew how to talk about himself. His grandmother used to take him to the local movie house for the Saturday matinee. 'Then all the next week,' he said,

> I'd live that picture. If it was a war picture I'd
> dig foxholes; if it was sword-fighting, I'd poke
> the cow with a stick ... it was just after the Dust
> Bowl, and sometimes I used to say that the first
> light that I saw was in the movie theatre, because
> the sun was just a little glow. And being in Kansas,
> there's nothing really to look at. And right away,
> it hit me ... The world on the screen was the real
> world, and I felt as if my heart would explode,
> I wanted so much to be a part of it. Being an actor
> was a way to be part of it. Being a director is a
> way to own it.

But then another time he recalls Elvis in Hollywood for his first movie, baulking at a scene in which he believed he had to hit his co-star: 'No, I can't hit a woman!' Hopper, I imagine, took a deep breath before explaining 'that you never actually hit anyone in a movie, that it was all faked, but the film was cut in such a way as to give the impression that it actually happened'. Being part of and owning the real world through acting and directing movies was more complex than his fantasy of a childhood fantasy come true suggested.

He began acting early in a theatre in La Jolla, where the likes of Dorothy McGuire were on hand to write the letters of recommendation that gave him a TV part at nineteen and then, almost immediately, a movie contract with Warner Bros. His first successful films (though he only had small parts in them) – *Rebel Without a Cause* and *Giant* – were steeped in 1950s cod-Freudian Oedipal narratives. He was, and in the way he looked back on his life increasingly became, a creature of his culture as well as an actor in it. Asked to describe his family life, Hopper says of his mother (the book has a large bibliography but the quotes are not annotated and rarely dated or attributed in the text): 'She was wild, very emotional, a screamer and a yeller. My mother had an incredible body, and I had a sexual fascination for her [*sic*]. I never had sex with my mother, but I had total sexual fantasies about her.' (The placing of 'total' suggests he said this late in life.) By the time the press wanted him to look back, he was living – and relating himself – as a legend, and a legend only partly of his own devising. He pulled into it stereotypes of bad boys, troubled genius and movie star narratives that were being developed in the early 1950s, and more or less fossilised by the end of the 1970s.

The story he told and retold of himself was made up of what he had missed, what he had lost and how his talents had been wasted by people in power who were too mediocre to understand them. Not very different,

I suppose, from the story any of us might tell, but more publicly told and more elaborately intercut between reality and the movies. He got stuck on the problem of having arrived too late, as each generation does, and being left to watch as the last of the great heroes disappeared. I still regret being just too late to sit in Les Deux Magots with Beckett or hang out at Shakespeare and Company with the Beats. Hopper missed mixing it with the hard-drinking rabble-rousers, Flynn, Bogart and Sinatra, while John Wayne, with whom he acted in *The Sons of Katie Elder* and *True Grit*, called him a Communist and offered to explain why he, Wayne, 'was worth a million per picture'. Hopper was, however, perfectly on time for the upcoming group of heroes, mumbling geniuses who had sat at the feet of Lee Strasberg at the Actors Studio in New York. But they left him behind for early deaths – in the case of Montgomery Clift and James Dean – or in Brando's case, just got lost. He had to make do with phantoms of forbidding stature, and legendary figures whose equal he claimed he would have been if they'd still been there to assent to his inclusion. Hopper met Dean while playing a gang member in *Rebel Without a Cause* (1955). His association with him during *Rebel* and the filming of *Giant* (also filmed in 1955) seems weirdly parallel to the hero-worshipping relationship Sal Mineo as Plato has to Dean's rebel, Jim Stark – except that in the movie Jim is nicer to Plato than Dean was to Hopper, and it's Mineo's character who dies. It's also true that Hopper didn't start out with any of Plato's insecurities: 'I was the best actor in the world, pound for pound – I mean the best *young* actor. I was really good, I had incredible technique, I was incredibly sensitive. I didn't think there was anyone to top me. Until I saw James Dean.'

Dean kept to himself, locking himself in his dressing room between takes and refusing to respond to Hopper's greetings. Hopper followed Dean around, and Dean did all he could to avoid him. Finally, Hopper grabbed him and shut them both in a car, demanding to know how to be as good an actor as Dean. Should he go to New York and see Strasberg? No, Hopper remembers Dean replying, 'you're too sensitive. Strasberg will destroy you.' Make what you will of both young men but bear in mind it's always Hopper's account you're reading. 'It was, in a strange way, a closer friendship than most people have, but it wasn't the kind of thing where he said, "Let's go out and tear up the town." Sometimes we'd have dinner. Also, we were into peyote and grass before anybody else. What we really had was a student-teacher relationship, the only one he ever had, as far as I know.' The sound of Plato hankering after Jim's attention is plainly audible. In *Giant*, Hopper watched Dean try to create the edgy Jett Rink by keeping his bladder full for a scene with Elizabeth Taylor, and then, after blowing his lines, dealing with his awe of Taylor by emptying his bladder in full sight of her, the crew and several thousand movie-struck onlookers. (A good moment to recall Laurence Olivier's comment to Dustin Hoffman, who had stayed up several nights to play a scene in which his character had stayed up several nights: 'Try acting, dear boy.') But then Dean died in a car crash, aged twenty-four, after, according to Hopper, stopping by the set to say to him: 'Today you were great.' Hopper lost a mentor, but gained a substantial ghost and a one-sided story on which he would rely for the rest of his career.

Hopper's early training in Oedipal awareness and petrol sniffing was useful support for his belief in his own remarkable talent. The notion of the angst-ridden, disturbed genius, and of the angst and disturbance confirming claims of genius, was as powerful in mid-twentieth-century America as it had been to the Early Moderns and the Romantics. Strasberg's daughter Susan remembers Hopper's disappointment after a psychiatrist he consulted told him he wasn't neurotic enough to need therapy. 'If I'm not sick, how can I be a good actor?' he moaned, to which she replied, either with sincerity or as an act of kindness: 'You *are* sick, Dennis. Believe me, you are!' Being crazy in the late 1950s and early 1960s was de rigueur for any major artistic genius. Crazy drunk, crazy drugged, crazy paranoid, crazy creative – it all helped to persuade you and others of your unique gift. Not everyone succumbed. While Hopper was still in his twenties, and noisily convinced that he was a better actor than Paul Newman, Joanne Woodward concluded (some time after hitting him on the head at a party with an antique copper bedwarmer): 'Dennis is a genius. I'm not sure of what, and I'm not sure Dennis knows of what. Certainly not acting. But he is a genius.' It wasn't just the acting: Hopper really was a zeitgeist man. He hung out with jazz musicians (apparently Miles Davis composed 'So What', on *Kind of Blue*, inspired by Hopper's repeated use of the phrase), with Allen Ginsberg and Peter Orlovsky and Andy Warhol and Roy Lichtenstein. He bought paintings that became a major Pop Art collection and took photographs that were published by glossy art and fashion magazines.

He had a good eye and a sense of what was going to last. Books, on the other hand, weren't an active enough expression of his artistic sensibility. Winkler describes how in a documentary on Hopper, instigated by Hopper, called *The American Dreamer* (1971), 'Hopper frolics with two girls in the tub. While the film shows a well-endowed nude woman sitting in a rocking chair, an off-camera Hopper philosophises: "I don't believe in reading. By using your eyes and ears, you'll find everything there is."'

Hopper followed Dean's example in wanting to be his own director to such a degree that after making life miserable for Henry Hathaway in his next film, *From Hell to Texas*, Warner cancelled his contract. Instead, he went to New York, lurked at the Chelsea Hotel, drank, took copious amounts of drugs and married Brooke Hayward, the daughter of a tragedy-prone Hollywood family. He did some television and a flopped stage version of *Mandingo* until Hathaway forgave him. In 1959, MGM signed a five-picture contract with him and he made some low-budget production-line movies, not at all seeming to be Dean's representative on screen, but working on his art collection and taking photos of artists while feeling 'in some strange way, I would be doing history a favour.' It was only a hiatus. 1968 was coming up fast and there was a story to be told.

The music in *Easy Rider* is just as good as I thought it was when it first came out, and the film in a few parts is better than I remembered. Whose film it was – that is, whose idea it was and who wrote it – has been so disputed in print and in litigation by Peter Fonda, Terry Southern, Hopper, and even Peter Coyote, that it looks like we'll just have to give the last man standing – that'll be Fonda or Coyote – whatever credit one or all of them deserve. It has its moments (though not nearly as many as *Electra Glide in Blue*, made a few years later with half an eye on *Easy Rider*). It conveys a sense of young Americans threatened by their own history, ripping up their roots and not so much finding themselves as getting lost for a while in familiar surroundings. The main pitch, according to Fonda, was to do dope, motorcycles and travel with some sex here and there, but to 'do all these things really honestly'. That was what we specialised in back then, doing it really honestly, whatever it was. We, and I daresay Fonda and Hopper, were sincere for the most part, by which I might mean young. Fonda and Hopper were going to remake the movies, break the old dead hand of the Hollywood industry and make independent visions of truth, just as the rest of us, high and spirited, were going to remake politics, social relations and, with the use of benevolent hallucinogens, reality itself. We have since learned how little sincerity and honesty has to do with making or remaking anything, but why not give us a little credit for naive effort?

What is most noticeable about the film – apart from Jack Nicholson's masterly cameo – is how unpleasant the Hopper character, Billy (think Billy the Kid), is from start to finish. His plain nastiness in almost all situations, including those that warrant none, is actually a bit of a relief played against Fonda's beatific and self-righteous Wyatt (think Earp), aka Captain America. But Billy's meanness and scariness are startling. It's possible to argue that it's what redeems the otherwise self-indulgent film. Billy and Wyatt were never going to change the world or even themselves: their bikes and the journey are funded by a cocaine sale (to Phil Spector, of all people) and freedom's just another name for dollars hidden in Wyatt's teardrop gas tank, a tourist trip to Mardi Gras, and a visit to the best whorehouse in New Orleans. We see a bit of free love and countercultural living on the way, but when Billy crows, 'We did it!' the night before they're blown away by rednecks, the ponderous Wyatt shakes his head: 'We blew it.' Billy has no idea what he means, because for him it was always about money, shiny machines, sex and popping into the carnival. I suspect that Hopper didn't really get it either. This is, surely, the only reading of *Easy Rider* that can make it an interesting film. It's seen as a road and a buddy movie and it does have a high proportion of roads, and of male compadres cavorting with whores. As Roger Ebert explains in an online review of the movie, 'One of the reasons that America inspires so many road pictures is that we have so many roads. One of the reasons we have so many buddy pictures is that Hollywood doesn't understand female characters (there are so many hookers in the movies because, as characters, they share the convenience of their real-life counterparts: they're easy to find and easy to get rid of).'

The result of a lot of stoned young people paying to see *Easy Rider* was that Hopper was allowed to direct *The Last Movie*, which turned out to be the last word in expensive, incoherent, drink and drug-fuelled art or chaos. Hollywood was not impressed with the new moviemaking and neither were the punters. Hopper got sent into the wilderness once again, this time to a mansion in Taos with a headful of paranoia, as well as guns, drugs, a partying entourage and a lot of money from the proceeds of *Easy Rider*. His marriage was over. He married Michelle Phillips of the Mamas and the Papas instead for about a week before she fled, then sank into a not-so-creative craziness with the daily help of three grams of coke, thirty beers, an untold amount of tequila, smoothed over with quantities of grass. After a suicide attempt and rehab, Wim Wenders cast him as an emotionally flat but lethally friendly Tom Ripley in *The American Friend* in 1977, probably his best movie and performance so far. Two years later, he was back to his old self in real life and on film in *Apocalypse Now*, as the funny, babbling, speeding and venomous photographer who provides the unpleasant comic relief in the midst of Kurtz/Brando's final madness. More lost Hopper years were spent getting crazy and getting straight before he decided to blow himself up in public as a way of proving he was indeed a true artist. It might have been a suicide bid, but his notion that sitting at the centre of a circle of exploding dynamite would put him in a safe vacuum turned out to be correct, so he survived even if his artistic credentials weren't much enhanced. Eventually, in 1984, after the drink, peyote, cocaine and LSD he took in order to fuel his creative muse had made a paranoid mush of his mind and he heard the telephone wires talking to him while sitting in his room holding a gun, ready to shoot the first person who came through the door, he was committed to a mental institution, where he was treated with major antipsychotics and his daughter was told he might never recover. He more or less got the message: 'In my mind, I was an artist and writer. The reality was that I was just a drunk and a drug addict. It wasn't helping me create.'

It turned out that he only had to be himself. A couple of months after coming out of rehab, he got the part of Frank Booth in *Blue Velvet* (1986). Straightaway he called David Lynch to reassure him: 'David, don't even worry about casting me in this. You did the right thing because I *am* Frank Booth.' Lynch turned to his lunch companions, Isabella Rossellini, Kyle MacLachlan and Laura Dern: 'I just talked to Dennis Hopper, and he said he *is* Frank Booth. I guess that's really good for the movie, but I don't know how we'll ever have lunch with him.' Booth's histrionic violence and self-pity, to say nothing of his constant and amazingly expressive use of the word 'fuck', are chilling, both for his *Henry: Portrait of a Serial Killer*-like authenticity and his night-terror menace. The collision of dream and reality horror is perfect. And he did it all cold sober, apparently.

After that, he was stuck with the dwindling shadow of Frank Booth in generally terrible movies reprising his most-vicious-evil-bastard-in-the-world performance; at least in *Speed* he caricatures his inhuman monster into camp comedy. He earned money, collected art, painted, did voice-overs for animated TV and movies, appeared on innumerable talk shows, and became a solid, sober citizen: a Republican who promoted both Bush administrations with all the self-satisfaction of a Billy who had not been shot and left for dead by the side of the road, but lived on to put his drug money to work in the system, change his fringed buckskin jacket for a decent suit while, it seems clear, continuing to be who he really always had been. He grew old like movie stars do and spent his last days with terminal cancer also as many seem to do, amid an inheritance battle between the children by his former marriages and his wife of fourteen years and mother of his young daughter, whom he was trying to divorce to get around a prenuptial agreement allowing her any money. It made for good gossip. Victoria Hopper claimed that he was being held incommunicado by his other children, one of whom was 'pulling her father out of his bed and driving him to the divorce lawyers', while the Hopper family were granted a restraining order against Victoria to prevent her from 'harassing, attacking, striking, threatening' Hopper or his grown-up children. A fairly dismal end, but who knows how James Dean's life and work would have gone? In retrospect Hopper looks more like the diminished latter-day Brando, though he never showed that he had Brando's truly remarkable early gifts, only his capacity for vanity and self-indulgence.

22 March 2012

I Haven't Been Nearly Mad Enough

'Madness is a childish thing,' Barbara Taylor writes in *The Last Asylum*, a memoir of her two decades as a mental patient. The book records her breakdown, her twenty-one-year-long analysis, her periods as an inmate at Friern Mental Hospital in North London, and in addition provides a condensed history of the treatment of mental illness and the institutions associated with it. Taylor was in the bin during the final days of the old Victorian asylums, before they were shut down in the 1990s, and their patients scattered to the cold liberty of the underfunded, overlooked region of rented accommodation or life on the street known as 'community care'. Loony bins. 'Bins', we called them for short, as Taylor does, just as we called mental illness 'madness' and 'being crazy'. We recall our secret stashes of meds we'd only pretended to swallow and were keeping in bulk for a rainier day, and reminisce together about the time we tipped too far into our roles and were held down by half a dozen nurses while another injected us with a major tranquilliser. ('Haloperidol?' 'No, chlorpromazine. The first time, anyway.' Comparative demerits then explored.) In public the conversation has the same steely glint of challenge in one direction and moue of camaraderie in the other that you sometimes see when Jews tell stomach-curdling Jewish jokes, while the uncircumcised grope in their bag of possible socialised reactions for a way to respond.

I say 'we', because reading *The Last Asylum* was an uncanny experience for me. I spent inmate time in several asylums, mostly in the late 1960s, long before Barbara Taylor's breakdown (although we are of a similar age), later in Friern itself, only a few years before her various stays there, and also in the controversial 'patient-run' Paddington Day Hospital, mentioned by Taylor as the model for the Pine Street Day Centre that she attended, both of which were closed down as a result of the fear they aroused in the authorities. (I decided, after several conversations with professionals about those times, that when talking about institutions you can distinguish between inmates and staff because the former were 'in' them while the latter worked 'at' them.) As I read, I saw myself flitting through the pages of Taylor's account like a precursor-ghost, or perhaps more a tetchy sprite, engaged in a debate with her text, ticking off the similarities between her experience and mine and weighing up the differences. Once I bumped into my own name and a description from my first novel of a ward round I suffered during my own very brief stay at Friern, which I fled to evade the threatened sectioning that would have allowed them to put me under lock and key and submit me to the treatment of their choice. ('Mm, lobotomy or ECT, it's a toss-up … ') I thought it a mistake to miss out the most objectionable thing about that experience of twenty or so suited doctors and social workers sitting in a circle interrogating me: on the coffee table in the centre of the circle, the open gold cake box with a half-finished cream gateau inside that no one thought to offer me.

This, then, is not even a pretence at a neutral, objective review. On the contrary, I was struck by the thought that rather than a professional, or even adult reading, I was grabbing a miniature shadow analysis for myself. I observed my responses to Taylor's suffering (competitive), her experiences (comparative) and her analyst's heroically determined interaction with her (part impatience, part envy), and found them looking more and more like the transference and counter-transference that analysts and analysands speak of with such awe. At any rate, the Poet said he'd never seen me so exercised about a book I was reviewing when he got back from work to find me spluttering, 'I should have been MUCH madder than I was. I haven't been NEARLY mad enough.' ('Probably not. A bit late now, eh?' he said, hopefully.) 'She describes what the worst of her anguish feels like, but it's what I feel like every hour of every day. *I* need analysis, five days a week for twenty-one years or the rest of my life, AT LEAST, whichever is longer.' ('You can't afford it, and I'm about to retire,' he said.) 'And I want to be LOOKED AFTER by a coterie of close, concerned friends.' ('What friends? You haven't got any.') 'And phone my shrink in the middle of the night and when he's on holiday demanding that he help me.' ('You don't much like being dependent.') 'But I SHOULD have been! I've been cheated out of a proper madness.' Then, as if my fifty minutes were up, I heard myself, the supposedly detached reviewer, me-me-me-ing, furious and wounded, deprived, jealous and greedy. It was quite startling. When I came across that sentence, 'Madness is a childish thing,' I thought of H, from my nine months in the Maudsley at the end of the 1960s, with whom I still argue about which of us was *really* mad or maddest when we were best friends in the bin. 'You were really mad, I was just, you know, angry.' 'No, you were much madder than I was. I just couldn't express myself. Actually, you still are madder.' It's never quite clear whether my claim (or hers) to be the saner is a statement of superiority or a confession of failure. It comes back to me vividly that part of being mad, as I understood it, was that you never felt mad enough or properly mad, compared to others who were *genuinely* suffering. Or you suspected that you were probably only acting mad, while the others were actually mad, and felt extreme guilt as a result; an impostor, and a loser in the anguish stakes. Others have told me it was the same for them.

As ever, living, reading and thinking around the subject, I return to the complete mystery of why some people are knocked flat and incapable by what seem like only the mildest of dysfunctional backgrounds, compared to others whose childhoods were devastated by cruelty and deprivation, let alone those who grow up with famine and war, yet seem to find a way to live their lives as if they were their own. And all that space in between the extremes of near harmlessness and full-blown misery: the whole regular family muddle and mess that everyone has to survive, or not. Like physical pain, which each individual is asked to assess on their own scale of one to ten, how much hurt you have received and how devastating it has been for you is too subjective to bear much comparison. I try not even to imagine the possibility of spending a crazed lifetime not just debating the one and ten of both kinds of pain against others' assessments, but forever redefining the four, five and six. Whatever hurts you hurts, and however damaged you've been is how damaged you are. Yet despite my intermittent insight into my crooked reading of her book, it was impossible to get through Taylor's singular and carefully structured account of her personal anguish and where it took her, without my childish, intrusive self chattering a comparative commentary. As with my own experience of psychotherapy, and life in general, self-knowledge on its own doesn't seem to change anything very much.

Taylor describes herself when she was at her most ill as totally panic-stricken, unable to tolerate being herself. Being intolerable to oneself is a feeling I know, one that seems almost impossible to convey effectively. You try this way and that to write it, or describe it, but always fail to do more than point at the name of the experience. Perhaps in an attempt to get closer to the physical and emotional reality of it, Taylor intersperses her chronological narrative with notes or recollections of sessions with her analyst, V, whom she saw at his consulting room five days a week, before, throughout and after her periods in hospital. On one of these worst of times, she lies on the couch, with V sitting behind her in the prescribed way, desperate to convey her feelings and to get V to do something to help her:

> *What am I going to do? I can't live like this;*
> *I can't be me any more; I can't be like this, I can't*
> *survive outside hospital! ... Where are you?*
> *Where are you? Oh, what am I going to do?*
> *I can't live like this ... I CANNOT FEEL LIKE*
> *THIS! It is impossible to feel these things and live!*
> *Who will help me? I want to die! Where are you?*
> *Do something for me!*

The condition Taylor speaks from is familiar, and is the most terrible condition on earth, for all one's awareness, even at the time, of what in all conscience appears to be the much greater real-world sufferings of the poor and oppressed. Her analyst lets Taylor know that he recognises the degree of her desperation: '"The worst feeling in the world" was how V described this naked defencelessness to me. "People will do almost anything to avoid feeling it."' She speaks of her 'stranded, homeless' feelings: 'Homeless feelings are boundless; they sweep all before them.'

This hopeless, helpless narrative is one I recognise very well. It runs on and on in me, like a mantra, unvoiced much of the time, in dreams and anxieties or simple visceral *feeling*, and has done for as long as I can remember. Sometimes, in my madder (saner?) moments, I've spoken it out loud, as Taylor does, demanding help, unreasonably because I know all the while that the help I want isn't available for the asking, or even there to be given, since I don't know what it is that could help, and I'm pretty sure that no one, psychoanalyst or psychiatrist, GP, lover or best friend, knows either, beyond their professional or humane conviction that talk and interpretation, medication or a cuddle will allow you to get an insight or a rest. It's the knowing you won't get help however urgently you want it that ratchets the feeling up into madness, a spiral that runs out of control. It is not that ghastly notion of the 'inner child' we hear so much of, but Taylor's 'madness-is-childish' that speaks, howls this stuff, while the despair, non-mad-non-child, knows no one can possibly ever care enough or do enough, however much they want to, even though it's their job and you pay them, or they love you for some reason, or simply would do anything to get some respite from your demands. The despair comes from knowing that no one is going to help, that only finding some way of getting on with it is going to help, and that getting on with it is the very last thing you are capable of. Except that you must. But you can't. (See Beckett, if you will.) There's nothing moral about it, it's just the adamantine way of the world. In such a state, and I would say, such a near truthful state, the reason anyone gets to this ten of interior suffering isn't really the thing that needs most urgently to be dealt with, yet it is precisely the job of psychoanalysis to investigate just that.

Taylor was brought up in Canada in the 1950s by self-involved, actively socialist parents. She was and still is a respected academic historian of radical movements and feminism from the eighteenth to the twenty-first century. How she got any work done or proceeded in her career is baffling. For two decades she battled intolerable feelings of rage and deprivation, as well as punishing nightmares, and used drink, drugs and sex copiously in her attempts to escape it all. She acknowledges that she was surrounded by devoted friends and feminist comrades who looked after her, helped her, kept her alive. In addition, all through her hospitalisation and her worst moments of self-loathing, she managed to visit V five days a week. Which is to say that she had some fundamental optimism that she could be helped by psychoanalysis. It isn't clear whether the pain from her childhood that she investigates in her analysis is the result of thoughtlessness or actual cruelty on the part of her parents. She was looked after by nannies from the local unmarried mothers' home, all of whom had just given up their babies for adoption. Their silent grief, which must have suffused the house, was never acknowledged or discussed by her mother: 'And why not give a girl, who has just lost her child, responsibility for your own little ones?' The young women came and went, giving Taylor much to grieve about, too, their losses and hers. It emerges through the book, and the analysis, that her parents were intellectuals and writers manqué. Taylor felt the pressure on her to win prizes, to be a writer – which is apparently what all thinking and politically active people aspire to and require from their children. She recalls moments of aggression from her father and too much intimacy in the way his hand touched or brushed against her as an adolescent; he was openly a philanderer, which caused third parties to appear in the house, father's and mother's lovers, their role also not spoken about. Her mother, she recognises, was self-centred and disappointed, and disappointed too in her daughter who wasn't the genius her parents required, and who wasn't wanted in their dramatic romance and political activism. She comes to realise that she was imperfectly loved and cared for. She developed tics and compulsions. She tried to fill up the void with eating, drinking, sex and drugs. 'I am starving. Nothing I put into me satisfies me. I could devour the world, but I chew myself (my nails, my hair) instead. When I eat, I keep on eating. There is no repletion, no stopping point.'

V does what analysts do and offers his patient interpretations that relate to their immediate situation in the consulting room and repeat the past the analysand is stuck in:

I think you want to feel fed. But you are afraid.
Fed?
Yes, fed. Full, satisfied.
(Long silence) *Why afraid?*
Because if I ever find out that you feel fed by me,
I will make you suffer for it ... You believe that I
would stop doing whatever I had done that satisfied
you. That's what you think would happen ... Stop
analysing you, stop feeding you, stop seeing you ...
That would be your punishment for feeling well
fed by me.

At this point in the therapy I've had, I've always muttered something like 'You, you, you. This isn't about you ... Yes, I *know* my hunger is about more than being hungry! And?' and refused to get aboard the interpretation train to a place where I might perhaps fully grasp my situation and ... feel better. (The gap between understanding my situation and feeling better is precisely what has always fed my distrust of the analytical situation.) Taylor is more compliant, more able to take or get what is offered and use it. Is it that essential optimism which helped to keep her on the couch? And what is that optimism: just what you've got or haven't got? She does get angry and argues at first and then takes time to see the truth of the interpretation. To me those twenty-one years, five days a week seem such a very long time to take to get the point where you see that imperfect love in childhood makes you forever dissatisfied and distrustful, or that eating too much is about being emotionally unfulfilled, but then I am a thoroughly failed analysand, and she is quite clear that she wouldn't have survived without V's commitment to taking her through her compulsions and terrors in the way he does.

Much of her madness is expressed through self-hating, vicious and violent nightmares. She brings her dreams to the consulting room and V urges her towards interpretation. A washing compulsion that goes back to childhood and returns in her dreams, contains, he suggests and she concurs, a knowledge of her father's open philanderings, his chasing away of a nanny, a knowledge 'so deeply hidden that it took almost a decade of psychoanalysis to disinter it, its presence marked only by its filthy seepage into my dreams and on to my disgustingly filthy face'. Her obsession with dirt is the subject of a later conversation with V. Perhaps she has filthy thoughts, he suggests. *'The sort that you feel on your face. On your dirty face.' 'My dirty face ... why my face?' 'I don't know. Dirty looks?'* Taylor queries this. V replies: *'Your mother's looks? The way your mother looked at you when you were a baby?'* What are you asking me? Taylor demands. *'I'm not asking you, I'm making a suggestion. I'm suggesting that your mother might have given you dirty looks; looks that made you feel dirty ... When you were tiny, when she was feeding you. She found it difficult feeding you ... it upset her. She gave you dirty looks.' 'How do you know such things??'* Taylor replies. *'You don't know such things!' 'Of course I don't know such things! (Deep sigh) I'm suggesting this as a possibility; that she was disturbed and distressed, and that you felt this, and it disturbed you very much.'*

Again, madness-is-childish me stamps her foot and starts to look sullen. So here we all are, none of us able to have the faintest idea what her mother's face looked like when she was breastfeeding, so there's no right or wrong, only an interpretation of a dream, which, apparently, will do. It's just a story (one among several, dozens possibly) that neatly accounts for the dream image and which is acceptable to Taylor. This is, I suppose, how analysis works, not so much by digging into and revealing the truth about the past but finding good enough interpretations of the past in the present to provide a satisfying explanation. We all, in analysis, writing or simply chatting to each other, tell our stories according to, or so that they add up to, our neuroses or psychoses. It isn't lying. It's teleology. But I never get past the 'How the hell do you know?' stage. Meaning, what if it's wrong? Or perhaps worse, what if it's right? So what? And? So I'm suffering from my mother's lack of love for me. I know! What shall I do about it? What *is* there to do about it? I've never read an account of an analysis that really describes in any detail where or how the analysand goes from there, whether it's strictly speaking true or a good enough analogy for what the patient is experiencing. I still don't see how a satisfying explanation alters the fact of the felt lack or deprivation and the subsequent depleted behaviour in the world. You are still and always will be deprived of that notional love and safety you were supposed to have in order to be a balanced person. Anyway, don't we all know by now that we're none of us sufficiently or properly loved, one way or another? So why am I or is she or he in such a state about it? And what exactly is to be done? It isn't clear in Taylor's account either how exactly the analysis worked, although she uses the word 'cure', indeed it's a chapter heading. It worked for her; there's nothing more Taylor's book is claiming for analysis. There aren't three of us in this telling of an analysis. My perplexity is my own.

What I completely recognise are Taylor's descriptions of the bin, her stays in Friern and her time at the Pine Street Day Centre and halfway houses. In her potted history of the asylum in general and Friern in particular, she describes the late eighteenth-century movement to reimagine the mad: places with decent optimistic conditions of airiness and light were built to house them and they were recast from Calibans to patients to be treated with rationality and humanity. Then, with a loss of interest in weakness and need, and the collapse of the idea of progress, the monumental asylums became monstrous institutions, dilapidated, overcrowded, with back wards inhabited for decades by neglected, tormented patients, the broken-down state of the fabric echoing the casual brutality of many of the staff and very little in the way of therapy apart from the chemical cosh. When Taylor got to Friern Hospital, the apotheosis of the Victorian asylum, it was already slated for closure. It knew it was dying and had been the subject of public scandals in the late 1960s and the 1970s when patient coercion and abuse were revealed to have been regular occurrences. Taylor got there three years after I'd been for my overnight trip. I remember the famous corridor she describes, the longest madhouse corridor in the country. (I only got halfway down it before I found a linen cupboard with a window to hide in.) Some of the patients who walked up and down its length, very slowly – there were no collisions – looked as if they had been doing it and getting nowhere without anyone noticing for many years.

The other side of all that is the warmth and camaraderie of the bin, which Taylor describes so well. It was a place, she says, where people looked out for each other, and often knew each other's needs better than the staff. In the Maudsley, we played a game after lights out in which we held a nightly 'staff meeting', voices in the dark as we lay in bed, assessing the progress of our experimental treatment of staff who we pretended were patients pretending to be staff. How well had they done that day, what setbacks had we noticed, should we alter our pretend-patient behaviour to improve their treatment? It was a kind of joking, knowing inmate conversation you only find in twenty-four-hour institutions. Taylor describes nurses coming to patients to ask them to help out with someone in a crisis. I remember that, too. People protected each other, for the most part, and laughed a lot in a spirit of embattled camaraderie. It's the only time I've experienced such a powerful feeling of community, however fraught and fragile our relationships might have been. Taylor confirms this without neglecting the other truth: that being an inmate could also be scary, chaotic and threatening. She describes times when

I was too paralysed by pain to reach out to
anyone yet could not stand to be alone. So
I would join the smokers in the dayroom, placing
myself next to Magda if she were there. Magda
would glance over at me and sit on quietly; once
she took my hand.

Soppy, maybe, but it really was like that sometimes. But I also remember being told to 'be quiet. You're only a patient, keep your place' when I remonstrated with a nurse who was pushing a dementia patient into a chair though the patient was doing nothing more than wander round the room holding out a rolled newspaper to everyone she passed. Sometimes we were babes in the wood, sometimes vile schoolkids plotting mayhem. It was never boring. And if you were having a bad time, you could have it. Everyone knew why you were there.

This advocacy of asylum is a crucial part of Taylor's book. Friern was shut down in 1993. The Paddington Day Hospital and the Pine Street Day Centre were closed too. They had been places where people could spend all day; in Paddington they could do intensive day-long group therapy; in all of them they could work together or alone on projects, stare, do nothing, feel they were in a safe space, with the physical warmth of other human beings around, and though the fights and dramas were plentiful, they happened in a peopled world that tolerated you. All those places, all the old institutions disappeared; it was the great triumph of Thatcherite libertarianism. Instead, general hospitals have emergency psychiatric wards, with a limited number of beds and as fast a turnover of patients as antipsychotic drugs can sustain. Then, you're on your own with the pills, and the underfunded, understaffed, sometimes mythical care in the community. Taylor makes the case that what we lost was not just the institutions, which had their problems, though with a will (admittedly unlikely) these might have been solved; we lost our asylums, and (not only in the realm of madness) with them the essential idea of asylum: a place society provided where one could go when overwhelmed by the terrible 'stranded, homeless feelings' that V described as 'the worst feelings in the world'. Taylor points out that they were hardly luxurious by the time of her and my visits; grim, stony places, cracked and falling apart. But they contained. They held out the promise of containment, given the goodwill and understanding of those who ran and paid for them – essentially ourselves when we are feeling better. You could get relief from feeling socially obligated and guilty, because you were finally in a place that knew what you were and how you were, even if it couldn't do much about it. Sometimes you need to bury yourself, to be enabled to sit the worst out without the world pulling at you, asking you what the matter is, or reminding you of the things you should but can't be doing. It sounds like an almost absurd expectation in the current austerity/hardworking family rhetoric. But providing places of safety to people who are ill might not be economic madness. William Tuke and Philippe Pinel instigated 'moral treatment' at the Retreat and the Salpêtrière, believing that once they'd freed the mad from shackles, cruelty and isolation there was a possibility of alleviating suffering, even bringing about an improvement. Their liberalism may well have been theoretically at the service of repressive Foucauldian power, protecting the status quo, but in practice they offered some chance of treating people decently and giving them a space to exist when they feel they can't. When in the twentieth century, the libertarian anti-psychiatrists and the Thatcher/Reaganite libertarians had their strange meeting of minds, and set out to deconstruct mental illness and its institutions, they disregarded, deliberately or ignorantly, the often implacable suffering of individuals, and the need for places of safety. They shouldn't really be so hard to provide, given the will. Taylor's bins and day centres and mine were not the Priory, comfortable asylums for the rich or those with medical insurance, but shabby, run-down places providing asylum on a low budget for people who for a while or even permanently, couldn't get on out in the world. It's obvious that someone lying on the ground with a broken leg can't walk, so no one expects them to get up and pop into A&E to get it set, and then get on with their business, but it seems it is much harder for many to believe in the physical anguish, debilitations and incapacitations of mental illness, and see the need to offer relief.

6 February 2014

However I Smell

One of the problems of ageing is knowing when to start complaining about being old. I received an email not long ago from a woman who had read something of mine in which I described myself, at sixty-six, as old. She said she worked with elderly people and her eighty-five-year-olds call people my age young. What's more, they never refer to themselves as old. The point of my piece (written for a Swedish newspaper) was to report that I supposed I must accept that I was old because my hairdresser says, 'Ah, bless,' in response to whatever I say in answer to her questions. 'Are you busy today?' 'Just regular working.' 'Ah, bless.' 'How was the weekend?' 'A friend came to stay.' 'Ah, bless.' The other day, when she asked, I said: 'I'm being interviewed by a journalist from Poland.' 'Ah, bless.' I hear it too from shop assistants as they call out that I've left my purse on the counter. 'Ah, bless,' they say when I return to pick it up. I used to leave my purse behind in my younger days too (though not nearly so often), but I don't recall anyone ah-blessing me until recently. The ah-bless alters or confirms whatever it's responding to, and in my mind's eye (altered and confirmed) I see a small, nondescript old lady going bravely about her business. There are other signs that I am no longer young, but the ah-bless is the most open and public. Yet my Swedish correspondent said she found me 'sad and pathetic' for describing myself as old. So that's me told, every which way.

Recently, I read an article in the *Guardian* by Bronwen Clune, headed (for all the world as if no one had suggested it before): 'Women, it's time to age disgracefully.' Two weeks off her thirty-ninth birthday, Clune talked of herself as 'edging towards a worthlessness that society has constructed around my age'. Older women, she said (accurately), 'feel their volume fading'. She also quoted the artist Molly Crabapple's thoughts on turning a mere thirty: 'Staying alive has power. The years should give you competence and toughness along with the battle scars. You've survived.'

I'm not about to write to Mss Clune and Crabapple telling them they're pathetic for thinking of themselves as ageing. It's right and proper that they should try on their older selves rather than sit in the warm but rapidly cooling bath of thinking themselves simply young. It's decidedly irritating, but also rather tragic, when head-turning young women, not content with being what they presently are, take the time to look at you in triumph, never doubting that they are going to stay young forever – or perhaps they think the old and the young are born that way. The only defence against them is also a kindness: silence and knowledge. Even if we don't take the Stoics to heart and live every moment as if it were our last, we should try to mitigate the awful shock that comes later on when we can't fail to remember that the direction we live in goes only one way.

People are going to be cross with you for declaring agedness too soon as well as too late, but it's not that easy to identify the right moment. According to *Scientific American*, we ought to be able to sniff out where we are at. Researchers at the Monell Chemical Senses Center in Philadelphia examined sweat-stained pads from the armpits of a cross section of ages and, it appears, were able to tell by smelling them which had belonged to the old. It confirms what we all know but hesitate to say: old people smell. Apparently, it isn't an unpleasant smell – like 'cucumbers and aged beer' or comparable to 'old book smell' – but it's there. Could that be one of the signals my hairdresser is picking up when she gives me the ah-bless? It seems not. The age groups were classified as twenty to thirty (young), forty-five to fifty (middle-aged), and seventy-five to ninety-five (elderly). So far as science goes, I am in a no person's land and my critical correspondent is right: I'm merely on the nursery slopes of age. I do, however, qualify for the state pension, which when I was growing up was called the old-age pension. There were no senior citizens then, or silver surfers. If you had a bus pass or a pension, you were old. Younger people may not now hear the echo of 'old age' when the pension is mentioned, and I've noticed sales assistants flinching when I announce I have an 'old person's' rather than a 'senior citizen's' railcard. The state retirement age is going to change in response to an increase in life expectancy. But it will be too late to affect me, so in spite of the ebullient eighty-five-year-old Swedes I'll take my cue from the language I've grown up with and my hairdresser's style of passing the time of day with me, however I smell.

I am of the cohort which lived inside a gilded bubble when young, and who made a proper song and dance about it. Now that group is clearly beginning to think of itself as old, and you can be sure this won't happen quietly. In addition to Lynne Segal's *Out of Time*, we've had Anne Karpf's insistently buoyant *How to Age*; Angela Neustatter's hymn to the great gift that ageing brings, *The Year I Turn … A Quirky A-Z of Ageing*; *Frenchwomen Don't Get Facelifts*, in which Mireille Guiliano speaks up for the power of chic in ageing; and, coming soon, post-baby boomer India Knight's *In Your Prime: Older, Wiser, Happier*. Germaine Greer got in early to greet the menopause with a moonlit dance of delight in *The Change* (1991).

Segal takes us back to the early days of British second-wave feminism, embedding her book in her political activism and youthful reading of Simone de Beauvoir's self-loathing (or at best ambivalent) book about being old, *La Vieillesse*. Back then, in the early 1970s, we baby boomers threatened our elders with radical change without thinking that we would ever change ourselves. But we have changed, in the ineluctable way, and not, as we assumed, as a result of personal choice. The irony of 'I hope I die before I get old' was that we didn't believe for a second that we could become the old as we knew them. And we weren't just young, but young in a way no previous generation had been young. We used 'young' and 'old' as time-free categories. 'Young' meant new and different, able to see what the old couldn't (certain visionaries excepted): we had reinvented the terms to mean us and them. They, the old, would die out: we would change the world and remain forever ourselves, meaning forever young. (Which is not at all the same thing, Segal points out, as the untruism that 'whatever your age, you are no older than you feel.') Without the constraints and necessities of war or strong memories of having had to manage austerity, we could believe that there was a single something that we purely were, and always would be. We made a fuss about being young, without understanding how much being young enabled us to make the fuss. Now, we're going to make a fuss about being old and that's going to be rather less straightforward.

It's certain that only a small fraction of my generation were doing any of the wild and wilful things people think (that we thought) we were all up to and that the same fraction are probably the ones who are going to write, talk, march and legislate about getting old in order to let the world – and ourselves – know what we think about it. The young of our old age have expressed considerable resentment at the noise we have made about our activities in the 1960s and 1970s – just wait till we've all got our old age books out. By squinting slightly, I can see what a gloomy prospect that might be for you young 'uns but given that you will be rid of us soon enough, you might just as well put up with it. Read, don't read, it's up to you. It's our last shout. We will read one another, then notate, cross-reference and append our thoughts in our own books. When we're dead I suspect it will be as if we had never been. The feminists, the radical left, the communards: all will dissolve into a trivial pop-culture history called the Sixties, much slighter and less consequential than it thought itself to be. So bear with us. Those few of our parents, aunts and uncles who remain still disapprove of us. The young now disapprove of us too. Even some of our own demographic disapprove of us. So nothing, really, has changed for the self-loving unloved baby boomers.

Segal was part of a London-based group of feminist, socialist, communal-living consciousness-raising sociologists, psychologists and historians who were active in the late 1960s and 1970s, and in favour of radical social and political change. *Out of Time* isn't a memoir of that period, but a personally informed discussion of the politics and sociology of her own ageing and that of her generation and the attitudes people now have towards it. Although she depends a good deal on fiction, often problematically treating novels as if they spoke directly for their authors' feelings, the examination is more useful when rooted in her awareness and memory of having been an active, political young woman, and her experience of and feelings about being in her late sixties forty years later.

One of her primary concerns is the war between the generations. The one in which, to our surprise, we are now the old and tiresome. But this time, there are worse accusations being chucked around. We are the baby boomers, the demographic catastrophe waiting to happen that is now happening. Baby boomers lived their youth in a golden time. Far from having to go into tens of thousands of pounds of debt, we had free tuition and decent grants to live on while we received a higher education. The generation that bore us and lived through the hardships of war and austerity, while disapproving of us, also provided us with welfare benefits that allowed us to take time off from earning a living, to play with ideas and new ways (we thought) of organising socially and politically, of exploring other cultures, drugs, craziness, clothes and music. Now, this free time seems mythic. If we wanted jobs, there were plenty of them. If we didn't, we benefited in a way that would be called scrounging now (it was then, but no one stopped it). We are costing a fortune as we age and we'll go on to cost much more because medical science has promised us twenty more years of some sort of life than our parents expected.

Our pensions, the medical expertise and equipment, the time and energy needed to care and cater for a disproportionately large aged population: all this, the young have been told, is coming out of their earnings and limiting their well-being. We got grants to do up houses we bought cheaply. They can't get a mortgage. Workers to our queens, they are providing our good life, in suburbia, beside the sea, in sunny Spain, filling hospital beds, out of their taxes. We take our pensions, our cold weather payments, foreign holidays and cruises, while the young struggle to find jobs to pay for our needs, our strokes, our previously unhealthy lifestyles that caused the sicknesses which the impoverished NHS is obliged to cure. Segal, quite rightly, doesn't blame the young for their anger, but mostly the media for provoking it. 'Older people lived the "good life". Why should the young have to pay for it?' the *Guardian* asks. 'Crumblies should stop whingeing and claiming priority over a scant welfare budget. We created this me-first world, now we should give something back,' says seventy-four-year-old Stewart Dakers. The *Mail* warns that the 'Young face future of higher taxes to pay for parents who won't save, says BoE man.' Another article in the *Guardian* tells us: 'The one demographic group that has not seen its incomes fall since the recession is those over the age of sixty. Pensioner incomes have continued to rise on average, albeit very modestly.' Beware of the albeits. A relatively small rise in income during the recession doesn't mean a relatively high income level to start with. 'Over 20 per cent of those who live in poverty are pensioners,' Segal points out, 'rising to around 30 per cent if they are single women, with at least a third of that group being people in their sixties.'

Opposition between the generations is a perfect shield for a government under fire for cutting welfare while destroying the NHS, privatising education and doing nothing about the depletion of reasonably priced housing. Let the young blame the old not the coalition. In addition, there is the now institutionalised pressure from all around to 'age well'. Government and official bodies issue warnings about eating wrongly and not getting enough exercise. We are told to take our well-being and our ageing process into our own hands. The idea of ageing badly looms over us: those who become ill or develop age-related conditions are to blame for failing to keep themselves bright and sparky. They have grown wilfully old and expect the world to take care of them. It all plays into the neoliberal notion that the old are demanding welfare and medical aid for which the young have to pay. Dependency, more or less inevitable with increasing age, becomes something about which the old should apologise.

These political lies and half-truths are bad faith enough, but Segal's real wrath is for those 'scapegoats who have joined the chorus' of blame. She quotes Marina Warner: 'my generation is guilty of heedlessness, I can see that now.' Nick Broomfield agrees: 'We have left this country bankrupt.' Will Hutton: 'I'm at the heart of it – guilty as charged.' Essentially, those of the left who are now apologising are doing so for having failed. Blame the government, big business and the bankers, but we were the ones who failed to stop them. It was less a selfish generation than a naive one, for thinking then, as some still do, that it is possible to change the inequities of the world. 'I'm heartbroken that we were defeated, politically, culturally. I'm also sad for the next generation,' Warner goes on to say. What we had then was a 'kind of hopefulness, the energy that buoyed one up in those days [that] nobody with any kind of sophistication can really entertain now. You can't believe there is something to be done that can be done by you.' Maybe we were so high on our intentions that we failed to see the fog of Thatcherism creeping up around our ankles. As for costing the young money, it's a marvellous distortion of the point of a welfare state. Perhaps we should apologise for being alive at a time when medical science is advanced enough and will do its best to keep us alive. But that's also going to be true of the next generation.

It was our generation that came up with the phrase 'the personal is the political'. And Segal examines her own experience of ageing in that spirit. She speaks of her surprise at finding herself hesitating to state her age. If it never occurred to us that we would grow old, it also never crossed our minds that we would baulk at growing old. Feminists may or may not have chucked out constricting undergarments and razors when they were young, but none of them dreamed they would dye their hair to eliminate the grey, or cover up their arms to conceal creased and creped skin, or wonder: is this skirt OK for a woman of my age? When Gloria Steinem snapped back at the 'compliment' that she didn't look her age with 'This is what forty looks like,' no one thought that in later years it would still be thought flattering to say a woman looked ten years younger than she was. We knew we'd have sorted that nonsense out by now. We certainly haven't. Many working women are right to withhold their age or make out cosmetically that they are younger, because there is still a problem about growing old in the job market. But even apart from that practical reality (as real as women of childbearing age being thought to be 'worth less' to employers), the deluge of advertising and articles addressed to women, and increasingly to men, continues to insist on the need to look younger in order to remain desirable. Being desirable, and staying desirable for longer, is the main thrust of marketing for clothes, cosmetics, medication and food.

It turns out to be harder than we thought it would be. The ageing flesh is not so fascinating, erotic or irrelevant to our sense of ourselves as we had planned to make it. Segal points out that everywhere culture still teaches us shame and disgust at our ageing reflections, and makes it seem reasonable that men see older women in that way too. The older woman becomes invisible in public, just part of a crowd, while recalling how when young she was catcalled and handled by strangers as soon as she stepped out on the street. Like young women now, we were spectacle whether we wanted it or not. We were always visible, even when alone. It is almost impossible to be a young woman and not imagine yourself being looked at. Some of us tell ourselves that invisibility is an improvement, and so it can be, but the release comes with, it's accepted, a loss of our sexual selves. Visibility and our sexuality are relegated to the past, youthful self, and it's not surprising if those selves grown older breathe a sigh of relief at being free from the incessant gaze, the time-consuming achings of desire and the desire to be desired. But Segal doesn't really believe those women who claim to be relieved at being released from the grip of sexual longing. She quotes from Virginia Ironside's *The Virginia Monologues: Twenty Reasons Why Growing Old Is Great*: 'One aspect of this, she too emphasises, is "the freedom of no sex". Having had far too much sex in the past, Ironside explains, she is now "older, wiser and luxuriating in [her] single bed".' Irma Kurtz, who chose to become celibate at forty-eight, gets called out, as does Eva Figes, who spoke of women being 'liberated from foolish longings': 'She may be alone, but she is no longer lonely, since her body no longer craves what she cannot have.'

According to Segal, these 'pronouncements of cheerful sexual abstinence look much less compelling for anyone used to delving more deeply into the curious and bizarre world encompassing sexuality and desire'. Rejecting the idea that sexuality is simply 'some particular physical action or engagement that is no longer performed', Segal looks at it from multiple angles – 'psychoanalytic conjecture, clinical observations, discursive musings or unguarded personal reflection' – and finds that 'sexual feelings permeate an infinite cluster of keen, anxious, stifled, blocked, voyeuristic desires popping up in all the secret spaces within and between people'. We are, she seems to insist, merely masking our always existing but culturally inconvenient sexuality if we claim to rejoice in its loss. This seems less thoughtful than prescriptive. Why doubt that some people really are relieved to get the bed and the streets back for themselves, while others make the best of it or agonise or shrug it off? But contentment with their physical lot among the elderly is certainly not what the market wants, even if cultural taboos express universal disgust for geriatric sexuality.

Advertisers who don't want to lose the massive cohort of the 'retired' hint constantly that some kind of desire and satisfaction is possible after forty when they show us those Eurosmart couples wandering barefoot along a calm seashore at sunset, holding hands and smiling into the limitless unviewable distance (which is the land of afternoon television where life insurance companies and undertakers show advertisements spoken by elegant older men and women for a nicely arranged and sanitised funeral).

The miracle of sustained desire (a nice amount, nothing rampant) after the bloom of youthful flesh has started to wither is brought about for her by 'anti-ageing' creams and firming serums, chemical peels, cosmetic surgery and weight-loss programmes. He may need his grey touching up and a machine to clear his nostrils and ears of excess hair, but it's nearly all about keeping her nice enough for him, because we know it's hopeless if she lets herself go. That is, do you want to become someone who's past it? Because when it's gone, it's gone. Do you want to be like the man who on his sixtieth birthday said to me, with tears in his eyes: 'Now no one will ever fall in love with me again.' (Did they before?) So much of the material and cultural world tells us that we are our sexuality and the effect we have when we enter a crowded room, that unless you've got something else going for you (fame or wealth), or never had any effect on a crowded room anyway, there must be existential panic at its loss. What does culture tell us is beyond the age of desire? Witches, post-menopausal creatures, bent over, noses to chin, hormonal unreason, watery eyes, fallen flesh, voices screechy and scratchy with age and malice, that smell, being loathed and feared by everyone. And that most terrible of fates, being a single woman. We all risk loneliness in old age if we live long enough – it is a terrible thing to be the last of your friends to die – but there is a special dungeon of isolation for women alone, mad old bats, pathetic creatures, talking to themselves and their cats, waiting out their lives. Being alone is as much of a stigma to be feared as losing sexuality. Old, lonely, unwanted, invisible. We learn about these sorry creatures in the books we read as small children, we see them repeatedly on the television news, dying of solitude and neglect, even in the crowded day room of a care home.

'Orgasms are good for you,' Segal says, 'and good to have often,' though I don't think she's including the possibility that the older woman might like to have her orgasms as well as her bed to herself. After two decades of living with a younger man, she tells us, she became single when he left her for a younger woman. Like Beauvoir with her late love, Sylvie Le Bon, Segal has moved on. 'Looking around my own ageing feminist milieu, I can see that I am far from the only older woman who has enjoyed and, in my case, celebrated the delights of a heterosexual partnership that ended in her late fifties, who has subsequently found unexpected erotic pleasure in a relationship with a woman.'

Having women lovers makes sense. It always seemed to me to be what there was to look forward to once the tedious hang-up with youthful heterosexuality had played itself out. If you didn't want to keep the bed to yourself, you might well choose, I imagined, to share it with another woman, on the grounds that women have a wider understanding of love and sexuality than men, and they don't make so much noise in the bathroom.

Annoying as I imagine new-found, latter-day lesbianism in the older woman might be for lifelong lesbians, Segal points to Adam Phillips's review of Lisa Diamond's book *Sexual Fluidity: Understanding Women's Love and Desire*, in which 'he is convinced that she and others are right in suggesting that what is most "mysterious" about women's desire and relationships is that they are less narrowly focused and more flexible.' This is Segal's answer to Kurtz and Figes. She rejects their rejection of sexuality because she has found a way not to reject her own. You can stop assessing your desirability through the eyes of men, and discover that you and other women can desire together more and differently. But it won't be everyone's way and in reality, there is more to fearing age than a loss of desire, for all Segal's examples of sexually active elderly women, and her insistence that sexuality dances kaleidoscopically within us, however old we are.

Another definitive non-sexual way of knowing you're old is the moment when your doctor tells you that 'you'll have to learn to live with it,' or that whatever ails or pains you is 'the result of wear and tear'. You wait for the suggestion of a procedure, the next appointment, and then realise that you aren't going to be considered for it. You see a virtual shrug that says you are no longer young enough for a resource-strapped institution to be overly concerned with getting you back to full health. There are higher priorities, and they are higher because the patients are younger. It comes to you that whatever ailment you've got at this point is decay inflected by decay, in one form or another, and, to people who aren't you, only to be expected. It is, to put it simply, which they won't, a recognition of the beginnings of the approach of death. And it can come to you in many ways, none of them alone necessarily recognisable. Things happen, this and that, which don't in themselves mean anything, until the incremental signs pile up to the fact that there's nothing to be done that's worth doing. You are old, getting older, you won't get younger, you are physically wearing out. You will die, sooner rather than later. Some things about ageing, such as whether we mind showing our wrinkled arms or living alone, are perhaps a matter of choice and decision, but then there comes the ordinary decay and breakdown of the old body. Eventually it's out of our control and even our social and economic situation will affect only the conditions not the way in which we die. None of the gung-ho books on ageing has more than a brief mention of the proximity of death as one of the symptoms of old age to be dealt with. 'Acceptance', they say, without much elaboration, and then move rapidly on. Even if it won't kill you imminently, the degeneration of the body will alter and limit how you can live, whether you can get out, continue to work and travel. I can't think of anything about the reality of ageing which improves a person's life. The wisdom people speak of that is supposed to come to us in old age seems to be in much shorter supply than I imagined, and apart from that, it's a matter of how self-deceptively, or stoically, you are able or prepared to put up with the depletions, dependency and indignities of getting old.

Segal's solution to the reasonable pessimism of ageing is to carry on doing what she always did, within the limitations of her capacity. The trick is to see the then and the now not as the same, but as continuous, a series of selves, changed over time, but linked to an underlying self that has always been. These thoughts might be read as vague pleasantries, except that they clearly mean something real and practical to Segal. She leans towards Beauvoir's solution of decent ageing: 'One's life has value so long as one attributes value to the life of others, by means of love, friendship, indignation, compassion.' A sense of love and community, a life vested in equality and the rights of women, certainly adds up to a proper life, even a good one, but I'm not sure that a good life, even the best life, is enough compensation for the multiple ills of ageing and what seems the single piece of wisdom I've learned from my past – the fact that the world is immune to benign liberal longings. As conclusions that work for her, her conclusions are fine, but her more objective analysis of the situation of the old and the attitude of society to them is more stringent.

She quotes John Berger writing in his eighties: 'One protests because not to protest would be too humiliating, too diminishing, too deadly. One protests ... in order to *save the present moment*, whatever the future holds.' Berger's social optimism is always cheering, but here it conceals the shadows. The advice seems to me to be to do what will prevent you from despairing, because being old and having been young, we are very well aware of the world's capacity to remain utterly unchanged by our efforts. And that awareness alone is enough to make the end of life grim and disappointing unless you have the capacity to grin and bear it.

8 May 2014

POST-ITS, PUSH PINS, PENCILS

The subtitle of Nikil Saval's book is curiously inapt. *Cubed* is not a 'secret history of the workplace', but the not (entirely) secret history of a very particular kind of workplace. The main title is intended to pull that particular workplace into focus, I suppose, to narrow the vast number of possible workplaces down to a single square box (or latterly a three-walled lidless box) that will inevitably bring to mind the environment of the white-collar pen-pusher, although it has been a very long time since office workers reliably wore white collars or pushed pens to fulfil their duties. But even if we allow 'the workplace' to stand for 'the office', 'the history of a secret workplace' would have been a more accurate subtitle. What happens there? People can be said to 'work in an office' and no further explanation is required, but there's no real clue to what they do, unlike people who work in other places, who make things in a factory, mine in a mine, teach in a school, sell things in a shop. What are the millions of children who since the late nineteenth century have increasingly been told that one (or both) of their parents is 'at the office' to understand by that? At least that nothing is made, mined, taught or sold.

The office in which mid to late twentieth-century fathers and mothers worked, where they went every day and returned from at night, had for me as a child in the 1950s the enticing pull of spun sugar and coloured comics, and, even now, long after I learned the difference between the dream and the reality, the word still triggers a promise of delight. Occasionally, when I was allowed to accompany my father to an office that was once or twice his place of work, I went with joy as to Santa's grotto. The office had so much more to engage with than mere roundabouts and swings.

The secret beating heart of the dream office is the stationery cupboard, the ideal kind, the one that opens to enough depth to allow you to walk in and close the door behind you. No one does close the door – it would be weird – but the perfect stationery cupboard is one in which you could be perfectly alone with floor-to-ceiling shelves laden with neat stacks of packets, piles and boxes, lined up, tidy, everything patiently waiting for you to take one from the top, or open the lid and grab a handful. It's fully stocked with more than one of everything and plenty to spare. Sundries. In bulk. A dozen of; assorted; multi-buys; bumper bundles. Paper in quires and reams, flimsy, economy and letter quality, neatly contained in perfectly folded paper packets. Boxes of carbon paper. (Children, you interleave a crispy dark-blue onion skin between each sheet of paper, you align them bottom edge and long side, tapping the long and short sides sharply together on the surface of your desk, and if you type sharply you can get as many as six or eight copies, each slightly fainter than the one before.) Refills and spares. A cornucopia of everything you would never run out of. Paper glued into pads or notebooks. Lined and unlined. Spiral, perfect bound, reporter. Envelopes with and without windows. Ring binders. Snap binders. Box files. Sticky white circles to reinforce the holes made by paper punches. Paper punches. Green string tags to go through the holes. Labels. So many blank labels. White, coloured, all shapes and sizes. And a mechanical labeller with plastic tape to emboss. More than enough supplies so that if a thing is done wrongly, spoilt or not quite right, mistyped, misspelled, holes punched in the wrong place, pencil broken, you throw it away and get a fresh one from the stationery cupboard that never runs out because it is there always to provide more.

Perhaps this idea of the overflowing, generous stationery cupboard that permitted what was badly done to be dispensed with and a new start made was a source of my reprehensible and ill-timed tendency to rejoice in waste. The pleasures of the clean new page, or a stiff unmarked notebook, the sharp perfectly conical tip of an unused pencil, the crisp blank blue of an unmarked carbon or a black unstruck typewriter ribbon, cloth or plastic. All there, waiting to replace whatever had run out or run down or been botched. And photocopier stuff. Typewriter ribbons. Post-it notes. Push pins, tin tacks, staples, rubbers, rubber bands, Tipp-Ex tape and white-out paint like nail varnish. Boxes of pencils, biros, coloured pencils, rulers, cheaper by the dozen. The stationery cupboard, the smell and silence of office necessities. Whenever I find myself in an office – occasionally the one that produces this paper – I have to restrain myself from asking to be shown to the stationery cupboard so that I can gaze on it and inhale the scent. Part bookish, part chemical. Papery. Inky. Metallic.

Outside the sanctuary of the cupboard, the office equipment, the meta pleasures. Filing cabinets of drawers running on metal sliders, inside, hanging folders on

metal struts and plastic labels. Photocopiers. A swivel
chair with a silent but compelling gas lift. A desk with
drawers into which you might spend hours placing and
rearranging the requirements of a convenient office life.
And on the desk, a typewriter. Phone. A pencil sharpener –
one that clamps to the edge of the desk which you wind
like a mincer. Highlighters – perhaps there weren't any
when I was small. Ink. Quink. Was there another kind?
Sheaffer? Red, black, blue-black, turquoise. Paperclips,
stamps, rubber stamps with sections you turn to get the
date, a rubber thimble for counting off pages, stapler,
staples, thousands of them that break off so neatly like …
like what? I can't quite get it or nothing else is like
it. Trays. Holders. Stands. Sorters. Desk accessories.
Containers for which you have to buy the things you
hadn't thought of until you saw a holder for them.

But the actual work, what needs to be done with
all the desirable sundries, the reason for them, wasn't
clear. Obviously mostly it had to do with paper. Books
were kept and letters written, loose-leaf papers filed.
But what the letters were about, what was written in
the books that were kept, wasn't even vaguely known.
Some instinct kept me from demanding detail, perhaps
because of a correct suspicion that the actual business of
business was the very least of the pleasures of the office.
What is done in offices, to generalise, is pretty boring and
derivative, being at the hands-off service-end of those
other places of work where things got made, mined,
taught or sold. Work that is always about something
other than itself. Paperwork. Allowed to play, I typed
'Dear Sir' at the desk on the huge typewriter, sitting high
on the chair, legs dangling. And ended 'Yours Faithfully'
('Sincerely' only after a named 'Dear' – I learned that

very young), after which I squiggled an elaborate signature that bore no relation to the alphabet. In the space between I let my fingers run riot over the keys, to produce a gobbledygook body of the letter that probably made as much sense to me as most of the real correspondence would have. The accoutrements and contraptions of the office were the delight, the actual commerce remained not so much a secret as an unwanted answer to an uncompelling mystery. Like the most extraordinary couture, Alexander McQueen's designs, say. You delight in and admire them, gorgeously and dramatically displayed in the videos of professional mannequins on runways, but you don't want to see them in everyday action, being worn disappointingly as *clothes*, in real life, to dull receptions or dinners without the special lighting and the right pose (how many frocks are designed to be sat down in?), by people who have them only because they are rich.

I took the idea of a history of the office to be as attractive as the opening of the stationery cupboard, hoping it would tell me about the development of offices as such and nothing very much about the history of what it was that people actually did at those places of work through the ages, or, even less excitingly, why they did it. I wasn't disappointed. I still don't know what people do in offices, or rather, I haven't been required by Nikil Saval's book to trouble myself more than is necessary with such matters. At the beginning of the final third of the book we are referred to Drucker's ('for businessmen who read no philosophy, Drucker was their philosopher') conception of 'knowledge work', defined by Fritz Machlup as 'conferring, negotiating, planning, directing, reading, note-taking, writing, drawing, blue-printing, calculating, dictating, telephoning, card-punching, typing, multigraphing, recording, checking, and many others.' Yes, but why? Never mind, the question isn't pressing.

The story of the office begins in counting houses, where scribes kept their heads down accounting for the transformation of goods into wealth and vice versa. You might go as far back as ancient Egypt or stay sensible and look to mercantile Europe for the beginnings of bureaucracy, and the need to keep written accounts of business in one place. Saval gives a nod to the medieval guilds but settles on the nineteenth century as the start of the office proper, still in Europe, although this is an overwhelmingly American account of the American office. The closer you get to modernity in *Cubed*, the more the emphasis is on buildings and the more diminished the figure of the worker inside the buildings (until you get to the end and the buildings begin to disappear, although so too do the workers). It's not a mystery. The design and construction of entire purpose-built structures for office work is a modern phenomenon. Scribes, to stretch the notion of office work, wrote in scriptoria, rooms in monasteries which were built for the more general purpose of worshipping God and housing those devoted to the various tasks (among which the reproduction of scripture) involved in doing so. Clerks are more likely to be what we think of when we want to look at the early days of office work. They emerged from their religious duties to assist commerce in keeping track of business, where we recognise them as dark-suited, substantially present characters in Trollope, Thackeray and Dickens. The ready-made spaces these clerks worked in became 'offices', rather than special buildings defining the work they pursued. They kept their books and scratched out their invoices in regular private houses given over to business, and sat or stood at desks in rooms they shared with their bosses for both convenience and oversight – this too disappears and then returns in postmodernity when hierarchy is spatially, if not actually, flattened.

Proximity has always been an important issue for office workers, so much so that it eventually precluded any form of unionisation. Rather than organise to improve their pay and conditions, office workers chose to keep close to their superiors in the hope, not always forlorn, that they would rise in prominence thanks to patronage. Physical closeness applied in the Dickensian office, but there are other ways to achieve it. In *The Apartment* (perfectly depicting the apex of the American way of office life in 1960 as *North by Northwest* perfectly depicts the fantasised alternative), Jack Lemmon gets close to his boss, which gets him ever closer to a key to the executive washroom, by lending his apartment to executives for their extramarital assignations. Until love (or an understanding of his place in feudal America) turns him into his own refusing hero, or, depending on your interpretation, strips down his view of his possibilities to something more realistic, he is the ingratiating clerk: a staple of office narrative. The demeanour of the literary clerk was twice indelibly and differently depicted in the mid-nineteenth century. In just three years he turns inside out from that epitome of sly unctuousness, Uriah Heep (1850), to the enigmatic bombshell that is Bartleby, the absolute refuser (1853). Perhaps the two portrayals are not coincidental. In 1851, the Melville family read *David Copperfield* aloud as their evening entertainment.

The pre-twentieth-century office worker saw himself as a cut above the unsalaried labouring masses, and was as ambivalent about his superiors, who were his only means of rising, as the rest of the working world was about him. Dandyish clerks prided themselves on not being workers, on the cleanness of their job (thus the whiteness of the collars), and on being a step above the hoi polloi. They became a massed workforce in the United States, where the attitude towards the scribe and record-keeper changed, so that they came to be seen both as effete and untrustworthy, like Dickens's Heep, and as ominous and unknowable, like Bartleby, but without receiving the amazed respect of Melville's narrator. By 1855 in New York they were the third largest occupational group. Their self-esteem as their numbers grew was not shared: 'Nothing about clerical labour was congenial to the way most Americans thought of work ... At best, it seemed to *reproduce* things ... the bodies of real workers were sinewy, tanned by the relentless sun, or blackened by smokestack soot; the bodies of clerks were slim, almost feminine in their untested delicacy.' In *Vanity Fair*, the clerks are '"vain, mean, selfish, greedy, sensual and sly, talkative and cowardly", and spent all their minimal strength attempting to dress better than "*real* men who did *real* work".'

By the mid-twentieth century sex had created a new division within clerical labour. The secretary was almost invariably a woman and so was the typist, who worked in massed serried ranks, although (again to be seen in *The Apartment*) there was also a pool of anonymous desks for mute men with accounting machines, like Lemmon as C.C. Baxter. The secretaries lived inside a bubble of closeness to power, looking to burst through it into management or marriage, most likely the latter, geishas at work whose most realistic hope was to become domestic geishas, while the typists (originally called typewriters) and number crunchers clattering on their machines on their own floor merely received dictated or longhand work to type or add up, distributed by runners, and so were not likely to catch the eye of an executive to give them a hand up unless they were prepared to wait outside their own apartment in the rain.

The pools of workers as well as the interior design of offices were under the spell of Taylorism, the 1950s fetish for a time-and-motion efficiency that tried to replicate the rhythm enforced in the factories to which office workers felt so superior. The idea that things that need doing and the people doing them could be so organised that they operated together as smoothly as cogs in a machine is everlastingly seductive. Anyone who spends half a day reorganising their home office, rejigging their filing system, arranging their workspace 'ergonomically' knows this. It isn't just a drive for cost efficiency, but some human tic that has us convinced that the way we organise ourselves in relation to our work holds a magic key to an almost effortless success. Entire online magazines like *Lifehacker* and *Zen Habits* are devoted to time-and-money-saving tweaks for work and home ('An Easy Way to Find the Perfect Height for Your Chair or Standing Desk'; 'Five Ways to Spend a Saved Hour at Work'; 'Ten Tips to Work Smarter, Not Harder'; 'What to Think about While You Exercise'). At a corporate level, this meant erecting buildings and designing their interiors and work systems to achieve office nirvana. No time, no motion wasted. The utopian dream of architects, designers and managers comes together in the form-follows-function mantra, beginning with Adler and Sullivan's Wainwright Building in St Louis in 1891, although, as Saval points out, from the start it was really all about form follows finance:

> The point was not to make an office building per specification of a given company ... but rather to build for an economy in which an organisation could move in and out of a space without any difficulty. The space had to be eminently *rentable* ... The skylines of American cities, more than human ingenuity and entrepreneurial prowess, came simply to represent dollars per square foot.

The skyscraper, the apotheosis of form following finance and function, appears once the manufacture of elevators allowed buildings of more than the five floors that people are prepared to walk up. It was a perfect structure philosophically and speculatively to house the now millions of workers whose job it was to keep track of manufacturing, buying and selling – 'the synthesis of naked commerce and organic architecture' as foreseen by Louis Sullivan, mentor to Frank Lloyd Wright. The basic unit of the skyscraper is the 'cell': 'We take our cue from the individual cell, which requires a window with its separating pier, its sill and lintel, and we, without more ado, make them look all alike because they are all alike.' The International Style reached its glory period with the vertical cities designed by Sullivan, Mies van der Rohe, Philip Johnson, Henry-Russell Hitchcock. The Philadelphia Savings Fund Society Building, the Rockefeller Center, the UN Secretariat Building, Lever House and the Seagram Building were visually stunning statements of corporate power and prevailed by making the perceived virtues of repetition and monotony in design synonymous with economy and order. Even the need for a window in each cell was obviated with the invention of an efficient air-conditioning system and electric lighting, allowing more rational ways to provide light and air. However beautiful or banal the exterior, curtained in glass or blank with concrete, the buildings served as hives for the masses who performed their varied tasks to produce the evidence of profit. They were Taylorist cathedrals, and new techniques of ergonomics and personality-testing for employees compounded the organisational religious zeal, so that individuals more than ever before became bodies operating within physical space, whose 'personalities' were tested for the lack of them in the search for compliance and conformity. Business jargon added mind-conditioning on a par with air-conditioning, keeping everyone functioning optimally within the purposes of the mini-city.

The popular sociology books that began to appear in the 1960s criticising this uniformity were read avidly by the office workers who started to see themselves as victims. *The Lonely Crowd*, *The Organisation Man*, *The Man in the Grey Flannel Suit*, the movie *The Apartment* itself, described a dystopian conformity that mid-century business America had produced in entire lives, not just in the working day. An alternative was proposed by office designers such as Robert Propst at Herman Miller, who were still working on behalf of the corporations, but who saw Taylorism as deadening the creative forces that were beginning to be seen as useful to business, perhaps as a result of the rise of advertising. Open plan became the solution. The cell opened out to the entire floor space of the building and it became a matter of how to subdivide that space to suit the varied tasks each individual needed to do, while retaining openness; to create office interiors in which workers needed to move around to achieve their goals, ideally bumping into one another on the way to permit the fortuitous cross-pollination of ideas. Cubes arrived, boxes without lids for people, but humane, alterable and adaptable to their needs (or the needs of the business for which they worked). Lots of little adjustable cells inside the main cell. Walls became flexible and low enough to be chatted over. Herman Miller's Action Office and the concept of Bürolandschaft, the landscaped office, replaced the fundamental lonely cell and created its own kind of hell: 'unpleasant temperature variations, draughts, low humidity, unacceptable noise levels, poor natural lighting, lack of visual contact with the outside and lack of natural ventilation'. And in addition there was a felt loss of privacy that had people bringing in all manner of knick-knacks to their cubes as self-identifiers and status symbols.

Another kind of office work came along with the arrival of the dot-com revolution. Not paper work but screen work. Like advertising but growing crazily, not humdrum invoice-stamping and letter-writing, but innovative programming that required intense brainwork from young, ill-disciplined talent who needed to be kept at their screens as much as possible while being nurtured and refuelled on the job. Being young and not having any connection with the office work of the past, the new workforce was offered on-site playgrounds that kept obsessive minds refreshed but still focused. Hierarchies

POST-ITS, PUSH PINS, PENCILS

were loosened, or more accurately given the appearance of being loosened. Jeans and T-shirts replaced suits, all youthful needs (except sleep-inducing sex) were catered for: pizzas and carbonated drinks, basketball and brightly coloured nursery furniture for the young geniuses to lounge or nap on when they were exhausted with programming. The open-plan office moved towards 'main streets' with side offices for particular purposes, often themed like Disneyland with lots of communal meeting and playing places, scooters to get around, and built-in time for workers to develop their own pet projects. The Herman Miller Aeron chair, still so desirable, was a design response to the need to sit for long periods working at a screen. It's advertised as being ergonomically created for people to sit comfortably on stretchy mesh for up to twelve hours at a time.

In advertising, Jay Chiat decided that office politics were a bar to inspirational thinking. He hired Frank Gehry to design his 'deterritorialised' agency offices in Venice, California in 1986. 'Everyone would be given a cellular phone and a laptop computer when they came in. And they would work wherever they wanted.' Personal items, pictures or plants had to be put in lockers. There were no other private spaces. There were 'Tilt-A-Whirl domed cars … taken from a defunct amusement park ride, for two people to have private conferences. They became the only place where people could take private phone calls.' One employee pulled a toy wagon around to keep her stuff together. It rapidly turned into a disaster. People got to work and had no idea where they were to go. There were too many people and not enough chairs. People just stopped going to work. In more formal work situations too, the idea of the individual workstation, an office or a personal desk, began to disappear and designers created fluid spaces where people wandered to settle here and there in specialised spaces. For some reason homelessness was deemed to be the answer to a smooth operation.

The great days of office buildings dictating where and how individuals work within them may have gone. There are new architects and designers who collaborate with the workers themselves to produce interiors that suit their needs and desires. 'Co-design' – allowing the users of a space to have an equal say in how it is organised – is a first sign that buildings, sponsored by and monuments to corporate power, might have lost their primacy over the individuals engaged to work in them. But if the time of grand structures is over, it's probably an indication that corporate power has seen a better way to sustain itself. The shift away from monolithic vertical cities of work and order might be seen as the stage immediately preceding the disappearance of the office altogether and the start of the working-from-home revolution we've been told has been on its way ever since futurology programmes in the 1950s assured us we'd never get out of our pyjamas within the year.

Fantasies of working from home, as people began to see round the corner into a computerised future, were forever being promised but never really came to anything. The idea made management nervous. How to keep tabs on people? How were managers to manage? And it alarmed office workers. It wasn't perhaps such a luxury after all not having to face the nightmare of commuting or those noisy open-plan dystopias, when confronted instead by the discipline needed to get down to and keep at work at home, operating around the domestic needs of the family, and having no one to chat to around the water cooler that wasn't there. Even now, when the beneficial economics of freelancing and outsourcing has finally got a grip on corporate accountants, there is something baffling and forlorn about the sight, as you walk past café after café window, of rows of people tapping on their MacBook Air. There for company in the communal space, but wearing isolating headphones to keep out the chatter, rather than sitting in their own time in quiet, ideally organised, or lonely, noisy, cramped home offices. Cafés with free Wi-Fi charge by the coffee to replicate a working atmosphere in what was once a place for daydreaming and chat. The freedom of working from home is also the freedom from employment benefits such as paid holidays, sick pay, pensions; and the freedom of permatemp contracts or none at all and the radical uncertainty about maintaining a steady income. These workers are a serious new class, known as the precariat: insecure, unorganised, taking on too much work for fear of famine, or frighteningly underemployed. The old rules of employment have been turned upside down. These new non-employees, apparently, need to develop a new 'self-employed mindset', in which they treat their employers as 'customers' of their services, and do their best to satisfy them, in order to retain their 'business'. The 'co-working' rental is the most recent arrival. Space in a building with office equipment and technical facilities is hired out to freelancers, who work together but separately in flexible spaces on their own projects, in a bid 'to get out of their apartments and be sociable in an office setting'. Office space has returned to what it really was, dollars per square foot, which those who were once employees now pay to use, without the need for rentiers to provide more than a minimum of infrastructure. The US Bureau of Labor Statistics projects that 'by 2020 freelancers, temps, day labourers and independent contractors will constitute 40 per cent of the workforce.' Some think up to 50 per cent. Any freelancer will tell you about the time and effort required to drum up business and keep it coming (networking, if you like), which cuts down on how much work you can actually do if you get it. When they do get the work, they no longer get the annual salaries that old-time clerks were so proud to receive. Getting paid is itself time-consuming and difficult. It's estimated that more than 77 per cent of freelancers have had trouble collecting payment, because contractors try to retain fees for as long as possible. Flexibility sounds seductive, as if it allows individuals to live their lives sanely, fitting work and leisure together in whatever way suits them and their families best. But returning the focus to the individual worker rather than the great corporate edifice simply adds the burdens of management to the working person's day while creating permanent anxiety and ensuring employee compliance. As to what freelancers actually do in their home offices, in steamy cafés, in co-working spaces, I still have no idea, but I suspect that the sumptuous stationery cupboard is getting to be as rare as a monthly salary cheque.

31 July 2014

A Diagnosis

The future flashed before my eyes in all its pre-ordained banality. Embarrassment, at first, to the exclusion of all other feelings. But embarrassment curled at the edges with a weariness, the sort that comes over you when you are set on a track by something outside your control, and which, although it is not your experience, is so known in all its cultural forms that you could unscrew the cap of the pen in your hand and jot down in the notebook on your lap every single thing that will happen and everything that will be felt for the foreseeable future. Including the surprises.

I got a joke in.

'So – we'd better get cooking the meth,' I said to the Poet, sitting to one side and slightly behind me. The Poet with an effort got his face to work and responded properly. 'This time we quit while the going's good.' The doctor and nurse were blank. When we got home the Poet said he supposed they didn't watch much US TV drama. It was only later that I thought that maybe, ever since *Breaking Bad*'s first broadcast, oncologists and their nurses all over the Western world have been subjected to the meth-cooking joke each time they have applied their latest, assiduously rehearsed, non-brutal techniques for telling a patient as gently but honestly as possible, having first sized up their inner resilience with a few apparently innocent questions ('Tell me what you have been expecting from this appointment'), that they have inoperable cancer. Perhaps they failed to laugh at my – doubtless evasive – bid to lighten the mood, not because they didn't get the reference, but because they had said to each other too often after such an appointment: 'If I hear one more patient say they should start cooking meth, I'm going to wrestle them to the ground and bellow death into their faces – "Pay attention, I'm fucking telling you something important!"' I was mortified at the thought that before I'd properly started out on the cancer road, I'd committed my first platitude. I was already a predictable cancer patient.

Then again, what if I had taken the other option, and sat in dignified silence for a moment collecting myself, which I'm sure is how one would describe the short hiatus, and then asked serious, intelligent questions about the nature of the treatment the Onc Doc was suggesting, not to 'cure' me (he had slipped that in right at the start for me to run with or blank out, as I chose), but which had a 20 to 30 per cent chance of producing a remission for an unguessable period? After listening as carefully as my muddled head could manage to his answer (three cycles of chemotherapy, a scan, a course of radiotherapy, taking us up to Christmas, almost, then we would see), I would then be obliged to ask the next, inevitable 'how long' question, hedged about with all the get-out clauses for Onc Doc, who after all wasn't to blame for my cancer.

'Of course, I understand it would be unreasonable of me to expect you to know, with any certainty, when I'm likely to die if I have the treatment. I'm sure it's different for everyone, and only based on statistics, but could you perhaps give me a general idea: years ... months ... weeks?'

The print size in my mind decreased with time's incremental decline, and as I arrived at the last word – *weeks* – it suddenly struck me, with all the force of the fullest sense of the word 'struck', that this could actually be his answer and not just the logical next time period in my sentence. Every cell in my body, except those responsible for maintaining a reasonable, calm exterior, was now Lindy Hopping at that possibility, the only one that hadn't occurred to me until that moment. *Weeks*. Still, the question itself was there waiting in line for me in the ready-made scripts file, for this unique to me but culturally familiar diagnostic moment, just after the Contemporary International Smart Cancer Joke.

Not that I've asked yet. I am getting ahead of myself. In fact, the Onc Doc, *my* Onc Doc as I now think of him, was drawing little circles, the results of my PET scan and bronchoscopy, on a ready-made outline map of a human torso, skinned and boned to show the lungs and lymph nodes, so that I could see the smallness of the tumour (good) in the lower left lobe, but also that it was too close to the pleura to be operable (not so good), and how its somewhat active cells (rather bad) had already travelled along two lymph nodes up to a third beside my oesophagus (more than rather bad). With that careful insertion of 'to treat, not to cure' in his suggested plan of action, he had in effect just told me I was going to die in his care, sooner rather than later. Now I had to decide, do I want to ask that obvious next question? And the one after that? (How long, then, without treatment?) I believe he knew exactly how these appointments went. Why should I make it easy for him, I now thought. It's quite hard to absorb rapidly the notion that someone forecasting your fairly imminent death might not be your enemy. More than that, the great weariness combined with the previously mentioned embarrassment, at the idea of asking question B or 2 and thereby setting the expected ball of clichés rolling, was overwhelming. Instead of complying, I imagined I could instead nod a thank-you and take my leave of the doctor and the nurse. The Poet would leave with me, and we'd never mention it again. The Woman with No Name approach. A short shriek of Morricone, after the door has closed behind us. But that wouldn't do, either. After the heroic moment there would be the hour-by-hour living. Everyday life, even a shortened one, doesn't permit heroic blankness in the way film does. Say, Leone's long, long close-up of Eastwood's or Fonda's impassive face; the Warhol movie of John Giorno sleeping for five hours and twenty minutes; Jarman's seventy-nine-minute single shot of saturated blue.

Or I could do nothing. I could sit in sadistic silence waiting for whatever is next on his list of diagnostic appointment moves for all occasions.

'Yes? And?'

Sullen rudeness is a possible option handed to us cancerees. It would institute a period of bad behaviour as one's own private, glumly gleeful saturnalia, world turned upside down, lord of misrule regulated havoc, for a short period before the great slog of getting on with it began again, cancer or no cancer. I probably couldn't sulk unto death, no matter that I'm one of the foremost sulkers on the planet. I'd get hungry. Or want to watch TV. Or even have an itch I had to scratch, and any such desire immediately and fatally cracks the implacable wall of sulk. Another route through the carefully tended maze of standard responses looks like the most spontaneous, although it really needs to be yelled by Jack Lemmon, tortoise-style, sticking his neck right out, inches from Onc Doc's face. 'You're telling me I've got CANCER? That I'm going to DIE, because don't think I don't know that INOPERABLE means it'll spread along the tracks from lymph node to nymph load (I'd apologise for that, but I'm not sorry). You've just said you reckon, with all your hedging and ditching, that I'm going to be DEAD IN THREE YEARS. If I'm LUCKY. Have I got that RIGHT?'

Actually, he said 'two to three years'. (The *weeks* moment passed, leaving me less cheered than I ought to have been.) But I've taken the long view to stop any quibbling. I do wonder, now he's laid the numbers out, with all the ifs and buts and maybes, how he manages his probability predictions. Does he pop an extra year on after 'or' for luck, like one for the pot? Or does he shift the lower end of the prediction a little towards the future to soften the felt brevity of a single year to someone whose time is slipping past at the speed of a sixty-seven-year-old's perception? Perhaps he's always as scrupulously accurate as possible in these situations, because, although he would like to offer a false glimmer of optimism, which is said to be as good as a placebo, he doesn't want to risk my ghostly or my next of kin's litigious fury if I died a day short of his over-generous soonest prediction. So I should believe him because fear of a lawsuit makes doctors realistic and therefore trustworthy. This not crazily short but vague two-to-three-years is a difficult real-life calculation for me. On the one hand, to die pushing seventy years of age is no great tragedy, even if my id would like to know what the fuck age has got to do with being rubbed out. Even so, such reasonableness doesn't take account of the kind of thoughts that run swiftly through my mind. Two to three years. Will the battery on the TV remote run out first? How many inches will the weeping birch grow, the one planted by the Poet for my sixtieth birthday (soppy old radical versifier)? I suppose I won't need another cashmere sweater to keep me warm come the planet's apocalypse, the ones I've already got will survive the moths for a couple of years or even three should it come sooner than my own apocalypse. I very much regret the disappearance of a website I once bookmarked called Sensible Units. It took a scientific unit of quantity and resolved it into units that are much more easily or entertainingly imagined. Who knew that 1 cm of depth is equivalent to twenty-nine human female fingernail thicknesses? Or that eighty gigabytes can be visualised as 110 CDs or twenty-five human genomes?

So, when my Onc Doc announced that I had cancer, inoperable cancer, and that there was no cure, but some lengthy and famously unpleasant treatment that might get in the way of its speedy (the word 'aggressive' comes to mind but wasn't actually said) progress, I chose the threadbare joke, from the already ready possible options. Because I had to choose something. But, as well as doing what I had to do in my new role, and for more than any other reason, it was a short-term panic-stricken solution for the flood of *embarrassment*, much more powerful than alarm or fear, that engulfed and mortified me at finding myself set firmly on that particular well-travelled road. I am and have always been embarrassed by all social rituals that require me to participate in a predetermined script. It may simply be that I am not a natural actor. That would account for the funk. Perhaps, having been handed this inescapable part, I was suffering from stage fright. It goes deep. I can perform at other people's dinner tables like a chattering magpie, arguing and picking up on the conversation to make a joke or say something smart. Then I go home covered with a layer of self-disgust as if I'd been rolling in donkey shit, and for a day or two afterwards, I stay in bed with the covers over my head in shame. In public and prescribed ritual, I have no easy get-out, but I can't just get on with it. The only way I can manage – gracelessly – is to keep my head down, my eyes low, dig my fingers hard into my palm, and move my mouth a little, like John Redwood singing the Welsh national anthem, while other people enjoy themselves intoning the required utterances. Ever since I was a child, it's been like that.

'You have to say, "I wish you long life," and shake his hand,' my father told me on our way to visit a relative sitting shiva. The rest of the journey was an agony of anticipation. I knew I couldn't say those words. I wouldn't be able to get them out. They were ridiculous, not what I'd really ever say to someone else. Not what small children would say and do, and it seems I could only play one role at a time. I've never been able to make my face work properly while repeating a set speech. Also, it seemed mean-spirited towards the newly dead to hope the mourner lived longer, who after all already had. 'It's what you do. Just say it and then go and get a smoked salmon bagel.' I could almost see that the anguish of the occasion was not actually mine but belonged to the bereaved. Still, I couldn't bear to think about doing it. It wasn't what I would say, therefore I couldn't say it. I think also, it was expected of me, and therefore I couldn't do it. I wonder what would have happened if I hadn't been instructed. Would I have taken his hand and said something suitable? What could that be? I might just have said, as I would now, 'I'm very sorry.' Why wasn't I allowed to do that? Because. We arrived and I took the hand offered me, but failed to look into his eyes, which, because of the low seating arrangement for chief mourners, were level with mine. I think I stared off to one side. And I managed only a mumbled noise, a strangled moan. Nothing that could be mistaken for 'I wish you long life.' I'd failed and although I knew I was in trouble, I was relieved not to have said the words out loud, while people watched me and smiled at the sweet little girl maintaining the grown-up tradition with archaic words translated from the Yiddish.

Growing up hasn't helped. Marriage ceremonies have been as difficult, even though I was an adult. The first was a blur, although I remember the fingers digging into my palm, and handing over my gold opal ring to my betrothed, just before we went in to be 'done', so he could slip it on my finger with the opal at the back, because we hadn't got round to even thinking about a ring until the morning of the registry office ceremony. Certainly, I was embarrassed and tied in knots by the corniness of the whole performance. Roger didn't mind, he always enjoyed me disconcerting his parents. By the time of my second marriage, well into my dog days, I had enough confidence to ask the registrar who was to perform the ceremony if I could just say 'Yes' when it got to the bit where I was required to say 'I do,' and to miss out repeating the affirmations about better or worse, sickness and blah blah blah, already much minimised by me and the Poet. She looked at me as if I'd kicked her favourite bunny. 'We *are* allowed to give people permission to do that,' she said. 'But only when they're terminally ill and have difficulty speaking.' I stopped myself from saying that I wasn't feeling too perky, actually, and who knows what it might turn into. Properly shamed, I went through with it, sotto voce and choking back some but not all the nervous giggles that always rise up when I'm forced to participate in ritual. The Poet said I behaved childishly and I completely agreed. I decided I was definitely not going to do that again, no matter how practical it might be.

Now I was faced with the prospect of a rather lengthy (in one view) public/private performance by which to be excruciated. A sudden death requires others to deal with the difficulty of ritual. A stroke, a heart attack. Then it's all someone else's problem. But this diagnostic appointment was the announcement of yet another version of the show going on the road in which I was to star. I had been formally inducted into Cancer World. (Mixing my metaphors, I'm afraid. Which should it be, the theme park or the lack of variety show?) I was handed my script, though all the lines were known already and the moves were paced out. There are no novel responses possible. Absolutely none that I could think of. Responses to the diagnosis; the treatment and its side effects; the development of cancer symptoms; the pain and discomfort; the dying; the death. Do I have to start a campaign? Wear a badge, run, climb walls, swim inordinate lengths, dance the tango for a very long time, in return for money for cancer research? Whatever that is. Does the money go to the drug companies? To university labs? To Jeremy Hunt? What is this crowd-funded research, where is it happening? Am I going to appear calm in the face of destiny? Actually cheerful, with people saying I was wonderful? Should I affirm my atheism or collapse into religious comfort? Or should I turn my face to the wall? And when the symptoms kick in, will I suffer in silence, quote Epictetus and Marcus Aurelius, or will I refuse to go gentle and make an almighty fuss ('Excuse me, *I'm* the cancer patient here!'). Dear God, not a bucket list? Really, there is nothing that I want to do before I die, except perhaps just lie back and enjoy the morphine, daydreaming my way to oblivion.

One thing I state as soon as we're out of the door: 'Under no circumstances is anyone to say that I lost a battle with cancer. Or that I bore it bravely. I am *not* fighting, losing, winning or bearing.' I will not personify the cancer cells inside me in any form. I reject all metaphors of attack or enmity in the midst, and I will have nothing whatever to do with any notion of desert, punishment, fairness or unfairness, or any kind of moral causality. But I sense that I can't avoid the cancer clichés simply by rejecting them. Rejection is conditioned by and reinforces the existence of the thing I want to avoid. I choose how to respond and behave, but a choice between doing this or that, being this or that, really isn't freedom of action, it's just picking one's way through an already drawn flow chart. They still sit there, to be taken or left, the flashing neon markers on the road that I would like to think isn't there for me to be travelling down. I am appalled at the thought, suddenly, that someone at some point is going to tell me I am on a journey. I try but I can't think of a single aspect of having cancer, start to finish, that isn't an act in a pantomime in which my participation is guaranteed however I believe I choose to play each scene. I have been given this role. (There, see? Instant victim.) I have no choice but to perform and to be embarrassed to death. I wish you long life.

We'd hardly got home before I said: 'Well, I suppose I'm going to write a cancer diary.' The only other thing I might have said was: 'Well, I'm not going to write a cancer diary.' Right there: a choice? I'm a writer, have been since I was small, and have earned my living at it for thirty years. I write fiction and non-fiction, but it's almost always personal. I start with me, and often enough end with me. I've never been apologetic about that nor had a sense that my writing is 'confessional'. What else am I going to write about but how I know and don't know the world? I may not make things up in fiction, or tell the truth in non-fiction, but documentary or invented, it's always been me at the centre of the will to put descriptions out into the world. I lie, like all writers, but I use my truths as I know them in order to do so.

'I wonder if I am not talking yet again about myself. Shall I be incapable, to the end, of lying on any other subject?' I used this quote from *Malone Dies* as the epigraph to my non-fiction so-called travel book *Skating to Antarctica*, though it would have been apt, to my mind, at the front of any book I've written, fiction or non-fiction, memoir or travel, history or fantasy. *Skating* concerned a voyage I took around the Antarctic peninsula and the story of my rather brief, rackety relationship with my mother. 'You know,' I'd say gaily to people who asked what it was about. 'Icebergs, mothers.

That sort of thing.' I couldn't even describe the most extraordinary landscape on the planet without reference to myself and my life outside the Antarctic cruise. I can't use my eyes to see things without my eyes knowing that what they see is conditioned by what I've known and what I've been. Ditto my mind to think things. So be it. I'm a writer. I've got cancer. Am I going to write about it? How am I not? I pretended for a moment that I might not, but knew I had to, because writing is what I do and now cancer is what I do, too.

And then the weariness. A fucking cancer diary? Another fucking cancer diary. I think back to cancer diaries I have read, just because they're there. You don't seek cancer diaries out, they come at you as you turn the pages of magazines and newspapers or thumb through Twitter and blogs. How many have I read? I can't remember, but they've spanned decades. I recall Ruth Picardie, a young woman in her thirties, with small children. John Diamond, married to Nigella Lawson and dying stylishly. Ivan Noble, a BBC science and technology writer; Tom Lubbock, art critic; Susan Sontag, although not exactly a diary, mined her cancer for a famous essay about the cultural nature of illness. Those stood out, they were all professional writers and most wrote their diaries as occasional or regular series for newspapers or online blogs. Can there possibly be anything new to add? Isn't the cliché of writing a cancer diary going to be compounded by the impossibility of writing in it anything other than what has already been written, over and over? Same story, same ending. Weariness. The odd thing is, narcissistic writer though I am, I have always thought of writing straight autobiography as incredibly tedious. I couldn't put hand to keyboard without there being something else, some other component in the narrative than just my personal history. In 1984, while I was in a deep and long depression, largely, I think, about how I wasn't being a writer, my previously adoptive or foster mother, Doris Lessing, would say, in her matter of fact, impatient way: 'Well, just write down your life story. It's interesting enough, and there are editors who can deal with sorting out your sentences and that kind of thing.' She wafted her arm in the air to show me how easy it would be. It was intended to encourage me. It made me even more silent with despair. I wasn't interested in just being published. I wasn't even interested in writing something 'interesting enough'. I was a writer and I couldn't understand why I wasn't writing. The answer was, I think, that I hadn't understood how writing gathers everything into itself to make a satisfactory piece. My story, someone else's story, a place, an idea, a dream, human anatomy, the mind acting on the world, vice versa, some or all and more yet unthought of, had to be combined in the right amounts in order to make a book, an essay, fiction, non-fiction, history, comedy, whatever, *work*. I was enough of a writer to know that writing the story of my interesting childhood was not being a writer. I was enough of a writer to be dismayed that Doris, having known me by then for nearly two decades, didn't know that about me. I was also, in spite of my depression, quite insulted that she thought my sentences needed such tending.

In my experience, writing doesn't get easier the more you do it. But there is a growth of confidence, not much, but a nugget, like a pearl, like a tumour. You learn that there is a process, and that it doesn't very much matter *what* you write, but *how* you do it, that is crucial, and that nothing I wrote, or you wrote, is ever going to be the same as what she wrote and he wrote, unless, as Truman Capote said, what you're dealing with isn't writing, but typing. So I've got cancer. I'm writing.

11 September 2014

AFTERWORD

A closed door and a very present absence are a familiar thing to any child of a writer.

'When this door is shut, Chloe, it means I'm working. Don't knock, don't fiddle around outside the door, don't push anything under it. I *need* to work. I'm not available.'

I would continue to fiddle, sing songs too loudly and poke my head around the door to ask a 'very important question' about something that could wait.

And then I would smile, anticipating her next, more animated, response. 'Chloe, I *need* solitude. I *need* to write. To *think*. I can't always be at your beck and call.'

Ooh, it would irritate me. Especially that word 'solitude', which I felt had been given such unimpeachable value, but was also a way of saying 'fuck off'.

My mum's shut-door mode would continue while she made tea to see her through the afternoon. Head down and hazy-eyed, she would be in the kitchen but also away, somewhere else. And thank God. Without that closed door and her dedication to solitude we would both have been in trouble. Jenny wasn't messing around. She did need to write. So, although I enjoyed the fact that I could rib her about this need and that she allowed for it a bit, there was also something very comforting about having such a productive mind around putting sane and ordered words on to a page. Better than my image of the alternative, had the solitude that fuelled the writing been denied. Torment, disturbance, struggle, and – possibly – a familiar urge to end that struggle.

It was only after a long and serious bout of depression in the 1980s, and only after the therapist who was seeing her through it gave a straight answer to her constant talk of wanting to write, saying 'Well, you had better just get on with it, hadn't you?' that Jenny wrote her first novel, *Nothing Natural*. Writing then became her profession. She was thirty-seven, and between the ages of thirty-eight and sixty-eight, when she died, she became far more well headed.

My mum has called me her rock, and I think my presence did help her a lot. But Mary-Kay Wilmers, who edited this volume and who edits the *London Review of Books*, was another rock for her. By the time she started writing long essays for the paper in 1992, Jenny had written five novels and a column called 'Off Your Trolley' for the *Sunday Times*, which was a bit about supermarkets, but mainly about her. It was a good gig. My friends and I thought so, as we got to taste-test bourbon biscuits and custard creams, and my dad thought so as he got to go to the opening of the local Waitrose (for him, a bucket list moment). But there was something about Mary-Kay's commissions – a looser form, more words and therefore more detours – that fitted perfectly with Jenny's mind.

Doris Lessing took my mum on in the 1960s, giving her a home and support, and I think Mary-Kay did something similar in the 1990s. In Mary-Kay she found a friend she respected and liked spending time with. A visit from Mary-Kay wouldn't send her to bed for days afterwards; it was a pleasure rather than an endurance. That alone was a big and surprising thing. But Mary-Kay could also see what my mum could do, and offered her more and more work, giving her books to review, mainly about people, which allowed Jenny to use herself and the subject to show and explore life's complications. So, for me, my mum was alone in her study, but in her mind, she was with the subject of the book, interrogating them, and interrogating how they were interrogated by the author of the book. Often – no, always – using her particular memory-suffused self to do so. The essays are about what they are about, but they are, essentially, about Jenny.

The first essay, and the first of this book, would have been chiselled and tweaked to perfection but would have also come naturally to her. It doesn't seem to be hard fought, this new, open and honest(ish) diary-like piece. I remember the few weeks she wrote about, the man who lived with us for a couple of years before moving out, our cat's stomach problems, her trip to see the orangutans. Each event was used to introduce and describe herself, but anything would have done. It would have been the same essay if nothing had happened besides a trip to buy a frock somewhere familiar in Hampstead. Like a rapper's first song, or a painter's first self-portrait, what she was saying was: I'm Jenny Diski and this is the way I do it.

Over the twenty-five years that she wrote for the *LRB*, this long-essay form, pretty much available only to *LRB* writers and therefore desperately coveted, gave her a way to – how she would hate this expression – express herself. And while she slipped into the form as easily as she slipped into her daily bath, the writing space that came naturally to her was, like her bath, a place of rigour and hard, serious thinking. She knew the value of what she had been given. The *LRB* allowed for a different kind of writing, and a different more established writing life, and so each essay was worked and worked on. My mum had no idea if the commissions would continue. If anything would continue, and what came out of that terror was terrific writing.

The *LRB* was also where she published the story of her final years. As if that context and the permissiveness that was offered were so vital that it would have been absurd to express it anywhere else. As absurd to her as not expressing it at all. The last piece in this book was the first of her so-called Cancer Diary. These pieces steadily grew to the length of a book and were published as *In Gratitude*, just after her death in 2016. In these articles she wrote on the two remaining subjects that she hadn't yet explored on paper: dying, and Doris Lessing. But she had explored death.

Her Diary (Vol. 16 No. 12; 23 June 1994), in which she is so funny about the offer of a grave plot from a friend, also called Jenny, is a light reflection on an unfathomable reality. Neither Jenny nor Jenny got 'top bunk' in the Highgate plot. The other Jenny is alive. My mum decided against Jenny's plot, and the idea of a 'natural death' ceremony with a draughty coffin was discarded both in the piece and eventually in the future, when my mum came to choose what she wanted after death.

My partner and I, and Jenny's husband, Ian, ended up at a crematorium outside Cambridge. The coffin moved through the opened curtains and a single song played. Tom Waits's version of 'Somewhere', from *West Side Story*.

There's a place for us
Somewhere a place for us
Peace and quiet and open air
Wait for us somewhere

When she mentioned a few months before she died
that she wanted that song played, and only that song,
I thought 'Us?': that's not very Jenny. Not very solitary.
But of course, it wasn't. Part of the reason for that closed
door, was to provoke a knock.

Chloe Diski

CREDITS

All the essays included in this collection appeared in the
London Review of Books.

'Moving Day' originally published as 'Three Whole
   Weeks Alone', Vol. 14 No. 10; 28 May 1992
'Good Housekeeping' (Review of *The Shrine of Jeffrey
   Dahmer* by Brian Masters), Vol. 15 No. 3; 11
   February 1993
'He Could Afford It' (Review of *Howard Hughes: The
   Secret Life* by Charles Higham), Vol. 16 No. 7; 7
   April 1994
'Stinker' (Review of *Roald Dahl: A Biography* by
   Jeremy Treglown), Vol. 16 No. 8; 28 April 1994
'The Natural Death Centre' originally published as
   'A Plot in Highgate Cemetery', Vol. 16 No. 12; 23
   June 1994
'Sweetie Pies' (Review of *Below the Parapet: The
   Biography of Denis Thatcher* by Carol Thatcher),
   Vol. 18 No. 10; 23 May 1996
'A Feeling for Ice', Vol. 19 No. 1; 2 January 1997
'The Girl in the Attic' (Review of *The Diary of a Young
   Girl* by Anne Frank, edited by Otto Frank and
   Mirjam Pressler, translated by Susan Massotty), Vol.
   19 No. 5; 6 March 1997
'Mrs Straus's Devotion' (Review of *Last Dinner on the
   'Titanic': Menus and Recipes from the Great Liner*

by Rick Archbold and Dana McCauley, *The* 'Titanic' *Complex* by John Wilson Foster and *Down with the Old Canoe* by Steven Biel), Vol. 19 No. 11; 5 June 1997

'Did Jesus Walk on Water Because He Couldn't Swim?' (Review of *The Children of Noah: Jewish Seafaring in Ancient Times* by Raphael Patai), Vol. 20 No. 16; 20 August 1998

'Perfectly Human' (Review of *Lillie Langtry: Manners, Masks and Morals* by Laura Beatty and *Véra (Mrs Vladimir Nabokov): Portrait of a Marriage* by Stacy Schiff), Vol. 21 No. 13; 1 July 1999

'Stinking Rich' (Review of *Branson* by Tom Bower), Vol. 22 No. 22; 16 November 2000

'My Little Lollipop' (Review of *The Truth at Last: My Story* by Christine Keeler and Douglas Thompson), Vol. 23 No. 6; 22 March 2001

'Don't Think About It' (Review of *The Girl from the Fiction Department: A Portrait of Sonia Orwell* by Hilary Spurling), Vol. 24 No. 9; 25 April 2002

'Fashion as Art', Vol. 24 No. 22; 14 November 2002

'It Wasn't Him, It Was Her' (Review of *Nietzsche's Sister and the Will to Power: A Biography of Elisabeth Förster-Nietzsche* by Carol Diethe), Vol. 25 No. 18; 25 September 2003

'XXX' (Review of *The Man Who Shocked the World: The Life and Legacy of Stanley Milgram* by Thomas Blass), Vol. 26 No. 22; 18 November 2004

'Mirror Images' (Review of *The Insider: The Private Diaries of a Scandalous Decade* by Piers Morgan), Vol. 27 No. 7; 31 March 2005

'My Word, Miss Perkins' (Review of *Literary Secretaries/Secretarial Culture* edited by Leah

Price and Pamela Thurschwell), Vol. 27 No. 15; 4 August 2005

'The Housekeeper of a World-Shattering Theory' (Review of *Martha Freud: A Biography* by Katja Behling, translated by R.D.V. Glasgow), Vol. 28 No. 6; 23 March 2006

'The Friendly Spider Programme', Vol. 28 No. 23; 30 November 2006

'Tunnel Vision' (Review of *The Diana Chronicles* by Tina Brown and *Diana* by Sarah Bradford), Vol. 29 No. 15; 2 August 2007

'Not Enjoying Herself' (Review of *Princess Margaret: A Life Unravelled* by Tim Heald), Vol. 29 No. 16; 16 August 2007

'Staying Awake' originally published as 'Trying to Stay Awake', Vol. 30 No. 15; 31 July 2008

'The Khugistic Sandal' (Review of *Jews and Shoes* edited by Edna Nahshon), Vol. 30 No. 19; 9 October 2008

'Toxic Lozenges' (Review of *The Arsenic Century: How Victorian Britain Was Poisoned at Home, Work and Play* by James Whorton), Vol. 32 No. 13; 8 July 2010

'Never Mainline' (Review of *Life* by Keith Richards, with James Fox), Vol. 32 No. 24; 16 December 2010

'Which One of You Is Jesus?', Vol. 33 No. 18; 22 September 2011

'Zeitgeist Man' (Review of *Dennis Hopper: The Wild Ride of a Hollywood Rebel* by Peter Winkler), Vol. 34 No. 6; 22 March 2012

'I Haven't Been Nearly Mad Enough' (Review of *The Last Asylum: A Memoir of Madness in Our Times* by Barbara Taylor), Vol. 36 No. 3; 6 February 2014

CREDITS

'However I Smell' (Review of *Out of Time* by Lynne
Segal), Vol. 36 No. 9; 8 May 2014
'Post-its, Push Pins, Pencils' (Review of *Cubed: A
Secret History of the Workplace* by Nikil Saval), Vol.
36 No. 15; 31 July 2014
'A Diagnosis', Vol. 36 No. 17; 11 September 2014

NOTE ON THE AUTHOR

Jenny Diski was born in 1947 in London, where she lived most of her life. She was the author of ten novels, four books of travel and memoir, including *Stranger on a Train and Skating to Antarctica*, two volumes of essays and a collection of short stories. Her journalism appeared in publications including the *Mail on Sunday*, the *Observer* and the *London Review of Books*, to which she contributed more than two hundred pieces over twenty-five years.

jennydiski.co.uk

NOTE ON THE TYPE

The text of this book is set in Linotype Sabon, a typeface named after the type founder, Jacques Sabon. It was designed by Jan Tschichold and jointly developed by Linotype, Monotype and Stempel in response to a need for a typeface to be available in identical form for mechanical hot-metal composition and hand composition using foundry type.

Tschichold based his design for Sabon roman on a font engraved by Garamond, and Sabon italic on a font by Granjon. It was first used in 1966 and has proved an enduring modern classic.